DOLLAR POLITICS: EXCHANGE RATE POLICYMAKING IN THE UNITED STATES

D1166953

I. M. DESTLER
C. RANDALL HENNING

Dollar Politics: Exchange Rate Policymaking in the United States

INSTITUTE FOR INTERNATIONAL ECONOMICS
WASHINGTON, DC 1989

I. M. Destler is Professor at the School of Public Affairs, University of Maryland, and a Visiting Fellow at the Institute. He is a former Senior Associate at the Carnegie Endowment for International Peace and the Brookings Institution. His previous books include American Trade Politics: System Under Stress *(1986) and* Our Own Worst Enemy: The Unmaking of American Foreign Policy *(1984).*

C. Randall Henning is a Research Associate at the Institute. He is the author of Macroeconomic Diplomacy in the 1980s: Domestic Politics and International Conflict Among the United States, Japan, and Europe *(1987) and a coauthor of* Can Nations Agree? Issues in International Economic Cooperation *(1989). He has lectured on international economic policy coordination at American University.*

INSTITUTE FOR INTERNATIONAL ECONOMICS
11 Dupont Circle, NW
Washington, DC 20036
(202) 328-9000
Telex: 261271 IIE UR
Fax: (202) 328-5432

C. Fred Bergsten, *Director*
Linda Griffin Kean, *Director of Publications*

The Institute for International Economics was created by, and receives substantial support from, the German Marshall Fund of the United States.

Printed in the United States of America
93 92 91 90 89   5 4 3 2 1

Library of Congress Cataloging-in-Publication Data

Destler, I.M.
    Dollar politics: Exchange Rate Policy-making in the United States
    Includes index
    1. Foreign exchange administration—United States.
I. Henning, C. Randall. II. Title.
HG3903.D47 1989
332.4'5673   89–19972

ISBN 0–88132–079-X

Contents

Preface

The Institute for International Economics has published a number of studies on the economics of exchange rates, with particular emphasis on the dollar, including *Deficits and the Dollar: The World Economy at Risk* by Stephen Marris, and *The Exchange Rate System* by John Williamson. Large portions of my own *America in the World Economy: A Strategy for the 1990s* and William R. Cline's *American Trade Adjustment: The Global Impact* deal with this subject as well. Another recent Institute publication, *Managing the Dollar: From the Plaza to the Louvre* by Yoichi Funabashi, is a path-breaking journalistic account of the international monetary negotiations of the past several years with an emphasis on their international political dimensions.

This newest study, *Dollar Politics: Exchange Rate Policymaking in the United States,* presents the first in-depth analysis of the domestic politics and procedures through which exchange rate policy is made in the United States. Its focus is the enormous swings in the value of the dollar and official American policy toward the currency in the 1980s: the dollar's sharp rise, encouraged by official "benign neglect," in the first half of the decade; the reversal of that policy and the successful effort to sharply weaken the currency via the Plaza Agreement of September 1985; and the subsequent stabilization phase initiated by the Louvre Accord of February 1987. The authors ask how the American decision-making system permitted and accommodated such shifts in domestic policy, and seek lessons for the future from the experience.

Dollar Politics is the joint work of two political scientists with extensive experience in analyzing international economic issues, I. M. Destler and C. Randall Henning. It reflects continuing Institute interest in the *process* of international economic policymaking and how it might be strengthened. A book with a similar emphasis was Dr. Destler's *American Trade Politics: System Under Stress,* published in 1986 by the Institute and the Twentieth Century Fund, which won the American Political Science Association's Gladys M. Kammerer Award in 1987 for the best political science publication in the field of US national policy. Dr. Destler, formerly a Senior Fellow at the Institute, is now a Visiting Fellow here and Professor at the School of Public Affairs at the University of Maryland.

Dr. Henning, whose earlier publications include *Macroeconomic Diplomacy in the 1980s: Domestic Politics and International Conflict Among the United States, Japan and Europe,* published in 1987, is a Research Associate at the Institute. *Dollar Politics* draws heavily on his extensive research in this subject area, and on his interviews with a large number of officials in executive agencies, the Congress, and private corporations. I want to join with the authors in thanking all those who gave so generously of their time and experience in that way.

The Institute for International Economics is a private nonprofit institution for the study and discussion of international economic policy. Its purpose is to analyze important issues in that area, and to develop and communicate practical new approaches for dealing with them. The Institute is completely nonpartisan.

The Institute was created by a generous commitment of funds from the German Marshall Fund of the United States in 1981 and now receives about 15 percent of its support from that source. In addition, major institutional grants are being received from the Ford Foundation, the William and Flora Hewlett Foundation, and the Alfred P. Sloan Foundation. A number of other foundations and private corporations are contributing to the increasing diversification of the Institute's resources. A grant from the Sasakawa Peace Foundation in Japan helped support this study, whose results will be integrated with similar projects now being conducted in Europe and Japan in an effort to improve the prospects for more effective international cooperation on economic and financial issues.

The Board of Directors bears overall responsibility for the Institute and gives general guidance and approval to its research program, including identification of topics that are likely to become important to international economic policymakers over the medium run (generally one to three years) and which thus should be addressed by the Institute. The Director, working closely with the staff and outside Advisory Committee, is responsible for the development of particular projects and makes the final decision to publish an individual study.

The Institute hopes that its studies and other activities will contribute to building a stronger foundation for international economic policy around the world. We invite readers of these publications to let us know how they think we can best accomplish this objective.

C. FRED BERGSTEN
Director
August 1989

Acknowledgments

Many people have contributed generously to this project. At the risk of inadvertently omitting important contributions, we would like to acknowledge some of those people here.

We would like to thank, first, the many people who granted us interviews. Rather than distinguish painstakingly between interviews conducted on an attribution versus not-for-attribution basis, we have chosen not to formally cite any of our interview sources in the book. Needless to say, however, the input of government, congressional, corporate, and trade association officials has been vital not only to our reconstruction of events but more fundamentally to our understanding and analysis of policymaking. Speaking to these committed and talented people has been one of the most enjoyable aspects of this project.

Second, we would like to thank our colleagues at the Institute for International Economics for their assistance and encouragement over the course of the project. In particular, C. Fred Bergsten generously offered his support, time, and insights to our study, and commented in detail on virtually every part of our manuscript. Kimberly A. Elliott, C. David Finch, Daniel Frisch, Stephen Marris, Peter Uimonen, and John Williamson, among others, also offered their incisive comments.

We are grateful as well to many other people who gave us feedback in one form or another on early papers and the penultimate manuscript. Those include Ravi Bulchandhani, Benjamin J. Cohen, Stephen D. Cohen, Stephen Cooney, Jessica Einhorn, Ava Feiner, Barbara Fliess, Lawrence A. Fox, Jeffrey A. Frankel, Judith Goldstein, Joanne Gowa, David Hale, Shafiqul Islam, Allan Mendelowitz, Lee L. Morgan, Henry R. Nau, John S. Odell, Scott Pardee, Lee Price, Jeanne Roslanowick, Leonard Santos, Joanna Shelton, and Edwin M. Truman. Peter B. Kenen and Robert Solomon, in particular, read the entire manuscript and offered extensive comments. Two anonymous reviewers also offered extensive constructive criticism. We, however, remain entirely responsible for any errors or omissions in judgment or fact that might remain in the book.

We acknowledge the hard work of our able assistants, Deborah Crowell, Drew Larson, Martina Lopez-Noguerol, Cindy McKaughan, and Helmut Rez, and wish them future success. Anthony Stancil competently managed our manuscript.

And finally, but far from least, we would like to thank our excellent editing and publications staff for improving our prose and turning our manuscript into a book: Linda Griffin Kean, Michael Treadway, and Terry Kannofsky.

Introduction

Since World War II the United States dollar has been the anchor of the global trade and financial system. Although other currencies have risen in importance, the dollar remains the prime medium for international trade, the main currency of denomination for international investment, and the standard against which other currencies are valued. Hence the dollar's exchange rate—what it is worth in Japanese yen, deutsche marks, or pounds sterling—is one of the most important prices in the world economy.

It has also become a critical price for the US economy. American firms and workers operate today in a global marketplace, and the great bulk of the goods they produce goes head to head with foreign-produced goods in domestic and international markets. The exchange rate is a major influence on who prospers in that competition, for if the dollar rises by 40 percent, this can be equivalent to a 40 percent tax on US exports and a 40 percent subsidy of US imports. Major exchange rate changes can also generate far-reaching, difficult-to-reverse shifts in the structure of the US economy.

Yet despite the exchange rate's central and growing importance to the US economy, official attitudes and policies have ranged from the constructive, responsible, and long-term oriented to the neglectful and shortsighted. All too often, US institutions and policy processes have failed to address the dollar as a policy variable and to consider it fully when setting other economic policies. Furthermore, there have been frequent changes in the government's exchange rate stance in the absence of changes in underlying US interests.

In the 1980s the exchange rate problem reached historic dimensions. In terms of the yen, the dollar rose from 203 at the close of 1980 to peaks of 278 and 263 in November 1982 and February 1985 respectively, dropped to 120 by December 1987, and then rose again above 150 by late May 1989, before receding in June and July. From its average in 1980, the dollar's overall international value rose 63 percent by March 1985, fell below its 1980 level by early 1988, and then rose 10 percent by the spring of 1989, only to decline thereafter[1] (figures 2.3 to 2.5).

Such swings for the dollar were without precedent in modern economic history, and they generated enormous pressures on US firms and workers. Hence the exchange rate became, for the first time in the postwar period, an important and visible issue in American politics. In the first half of the decade, the superstrong dollar drove US producers of traded goods into the political arena as never before, seeking policies to correct it and relief from its effects. In the years that followed, international efforts to bring down and then stabilize the dollar's value commanded center stage.

Exchange rate fluctuations did not spoil the positive achievements of the domestic economy on Ronald Reagan's watch. Those achievements were notable: After the 1981–82 recession, the US economy registered the longest peacetime recovery of the postwar era. Gross national product increased by 18.8 percent in real terms between 1981 and 1988 (by 20.7 percent from the trough of the recession). From 1981 through 1988, total employment rose almost 16 percent, as about 16 million additional jobs were created, while the unemployment rate fell from 10.6 percent in late 1982 to just above 5 percent in early 1989. Consumer price inflation fell quickly from double-digit rates at the turn of the decade (the fall was facilitated by the dollar's appreciation) and still remains low compared to earlier levels at just over 5 percent.

However, the good news was purchased at a price: disruptive swings in the dollar and, from 1983 onward, large and persistent current account deficits and a burgeoning foreign debt, which has now become the largest in the world. Reducing the trade imbalances and servicing that debt will require a compression of US consumption, investment, or both in the years to come. Then it will become apparent that, to a disturbing degree, the economic policies of the 1980s simply borrowed prosperity from the 1990s, through the mechanism of foreign capital inflows, exchange rates, and massive imports of foreign goods.

The dollar's exchange rate is thus intertwined with the success (or failure) of firms and workers, and with balance (or grievous imbalance) in the nation's overall accounts. It therefore poses a formidable challenge to government management of America's economy, of its international economic relations, and ultimately of its foreign relations more generally. Our institutions have not yet proved adequate to this challenge, as evidenced by swings in policy every bit as large and erratic as those taking place on the foreign-exchange markets.

The first Reagan administration foreswore virtually all official intervention in foreign-currency markets, treating the dollar's value as a free-market price like

---

1. According to the Multilateral Exchange Rate Measure of the International Monetary Fund, which calculates the dollar's value against all currencies, weighted for their importance to US trade. *International Financial Statistics*, various issues.

any other. At the same time, an extraordinary combination of tight monetary and loose fiscal policy generated a gargantuan inflow of foreign capital, driving the dollar upward. This laissez-faire attitude toward official influence over exchange rates reversed the Carter Treasury's late-1970s' practice of substantial intervention. The first Reagan administration's policies were in turn reversed in the second term, with Secretary of the Treasury James A. Baker III leading a dramatic, internationally coordinated effort to bring down the dollar's value. Then, after substantial dollar depreciation had been achieved, the Baker Treasury moved to yet a third policy, that of stabilizing the dollar within broad, albeit secret, target ranges. This exchange rate stabilization policy continued into the Bush administration, although the present Treasury Secretary, Nicholas F. Brady, has to date given it a lower priority than did his predecessor.

Such shifts in policy were not unique to the 1980s. Those of the Reagan era were particularly sharp, as officials were confronted with a volatile mix of unprecedented domestic fiscal deficits and international capital flows. But previous administrations had their policy swings also. The Nixon administration moved from "benign neglect" of international payments balances to sudden action to cut the dollar loose from gold and devalue the dollar; this move led to the demise of the Bretton Woods system of fixed parities. The Carter administration began by promoting dollar decline but later moved to major intervention to arrest and reverse that decline when it went too far.[2] Indeed, the United States appears almost unique among the world's major countries in the changeability of its exchange rate policy, and in the frequent insensitivity of that policy to the interests of producers of internationally traded goods.

Bretton Woods—and After

The roots of that uniqueness can be found in postwar history, and specifically in the passive exchange rate role established for the United States after the Bretton Woods Conference in 1944. As the international monetary regime agreed upon there evolved through the 1960s, every country but one could set current

---

2. Cycles between neglect and activism have been identified and explained in Benjamin J. Cohen, "An Explosion in the Kitchen? Economic Relations with Other Advanced Industrial States," in Kenneth A. Oye, Robert J. Lieber, and Donald Rothchild, eds., *Eagle Defiant: United States Foreign Policy in the 1980s* (Boston: Little, Brown, 1983), 105–30; C. Fred Bergsten, "America's Unilateralism," in Bergsten, Etienne Davignon, and Isamu Miyazaki, "Conditions for Partnership in International Economic Management," *Report to the Trilateral Commission* 32 (New York: Trilateral Commission, 1986), 3–14; C. Randall Henning, *Macroeconomic Diplomacy in the 1980s: Domestic Politics and International Conflict among the United States, Japan, and Europe*, Atlantic Paper 65 (London: Croom Helm, 1987), 50–52.

account targets independently of the others.[3] All other countries could revalue or devalue their currencies (with respect to gold and other currencies) under conditions of "fundamental disequilibrium" (although the consent of other governments through the International Monetary Fund—the IMF—was formally required, and such changes were expected to be relatively rare). But because US dollars were held as international reserves in addition to gold (the Bretton Woods regime was a gold-*exchange* standard), the United States was far more constrained from altering its exchange rate than were its partners. Although changes in the worth of the deutsche mark, the French franc, and the pound sterling were negotiated, and the Canadian dollar was permitted to float for extended periods, the US dollar remained fixed until 1971 at the level set at the end of the war. As Bretton Woods evolved, then, the United States came to serve as the passive "*n*th country" in the international monetary regime, its acceptance of the collective current account positions of all partner countries enabling the others' targets to be mutually compatible.

The development of domestic institutions of exchange rate policy under the Bretton Woods regime was geared toward sustaining the regime and America's role in it. This meant supporting the dollar even as it became progressively overvalued, and preventing a drain of gold from the United States as payments deficits emerged. Institutions and procedures for conducting an active exchange rate policy, in pursuit of trade and current account objectives, were not developed, nor were fundamental monetary and fiscal policies dedicated to sustaining the Bretton Woods arrangements. Combined with inflationary macroeconomic policies, this neglect sowed the seeds for America's exit from the regime.

When Bretton Woods was replaced by the floating exchange rate regime of the 1970s and 1980s, the United States was left without a rudder, without an institutional framework to establish an exchange rate policy embedded in a national economic strategy. If the most widely accepted academic case for flexible exchange rates had been vindicated by events, no institutional rudder would have been necessary. Floating rates would have reduced current account imbalances without governments having to alter domestic macroeconomic policies. But instead of being determined primarily by the flow of goods, exchange rates have been driven increasingly by capital transactions, as some

---

3. For excellent reviews of the operation of the Bretton Woods regime, see C. Fred Bergsten, *The Dilemmas of the Dollar: The Economics and Politics of United States International Monetary Policy* (New York: New York University Press for the Council on Foreign Relations, 1975), chap. 3; John Williamson, *The Failure of World Monetary Reform, 1971–74* (New York: New York University Press, 1977), chaps. 1 and 2; Benjamin J. Cohen, *Organizing the World's Money: The Political Economy of International Monetary Relations* (New York: Basic Books, 1977), chap. 3; Robert Solomon, *The International Monetary System, 1945–1981: An Insider's View,* 2d ed. (New York: Harper and Row, 1982).

economists anticipated even in the 1960s. These capital flows ballooned in volume, coming to dwarf transactions for the buying and selling of goods and services. Thus, flexibility has been accompanied by growing, not declining, imbalances and by much greater swings in the market values of currencies.

Responding to these new circumstances, US dollar policy has tended toward the expedient and short-term. Authorities' postures have fluctuated with the business cycle and balance of payments conditions, and with the policy priorities of specific administrations. Although the post–Bretton Woods regime is properly characterized as one of managed rather than free-floating currencies, in general other countries have managed their exchange rates much more consistently than has the United States.

The United States could long afford to treat the level of the dollar as a residual of other economic policies, domestic and foreign, and could tolerate institutions that generated passive or changeable exchange rate policies, because the United States was a relatively closed economy. Indeed, that is a primary reason why the United States accepted its passive role under Bretton Woods and withdrew support for the regime when its maintenance would have required domestically painful macroeconomic steps to buttress the dollar. Since then the US economy has become more internationalized, but US institutions and processes have not evolved commensurately. They remain fundamentally the same.

Taken together, the demise of Bretton Woods, the transformation of foreign exchange markets, and the internationalization of the US economy produced—in combination with domestic policies—the unprecedented exchange rate swings and current account deficits of the 1980s. The magnitude of these imbalances has made this a unique decade in comparison with those that preceded it. And the costs of exchange rate volatility and misalignment were substantial: at least one million US jobs lost in traded-goods industries; firms abandoning plants and lines of production, which could not easily be restarted when the dollar's value receded; the broader misallocation of resources triggered by changing and misleading exchange rate signals.

But because the underlying forces continue to operate, the disturbances of the 1980s may well foreshadow events in the 1990s and beyond. This danger is particularly great should the United States again eschew active management of the exchange rate and external accounts, and again formulate monetary and fiscal policies with scant regard for their external effects. Exchange rate neglect could prove even more costly in the future.

For as we enter the new decade, the United States is becoming, if anything, even more dependent on international transactions for its domestic well-being. Capital markets are increasingly global: foreign financial assets are increasingly substitutable for US assets in American and foreign portfolios. The movement of American and foreign investors in and out of US assets substantially affects not only American stock, bond, and other financial markets but the entire US economy. And trade competition among nations continues to intensify.

Meanwhile, as the value of the dollar becomes increasingly important to US economic performance, Japan and Europe are becoming more influential in exchange rate matters and more assertive in international financial institutions. Japan has become a global financial power. European monetary unification, now more than a distant dream, would create a larger, stronger competitor with enhanced bargaining power. As the yen, the mark, and perhaps one day the ECU (European Currency Unit) become more attractive international currencies, the United States might well find itself co-managing a truly multiple–reserve currency system.

This new external environment will be more demanding and less forgiving of US international monetary policy. Responding to it is likely to sharpen conflicts among domestic actors whose economic and bureaucratic interests are affected by the dollar. Government leaders will need to work with, reconcile, and aggregate these interests in ways that are credible to a stronger set of international negotiating partners and economic competitors. To extract cooperation from the other governments of the Group of Seven (G-7) advanced industrial nations, the United States will need to go beyond short-term exchange rate management: it must develop a capacity to make and deliver on commitments to change domestic macroeconomic policy as its contribution to international policy bargains. Such a capacity is critical to the operation of a target zone system or of any other regime that calls upon participating governments to employ a range of economic policy tools to keep exchange rates within agreed bounds. Strengthening *internal* economic policymaking will be essential to full participation in the international system, and—as this study will seek to demonstrate—governmental focus on the exchange rate is a necessary and important element in this process.

As a contribution to such ends, this book analyzes the politics, processes, and institutions by which US exchange rate policies have been set in the postwar period—the 1980s in particular—and makes recommendations for improvements.

Government, the Exchange Rate, and Economic Performance

This study rests on a simple premise: that the international value of the dollar is an important price for the US economy and can be significantly influenced by government actions, and hence should be an important focus for US policy. Particularly critical is the exchange rate's relationship to the balance on current account—the difference between what Americans pay for goods and services provided from abroad and what Americans receive for the goods and services they sell abroad.[4] If this balance is persistently negative, it means that Americans are borrowing to sustain their current economic choices; the interest bill will grow as long as that net borrowing continues.

Our premise raises two immediate questions. The first is whether the balance on current account is an appropriate target for government policy. The second is whether the exchange rate offers a useful lever for influencing it.

Some argue that current account balances are simply the "revealed preferences" of open economies for savings and investment, and that these preferences should be accommodated. As stated, the first part of this argument, based on an accounting identity, is a truism; but the second reflects a value judgment with which we differ.

Current account deficits and surpluses *can* be beneficial, of course, to the extent that they permit countries to lend excess savings or to borrow during temporary savings shortfalls. However, in our judgment many of these imbalances are *not* beneficial, and the US current account deficits of the 1980s are a case in point. Not only have they retarded the manufacturing sector and generated a mountain of external debt—both of which are appropriate concerns of the nation as a whole—but indeed they have been used to finance an ill-considered consumption binge during the 1980s.

Had the capital that this country borrowed from abroad been invested in productive resources, such borrowing might have been appropriate. If, for example, the United States had had an extraordinarily young population due to reach productive age within the next decade, or if a national emergency had required massive assistance for certain hard-hit regions or social classes, a deliberate national decision to borrow from abroad might have been justified.

But no such circumstances obtained. US investment in plant and equipment did not rise above historical levels during the 1980s; there was no considered rationale for redistributing consumption from the 1990s (and beyond) to the present. The United States borrowed from abroad in the 1980s because of a failure to come to grips with the federal budget deficit, compounded by a drop in private domestic savings. This borrowing was driven by domestic political deadlock and paralysis—manifest in government policy—not by a considered national choice.[5]

---

4. The balance on current account also includes international payments of interest and remittances as well as unilateral transfers.

5. Herbert Stein, *Presidential Economics*, 2d Touchstone ed. (New York: Simon and Schuster, 1985); David A. Stockman, *The Triumph of Politics: The Inside Story of the Reagan Revolution* (New York: Avon Books, 1987). For a treatment of the resulting external deficits, see Stephen Marris, *Deficits and the Dollar: The World Economy at Risk*, POLICY ANALYSES IN INTERNATIONAL ECONOMICS 14, rev. ed. (Washington: Institute for International Economics, 1987).

Some current account imbalances should be resisted, and it is an appropriate and indeed necessary role of the government to distinguish imbalances that are desirable from those that are undesirable. This is a proper subject for national debate and central decisions. The government should develop a current account target as part of a national economic strategy that explicitly considers the investment needs of the economy, realistically assesses future domestic savings, and derives from them national borrowing (or lending) requirements. This analysis would realistically address the desirability of the resulting debtor (or creditor) position and the trade-offs involved between sectors of the economy and across time periods. Government dissaving (or saving) would also be an explicit part of these calculations.[6]

The government should consider the exchange rate as one instrument to help achieve that current account target and prevent inappropriate deviations from it in the medium term. The exchange rate, therefore, takes on a role within a broader economic strategy whose ultimate goal is long-term *domestic* growth and prosperity. International cooperation focusing on the exchange rate is a collective means to this end for all cooperating countries.

But does the exchange rate have a role that is independent from monetary and fiscal policies and private-sector activity? And can the government actually affect the exchange rate without compromising other important objectives? Both questions have been the subject of extensive research in international economics. This is not the place (and we are not the people) to advance this research. Nevertheless, because our positions on these questions are central premises of our study, a few words about each are appropriate.

The debate among economists revolves around the effectiveness of so-called *sterilized* intervention. Intervention by central banks in the foreign-exchange market to purchase (or sell) the national currency for foreign currency reduces (or increases) the money supply. All economists agree that this *un*sterilized intervention does affect the exchange rate on a lasting basis. However, central banks prefer to offset the effects of intervention on the money supply through purchases (or sales) of domestic bonds, so as to protect their previously set money supply and interest rate targets. Many economists argue that because this sterilized intervention does not raise (or lower) interest rates, it cannot have lasting effects on exchange rates, because the main determinant of international capital movements remains unchanged.[7] Still, there are several reasons why

6. On current account targets and their relationship to exchange rates, see John Williamson, *The Exchange Rate System*, POLICY ANALYSES IN INTERNATIONAL ECONOMICS 5, rev. ed. (Washington: Institute for International Economics, June 1985), especially 19–25; C. Fred Bergsten, *America in the World Economy: A Strategy for the 1990s* (Washington: Institute for International Economics, 1988), especially chap. 4.

7. For examples of this critical view of sterilized intervention, see Martin Feldstein, "New Evidence on the Effects of Exchange Rate Intervention," *NBER Working Paper* 2052,

sterilized intervention can have significant impact.

First, there is substantial evidence that foreign-exchange markets operate under great uncertainty, suffer from a chronic lack of stabilizing speculation, and therefore exhibit herd behavior and speculative bubbles.[8] Market-determined exchange rates therefore do not always translate domestic savings-investment balances into appropriate current account positions. They have an independent impact on those positions, through trade competitiveness principally, and thus on *ex post* savings-investment balances. Government can improve the efficiency of the market by reducing uncertainty, providing stabilizing long-term speculation, and bursting bubbles preemptively. By so doing, it can make exchange rates into more reliable and credible price signals to producers and users of internationally traded goods and financial assets.

Second, the government's capacity to influence exchange rates is much greater than what a comparison of total daily trading volume to the relatively modest quantity of foreign-exchange intervention would imply. The currency markets are indeed broad and deep, with as much as $300 to $400 billion per day changing hands in the dollar market alone, whereas government intervention on a given day amounts to a few billion dollars at the very most. However, the figures for total private trading are *gross* transactions, representing positions that are taken and then reversed, perhaps several times in a single day, and that would not themselves have a sustained impact on exchange rate levels. Government intervention can be effective at the margin, if strategically timed and conducted so as to hurt those speculators who have strong market positions in the direction opposite that sought by the officials. Not all intervention is equally effective, of course: the government can more easily affect the rate when pushing toward a level that the fundamentals justify. It does the converse at its peril.

(Cambridge, MA: National Bureau of Economic Research, 1986); Feldstein, "Correcting the Trade Deficit," *Foreign Affairs* 65 (Spring 1987): 795–806. For a more favorable view see Peter B. Kenen, "Exchange Rate Management: What Role for Intervention?" *American Economic Review* 77 (no. 2, May 1987): 194–99; Shafiqul Islam, "The Dollar and the Policy-Performance-Confidence Mix," *Essays in International Finance* 170 (Princeton, NJ: Princeton University Press, July 1988); Thomas D. Willett and Clas Wihlborg, "International Capital Flows, the Dollar, and U.S. Financial Policies," paper presented at the American Enterprise Institute Conference on Monetary Policy in an Era of Change, Washington, 16 and 17 November 1988. For an in-between view see Jeffrey Frankel and Rudiger Dornbusch, "The Flexible Exchange Rate System: Experience and Alternatives," *NBER Working Paper* 2464, December 1987.

For good general works on exchange rate economics see John F. O. Bilson and Richard C. Marston, *Exchange Rate Theory and Practice* (Chicago: University of Chicago Press for NBER, 1984); Peter B. Kenen, *Managing Exchange Rates* (London: Routledge for the Royal Institute for International Affairs, 1988), chap. 2; Paul R. Krugman, *Exchange-Rate Instability* (Cambridge, MA: MIT Press, 1989).

8. See, for example, Krugman, *Exchange-Rate Instability.*

Most important, intervention and official declarations carry the threat that they will be reinforced with changes in monetary policy. Thus, intervention and public statements can have an impact independent of the follow-up (although the "fundamentals" must be changed periodically to keep these measures credible on this account). Furthermore, the effectiveness of such action can be greatly enhanced if it is undertaken by several governments acting in concert. We conclude, therefore, that although macroeconomic forces dominate over the longer term, there is scope for government to alter the exchange rate through means other than fiscal and monetary policy and capital controls, within certain margins over the short and medium run.

In summary, the exchange rate should be a matter of concern for government authorities for two primary reasons. First, it is an instrument to help achieve the desired current account balance, in the context of a broad national economic strategy that takes explicit account of the sources and uses of savings over the long term. Second, the exchange rate serves as a signal indicating when monetary and fiscal policy might be inconsistent with the desirable long-term current account position. Exchange rate deviations from this long-term trend should raise a red flag, initiating a review of these policies to determine whether they or the long-term projections of the saving (or lending) needs of the private economy should be changed. Rather than a goal in and of itself, the exchange rate is a vitally important instrument over which the government has substantial influence but not total control. Because it is so important, the institutions and processes by which the government weighs, or fails to weigh, the exchange rate merit careful analysis.

Direct and Indirect Exchange Rate Policy

Our study focuses particularly on two types of government actions:

- Direct exchange rate policy, or efforts to influence the exchange rate through public declarations and market intervention (including explicit decisions to eschew such efforts) and

- Indirect exchange rate policy, or the adjustment of monetary and fiscal policies to influence the price of the dollar.

By direct exchange rate policy we mean those actions whose explicit and overriding objective is to influence the market price of the dollar, including in particular official intervention in foreign-exchange markets and declarations concerning what value the dollar *ought* to have. Direct policy actions can also take the form of US pressure on foreign governments and central banks to intervene in the markets (or to desist from intervention), or to adjust exchange and capital controls, or to apply "moral suasion" or "administrative guidance" to major private actors. In contrast, indirect exchange rate policy consists of those adjustments of fiscal and monetary policies that have, as one explicit purpose, influence over exchange rates. The exchange rate acts as an important signal for adjustment of these other policies in order to maintain a desirable international payments position.

We must draw reasonable boundaries around the indirect policy category, however. Most important governmental economic actions have some exchange rate impact. If this study were to cast its net that widely, it would become indistinguishable from a study of overall US macroeconomic policymaking. Therefore, to maintain our specific focus, we limit the scope of our detailed examination of policymaking and policy advocacy to those actions *intended* to influence the exchange rate. But our description of the unfolding of the exchange rate issue during the 1980s is also concerned with other government actions with unusually sharp (even if unintended) exchange rate impact, such as the Reagan tax and spending "revolution" of 1981.

Current Policymaking Institutions

In sharp contrast to the swings in currency rates and official policies, there has been remarkably little change over the postwar period in the way that US exchange rate decisions are made and executed. This process has remained a strikingly private affair. It is controlled, as the United States enters the 1990s, by essentially the same "closed" institutions and processes that controlled it in the early postwar period and before. Although their decisions often incorporate broad economic considerations, these institutions are insulated from private and congressional pressures and are frequently not held to account for their decisions on exchange rate matters. Decisions about direct exchange rate policy are made and executed by a narrow group of officials led by the Secretary of the Treasury and including typically the Deputy Secretary or the Under Secretary for Monetary or International Affairs, and the Assistant Secretary for International Affairs.

Whereas the Treasury is responsible for exchange rate and international financial policies, the Federal Reserve Board has the task of setting domestic monetary policy. Despite this apparent division of labor, the Fed's actions strongly influence the effectiveness of foreign-exchange intervention and the viability of exchange rate targets and international agreements. This linkage, combined with the Fed's role as agent in all foreign-currency operations, makes the Chairman of the Federal Reserve Board an essential Treasury partner in exchange rate policy. In this role the Chairman is typically supported by one or two Fed staff (and sometimes Board) members in Washington and by the President of the New York Federal Reserve Bank and his Executive Vice President in charge of foreign-exchange operations. As the third member of the foreign currency subcommittee of the Federal Open Market Committee, the Vice Chairman of the Board is also included.

On most occasions, decisions about intervention in the foreign-exchange markets are made within this small group, and aside from the President, only senior members of this group can make authoritative public statements about desirable changes in the dollar's value or commitments to stabilize the dollar at a certain level. The White House becomes involved only occasionally, when the President wishes to address the exchange rate in public remarks or when a presidential statement is needed to impress the markets. But in most instances Presidents have left the matter to the Treasury. Procedures for review by broader bodies are weak, deliberations are secret, and there is rarely a publicly known timetable for decision making.

Congress, private groups, and the public at large loom in the background. Congressional support is necessary for major agreements, such as international monetary reform, and substantial commitments of national resources, to the IMF for example. But in most cases congressional influence is only indirect and delayed. It would be impractical to legislate directly on exchange rates. Consequently, Congress is consulted as a rule only after the fact on exchange rate policy decisions or when budgetary resources are needed.

In these respects (although not in the limited presidential engagement) the exchange rate policymaking process resembles national security decision making more than it does other policy processes with broad economic impact. The readiness to respond to crises and the arrangements for quick communication with other governments in the midst of turmoil also recall national security policy processes. The rationale for closed and secret policymaking on exchange rates is that government effectiveness in the markets depends on the ability to reach decisions quickly, avoid leaks, and act without warning.

In short, a Treasury-Fed duopoly reigns over US exchange rate decision making, with other actors—Congress, critically affected private interests, other executive branch agencies, even the White House—remaining on the periphery. The peripheral players did become more engaged in the mid-1980s, when the strong dollar's trade impact was most acute. Congress, through permanent legislation, has asserted anew its oversight prerogative vis-à-vis the Treasury. But after the Treasury shifted policy in 1985 to one of visibly promoting depreciation, the activity of private groups and the urgency of congressional concern diminished, leaving the core policymaking process only marginally changed.

The Plan of the Book

Are mere marginal changes in existing institutions and processes and involvement of nontraditional actors sufficient to cope with the enormous increase in international economic integration and capital mobility over the past three decades? Are these policy-setting mechanisms up to the challenge of the 1990s? Should the United States continue to leave exchange rate policymaking to the present closed system, segregated from broader domestic and international economic policy processes? Will those responsible for exchange rate policy and for negotiating international agreements on behalf of the United States have sufficient leverage over monetary and fiscal policies to be credible with foreign officials? This study seeks to shed light on such questions, using as its base an analysis of the rich and varied policy experience of the Reagan years.

We begin with an interpretive review of that experience. We examine, in Chapter 2, the policy of official neglect of the exchange rate during the first Reagan term, even as the rise of the dollar was inflicting enormous pain on a broad range of American producers. In Chapter 3 we explore the sudden shift to exchange rate activism in 1985, and particularly the contribution of the crisis in trade politics to this shift. Chapter 4 recounts the exchange rate management experience of the second Reagan administration: the managed decline of the dollar until early 1987, and the movement to dollar stabilization thereafter.

With the chronology complete, we turn to a closer analysis of policy-influencing interests and institutions. We begin at the center: Chapter 5 addresses the Treasury–Federal Reserve relationship, examining its general rationale and specific operations. We move then to the key groups that sought in the 1980s to penetrate, or at least influence, the inner circle. The subject of Chapter 6 is the Congress, driven to action by alarm over the trade imbalance and the pressures it generated from affected domestic producers. Chapter 7 then examines the role of the private sector, and especially of those same producers who were driven for the first time to take the international price of the dollar seriously and seek influence over it.

We conclude in Chapter 8 with an analysis of how US exchange rate policymaking might be strengthened for what awaits the nation—and the international policy coordination system—in the 1990s and beyond. We center our proposals in three areas:

- Exchange rate policy execution—particularly the closed system and the Treasury-Fed relationship;

- Exchange rate goal-setting—how the administration and Congress might better and more explicitly weigh competing perspectives and interests;

- Broad policy linkages—how exchange rate policymaking can be better integrated with other, inevitably intertwined policy processes, particularly those for monetary and fiscal policy.

At this writing, the overall domestic performance of the US economy remains satisfactory. The expansion continues, although at a more measured pace;

unemployment remains low; inflation, if somewhat above the levels of the mid-1980s, remains moderate. However, US external imbalances remain large: the current account deficit remains around $120 billion and is likely to rise again without new policy measures. There is continued stalemate in the policy area most critical to reducing those imbalances, namely, the federal budget deficit.

We cannot argue, therefore, that reform of exchange rate policy, or of exchange rate policy institutions, offers a simple, single cure for America's international economic ills. But the price of the dollar is an important element, both shaping and shaped by our broader macroeconomic condition. Hence we believe that the institutions and processes that affect the exchange rate are an important part of the policy landscape and an understudied one as well. With the analysis that follows we intend to establish the former point, and to help to remedy the latter.

Part I

An Interpretive Review of Policymaking in the 1980s

2

Exchange Rate Neglect, 1981–1984

When Ronald Reagan entered office in January 1981, he faced a bleaker set of domestic economic indicators than any new President since Franklin D. Roosevelt. Inflation was running at 12 percent, the "second oil shock" of 1979 having doubled the price of motor fuel. Unemployment was well over 7 percent, and the prime interest rate exceeded 20 percent.

As the White House developed and unveiled its radical program to redress these ills, however, US international economic indicators looked unusually good. The nation ran a modest current account surplus in 1980 and would do so again in 1981. The dollar had recovered from its lows of 1978–80, and its early 1981 level was consistent with maintaining international economic balance.[1]

International economic forces therefore were not an immediate problem for Reagan and his senior advisers in 1981 (in sharp contrast to the situation that would confront George Bush eight years later). They were free to focus on what they most cared about, economically and politically: domestic output, employment, and inflation rates. They could treat the exchange rate as a residual, and that, in practice, is precisely what they did.

The administration's prescriptions for these domestic ills reflected an agglomeration of the goals of the three main groups of economists—supply-siders, monetarists, and orthodox fiscal conservatives—represented in the new team: reduce taxes, control government nondefense spending, reduce inflation through tight monetary policy, and accelerate deregulation.[2] The President defended the national focus of his economic program by saying, "The most important contribution any country can make to world development is to pursue sound

---

1. John Williamson, *The Exchange Rate System*, rev. ed., POLICY ANALYSES IN INTERNATIONAL ECONOMICS 5 (Washington: Institute for International Economics, June 1985), figure A7, 106.

2. See Office of the President, *Program for Economic Recovery*, (Washington: Office of the President, 18 February 1981).

Table 2.1 US federal budget deficits, 1980–1988
(billions of dollars)

Fiscal year	Amount
1980 (Carter)	73.8
1981 (Carter-Reagan)	78.9
1982	127.9
1983	207.8
1984	185.3
1985	212.3
1986	221.2
1987	149.7
1988	155.1

Source: Council of Economic Advisers, *Economic Report of the President,* January 1989, table B-76.

economic policies at home."[3] A temporarily benign international situation allowed the administration this liberty, but the domestic actions taken in 1981 spilled over quickly into the international realm.

The Spillover of Domestic Macroeconomic Policy

The Reagan tax cuts and increases in defense spending swelled the US budget deficit. Despite fiscal adjustments in 1982 (labeled by disaffected supply-siders as "the largest tax increase in history") and in 1984, the federal deficit rose from 2.6 percent of GNP in 1981 to 5.4 percent in 1985. The full implications of the Reagan revolution for the structural fiscal balance became evident when, even as the economy bounced back from deep recession in 1983, fiscal forecasters, including Office of Management and Budget (OMB) Director David A. Stockman, projected huge deficits "as far as the eye could see." Reality bore these forecasts out, as the fiscal record of the Reagan years illustrates (table 2.1).

---

3. See "Remarks of the President to the Annual Meeting of the Board of Governors of the World Bank and International Monetary Fund," *Washington Post,* 30 September 1981. For a critical assessment of the development of international economic policy during the first few months of the Reagan administration, see Benjamin J. Cohen, "An Explosion in the Kitchen? Economic Relations with Other Advanced Industrial States," in Kenneth A. Oye, Robert J. Lieber, and Donald Rothchild, eds., *Eagle Resurgent? The Reagan Era in American Foreign Policy* (Boston: Little, Brown, 1987), 115–43. For a spirited defense of the Reagan policies, see Henry R. Nau, *International Reaganomics* (Washington: Center for Strategic and International Studies, 1984).

Figure 2.1 Short- and long-term interest rates, United States, 1979–1989

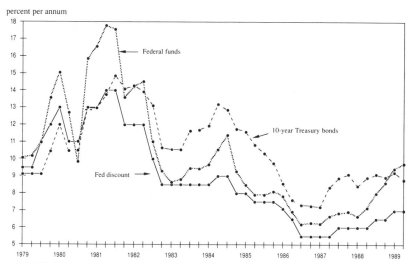

percent per annum

SOURCES: *Federal Reserve Bulletin*, July 1989; Council of Economic Advisers, *Economic Report of the President*, 1981, 1986, 1989; *International Financial Statistics*, various issues.

This exceptional fiscal laxity was joined by unusual stringency on the monetary side. The Federal Reserve had tightened monetary policy well before the Reagan administration took office, and the monetarists on the new economic team urged the Fed to hang tough despite record high interest rates and a deepening recession in 1981–82 (figure 2.1). The Fed finally eased monetary policy in mid-1982, and interest rates declined. However, the rate of inflation dropped by an even greater amount, from 12.4 percent in 1980 to 3.8 percent in 1982.[4] As a result, real interest rates remained very high (figure 2.2), spurred by increased government borrowing to finance the deficit and by the fact that neither the administration nor the Fed wanted to risk the hard-won gains against inflation by pursuing a monetary policy that might later prove overexpansionary. Propelled as well by foreign macroeconomic policies, internationally mobile capital therefore flowed toward high-yielding dollar-denominated investments in record volumes, catapulting the dollar upward.[5]

---

4. Inflation figures are given as the change in consumer prices, December to December. Council of Economic Advisers, *Economic Report of the President*, January 1989, 377.

5. For a full account and an analysis of the role of the macroeconomic policies of foreign governments, see Stephen Marris, *Deficits and the Dollar: The World Economy at Risk*, rev. ed., POLICY ANALYSES IN INTERNATIONAL ECONOMICS 14 (Washington: Institute for International Economics, August 1987).

Figure 2.2 Real and nominal long-term interest rates, United States, 1979–1989

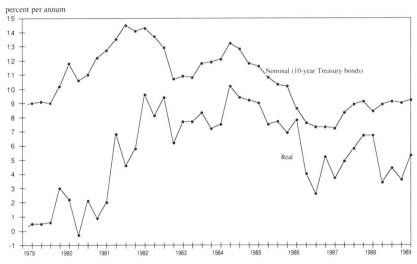

percent per annum

SOURCES: *International Financial Statistics*, various issues; *Survey of Current Business*, various issues.

The Policy of Nonintervention

With the rise of the dollar still in its early stages, Under Secretary of the Treasury for Monetary Affairs Beryl W. Sprinkel announced in April 1981 that the Treasury was ending the practice of regular intervention in foreign-exchange markets.[6] In the Carter administration there had been almost daily intervention in coordination with foreign central banks from 1978 on. With Treasury Secretary Donald T. Regan, this was to change: the Treasury would intervene only in the most disorderly of markets. The example Sprinkel offered—the buying of dollars after the March 1981 shooting of the President—indicated how rare the Treasury expected such exercises to be.

This nonintervention policy was not a necessary outgrowth of the administration's domestic orientation, but it was a plausible one. President Reagan's managerial style was to set strong, if not always consistent, guidelines and leave it to others to fill in the details.[7] His economic goals were domestic, and so it was

---

6. *New York Times*, 17 April 1981.

7. Regan recalls, "In the four years that I served as Secretary of the Treasury I never saw President Reagan alone and never discussed economic philosophy or fiscal and monetary policy with him one-on-one. From first to last at Treasury, I was flying by the seat of my pants." *For the Record: From Wall Street to Washington* (New York: Harcourt Brace,

up to his Cabinet and sub-Cabinet officials to deal with the international consequences. Not surprisingly, they did so in a manner consistent with their ideological predilections. Regan and the other senior economic advisers— including Budget Director Stockman and Chairman Murray L. Weidenbaum of the Council of Economic Advisers—were strong exponents of free markets. Thus, in interagency deliberations they endorsed the new hands-off policy on exchange rates. Officials at the State Department and the Fed, however, saw Sprinkel's announcement as antagonistic to foreign governments and unnecessarily restrictive of US policy.

The few members of Congress who watched exchange rate policy at that time were likewise skeptical. Representative Henry Reuss (D-WI), Chairman of the Joint Economic Committee, subjected Sprinkel to a prophetic cross-examination at a hearing held in early May 1981:

> Reuss: [S]uppose however, as certain spoilsports and wet blankets are saying, that your supertight money policy is going to retard growth and your very huge deficit-prone budgetary policy is going to raise interest rates. . . and those interest rates will make the dollar extra strong. . . . Would you intervene?

> Sprinkel: It is very doubtful that we would intervene in a circumstance similar to that. It is also practically impossible that the assumptions you have made would lead to higher interest rates. . . . [8]

Regan and Sprinkel also renounced declaratory policy: they would not make public statements signaling the direction they thought the exchange rate should move. They decided early on that they would not try to target the dollar indirectly by modifying the mix of monetary and fiscal policy—loosening money would risk inflation, they argued. Nor would they push to change fiscal policy; in fact, they denied, with regularity, that there were causal links among the budget deficit, real interest rates, the strong dollar, and the trade deficit.

Tax and regulatory restrictions on international capital movements would not be altered with the objective of shifting the dollar's rate, nor would the Regan Treasury pressure US allies and economic partners to revise their monetary or fiscal policies to achieve a lower dollar. Instead, using the strong dollar as leverage, the administration pressured allies, particularly socialist France, to tighten monetary policies to reduce inflation.

In sum, the Treasury would no longer do anything to make the dollar's value different from the unique rate determined by domestic and foreign macroeco-

---

1988), 142. For a broader analysis of Reagan's leadership style, see I. M. Destler, "Reagan and the World: An 'Awesome Stubbornness'," in Charles O. Jones, ed., *The Reagan Legacy* (Chatham, NJ: Chatham House, 1988), 241–61.

8. US Congress, Joint Economic Committee, *International Economic Policy*, hearings, 97th Cong., 1st sess., 4 May 1981, 27–28.

nomic policies and the plethora of private economic forces. It would not counteract speculative bubbles generated by the expectations of private actors unrelated to government policy and unjustified by the "fundamentals." Nor would it try to dampen extreme fluctuations in the exchange rate. And it certainly would not resurrect the gold standard for the dollar.[9] Except in those rare cases when fluctuations became "disorderly," the Treasury's new leadership believed, private agents were able to provide stability at least as well as government. The Regan Treasury apparently did not even develop a view of the preferred exchange rate level or movement for use within the administration.

Sprinkel argued that correctly setting the main domestic policies—deregulation, reducing the size of government, and above all maintaining steady money supply growth—was the best contribution the government could make to the private sector. The exchange rate was a by-product of these (and foreign macroeconomic) policy settings. The government could influence the exchange rate, but only at the cost of compromising fundamental policies, he argued. Other than that there was no effective way to manage the dollar. Sterilized intervention, in particular, risked public funds, discouraged private participation, and in any case could not affect the exchange rate on a lasting basis. Sprinkel and Regan did not like the soaring budget deficits, but they denied that they affected the international value of the dollar.[10]

Notwithstanding this analysis, the dollar moved dramatically. Driven initially by tight monetary policy, and then by a mix of very loose fiscal and moderate monetary policy, it appreciated, with temporary pauses and reversals, throughout the first Reagan administration (figures 2.3 to 2.5). The pattern varied somewhat by currency. For example, the peak against the Japanese yen was actually reached in November 1982, at 278 yen to the dollar; the rate then fell to 232 yen by the end of 1983. In contrast, the dollar rose from 2.25 to 2.72 German marks over the two years 1982–83. When the dollar reached its overall peak in late February 1985, it stood at 263 yen and 3.44 marks. At that point, on a

---

9. Secretary Regan used a special commission created to study the role of gold to punctuate his opposition to reestablishing gold parity and convertibility for the dollar, which would have required continuous intervention. The Gold Commission was created by Congress at the end of the Carter administration as a condition for an IMF quota increase and quickly became the hope of the "gold bugs" within the Reagan coalition. Its final report, however, did not endorse radical changes, was riddled with dissenting objections of commission members, and effectively ended further serious discussion of the issue. A majority of the commission, which Regan chaired, supported his position: "We favor no change in the flexible exchange rate system. In addition, we favor no change in the usage of gold in the operation of the present exchange rate arrangements." *Report to the Congress of the Commission on the Role of Gold in the Domestic and International Monetary Systems* (Washington: US Department of the Treasury, March 1982), I, 20.

10. Sprinkel's statements before Congress are cited in notes 8 and 13. For a more comprehensive statement see Council of Economic Advisers, *Economic Report of the President,* January 1989, chap. 3.

Figure 2.3 Yen-dollar exchange rate, 1980–1989

yen per dollar (monthly average of market rates)

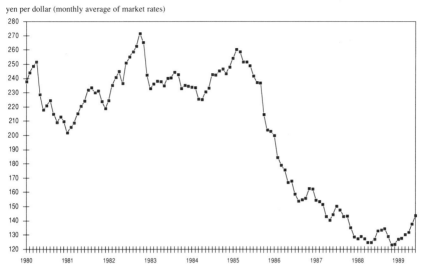

SOURCE: *International Financial Statistics*, various issues.

multilateral, effective basis, the dollar had appreciated over the average level in 1980 by 67 percent by the International Monetary Fund's measure and by 88.2 percent by the Fed's measure. Despite this unprecedented rise, the Regan Treasury intervened during only 10 episodes from the spring of 1981 through January 1985. The gross magnitude of this intervention was about $1.1 billion; net intervention was less than $1 billion—trivial by any meaningful standard.[11] (In contrast, during the 11 months following the Louvre Accord of February 1987, net US intervention totaled $9.9 billion.)

Over the same period, the central banks of the other G-10 governments intervened on the order of many tens of billions of dollars—and maintained tight monetary policies—to prevent their currencies from depreciating further against the dollar. Chafing under high interest rates, foreign governments complained vehemently about the American fiscal-monetary policy mix and nonintervention policy. They succeeded in placing the matter high on the agendas of the G-7 economic summit meetings at Versailles in 1982 and Williamsburg in 1983 and of the (then quietly held) G-5 meetings of finance ministers and central bankers, but they did not succeed in changing Reagan

---

11. "Treasury and Federal Reserve Foreign Exchange Operations," *Federal Reserve Bank of New York Quarterly Review*, various issues, Autumn 1981–Spring 1985. We count a few consecutive days of intervention as one "episode."

Figure 2.4 Mark-dollar exchange rate, 1980-1989

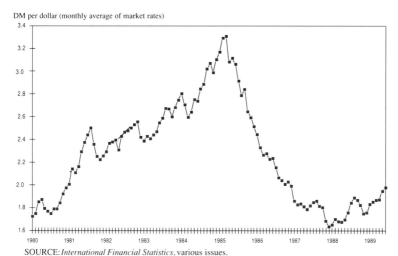

DM per dollar (monthly average of market rates)

SOURCE: *International Financial Statistics*, various issues.

administration policy.[12] (The United States, Japan, Germany, France, and Great Britain comprise the G-5. The G-7 includes Italy and Canada.)

Senior Treasury officials intermittently offered some public encouragement to those hurt by the strong dollar. Although Sprinkel continued to deny that it was analytically feasible to determine whether a currency was over- or undervalued, during 1982 and 1983 he occasionally predicted that the dollar would decline. When the low value of the yen became an issue in Washington, Sprinkel argued, vaguely, that Japanese trade and capital-market liberalization would be in the interest of the United States.[13]

---

12. C. Randall Henning, *Macroeconomic Diplomacy in the 1980s: Domestic Politics and International Conflict among the United States, Japan, and Europe,* Atlantic Paper 65 (London: Croom Helm, 1987), 13–23.

13. Sprinkel's assessments of the impact of Japanese capital-market liberalization on the yen-dollar rate were mixed. For examples of his testimony to Congress, see US Congress, House, Committee on Ways and Means, Subcommittee on Trade, *Fair Practices in Automotive Products Act,* hearings on H.R. 5133, 97th Cong., 2d sess., September and October 1983; *Current Exchange Rate Relationship of the U.S. Dollar and the Japanese Yen,* hearings, 97th Cong., 2d sess., 30 November 1982; *United States–Japan Trade Relations,* hearings, 98th Cong., 1st sess., March and April 1983; House, Committee on Banking, Subcommittees on International Trade and Domestic Monetary Policy, *Joint Hearings,* October and November 1983; Senate, Committee on Banking, *Federal Reserve's Second Monetary Policy Report for 1983,* hearings, 98th Cong., 1st sess., 21 and 28 July 1983.

Figure 2.5 Nominal effective dollar exchange rate index, 1980–1989

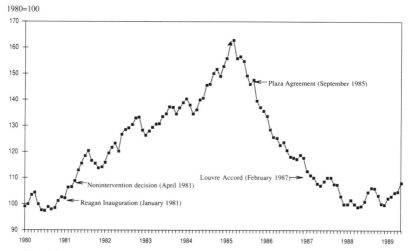

1980=100

SOURCE: *International Financial Statistics*, various issues. The index is based on weights derived from the International Monetary Fund's Multilateral Exchange Rate Model.

Secretary Regan strayed at times a little further from complete neutrality. On a couple of occasions he stated or implied that a depreciation of the dollar would be desirable, although the Treasury would do nothing to bring it about.[14] At the end of 1982, Regan surprised many observers by calling for a "new Bretton Woods" conference to discuss changes in the international monetary regime.[15] He and Sprinkel also agreed to conduct studies within the G-7 and G-10 deputies groups on the effectiveness of intervention and the international monetary system.[16]

These departures from pure laissez-faire attitudes reflected, among other things, disagreements within the Treasury over Sprinkel's policies and the ambivalence of Regan over dollar policy. Such declaratory "concessions" to foreign governments and American producing interests were also tactical, designed to deflect pressures and to keep the nonintervention policy intact.

---

14. *New York Times*, 29 March 1982; *Business Week: Special Report*, 27 June 1983.

15. *International Herald Tribune*, 7 December 1982.

16. The results of these studies are reported in "Treasury and Federal Reserve Foreign Exchange Operations," *Federal Reserve Bank of New York Quarterly Review* 8 (Autumn 1983): 48, and "Report of the G-10 Deputies on the Functioning of the International Monetary System," *IMF Survey* 14 (July 1985): 2–14.

Neither the occasional words of encouragement nor the results of international studies signaled or led to a change in the Treasury's bottom line on the exchange rate: the Treasury would not act to promote a depreciation, or even a "capping" of the dollar, in any way.

Indeed, from the standpoint of the tradeable-goods sector, the administration's declaratory policy actually became worse than neutral. Rather than simply remaining silent during the rapid appreciation of the dollar, the President and the Secretary of the Treasury came to celebrate it. During 1984, Regan argued that the strong dollar reflected the strong American economy, cited its beneficial effects on US inflation and foreign growth, and observed with complacency that the dollar might not begin to weaken for three more years.[17] Both he and the President continued to argue through the summer of 1985 that a strong dollar was a good thing. As late as September, the President declared that external deficits were not harmful to the economy, cheered foreign capital inflow, and challenged the assertion (based on US Commerce Department statistics) that the United States had become a debtor country.[18]

What accounts for this perverse shift in declaratory policy in 1984–85? Doubtless, one reason was that the strength of the economic recovery took the administration leaders off the political defensive. Until 1983, the actual fruits of Reaganomics had been sour, but during that year, the Reagan boom took hold, first economically and then politically. The Treasury, like the President, made more concessions to its critics when the economy was weak in 1981–82 than when the Reagan recovery was roaring in 1984.[19] "America was back," and celebrations of the strong dollar were consistent with this spirit of economic success. They also had a second, highly practical purpose. The burgeoning US demand for savings, both for private investment and to finance the budget deficit, generated a voracious appetite for foreign funds. Upbeat words from Washington might just help to attract them.

The Need for International Borrowing

By early 1983 it had become clear that a major by-product of the Reagan economic program was enormous, persistent budget deficits. In the absence of

---

17. *New York Times*, 1 and 23 February and 5 June 1984.

18. See White House, "News Conference by the President," press release, Washington, 17 September 1985, 8–9.

19. For a description of this pattern as it applied to fiscal policy, see David A. Stockman, *The Triumph of Politics: The Inside Story of the Reagan Revolution* (New York: Avon Books, 1987). Stockman observes that President Reagan was most responsive to pressure to compromise on taxes when there was bad news about the economy or when he was politically vulnerable.

a huge, offsetting increase in private savings, these deficits would—in a closed economy—have crowded out a substantial fraction of private investment. This would have driven interest rates much higher, dampened the economic recovery, and probably generated political pressure for a reversal of Reagan's economic policies.

For the open US economy of the 1980s, however, foreign capital was more than available—it was plentiful. In the words of former British Prime Minister Harold Macmillan, Reagan "called in the resources of the old world in order to finance the expansion of the new." As long as capital flowed in from abroad, the burgeoning budget deficit would not crowd out private borrowers, and interest rates would remain several percentage points lower than they would be otherwise.[20] By borrowing abroad, the administration could avoid or defer the choice, inevitable in a closed economy, among cutting spending programs prized by important constituencies, raising taxes, or crushing the interest-rate-sensitive segments of the economy.

The road the administration followed required squeezing traded-goods producers, however, and this economic logic was clearly perceived by some of the President's advisers. In a memo to the Cabinet in the spring of 1983, the new Chairman of the Council of Economic Advisers, Martin S. Feldstein, put the question directly:

> Would it be desirable to have a lower exchange value of the dollar? A weaker dollar would raise exports and reduce the substitution of imports for domestically produced goods. As such, it would be welcomed by those U.S. industries that are now being hurt by the strength of the dollar.
>
> But a weaker dollar and smaller trade deficit would also mean less capital inflow from the rest of the world and therefore a lower level of domestic investment in plant and equipment and in housing. The rise in the dollar is a safety valve that reduces pressure on domestic interest rates; the increase in the trade deficit allows the extra demand generated by the budget deficit to spill overseas instead of crowding out domestic investment.
>
> The question of whether it would be desirable to have a lower-valued dollar is equivalent to asking whether it is better to allow the temporary increase in the budget deficit to reduce domestic investment and interest-sensitive consumer spending or to reduce the production of goods for export and of goods that compete with imports from abroad. The answer to this question is clear in principle: it is better to reduce exports and increase imports. . . .

---

20. Stephen Marris estimates that private capital inflow held US interest rates as much as 5 percentage points lower during 1983–84 (*Deficits and the Dollar*, 44). See Chapter 2 of Marris's study for an analysis of the contribution of weak recovery in Europe and Japan to these capital movements. (The Macmillan quotation appears on page 1.)

> The basic fact is that the value of the dollar can be changed only by modifying the goals for our domestic economy.[21]

Feldstein was not arguing for foreign borrowing as intrinsically desirable, but rather as a temporary, second-best strategy. He was underscoring that the strong dollar was a necessary consequence of the capital inflows, which were themselves a positive development given the existing fiscal situation. However, both he and Federal Reserve Chairman Paul A. Volcker, as well as others outside the administration, warned that there were limits to the willingness of foreigners to lend to the United States, and that the budget deficits would be onerous indeed once that foreign capital dried up. Feldstein and Volcker argued that the solution to the strong dollar, the trade deficits, and the risks of dependence on capital inflows was to reduce the federal budget deficit.[22] But neither of them was in a position to reverse the administration's fiscal policy.[23]

The administration opted in practice in favor of the sectors of the economy "exposed" to interest rates, government spending, and taxes and against the sectors exposed to international competition. This was not, apparently, a conscious *political* strategy—we are not aware of anyone within the administration arguing, for example, that the interests of the tradeable-goods sector were to be given second priority to those of the interest-sensitive sector. Nevertheless, given the choices facing the administration in the middle of its first term, foreign borrowing was the path of least economic and political resistance, at least in the medium term.

Once the administration arrived at this solution, the Treasury pursued it with enthusiasm. Regan and Sprinkel moved in 1984 to use tax and regulatory changes at home and abroad not simply to increase borrowing from abroad but to permanently expand the pool of internationally mobile capital on which the United States could draw.[24] They were aided by David C. Mulford, the former

---

21. Martin S. Feldstein, "Memorandum for the Cabinet Council on Economic Affairs, Subject: Is the Dollar Overvalued?" 8 April 1983, cited in William Greider, *Secrets of the Temple: How the Federal Reserve Runs the Country* (New York: Simon and Schuster, 1987), 597.

22. Paul A. Volcker, "The Twin Deficits," *Challenge* 26 (March/April 1984): 4–9; Martin S. Feldstein, "Why the Dollar Is Strong," *Challenge* 26 (January/February 1984): 37–41.

23. Nor was Budget Director Stockman. See *The Triumph of Politics,* especially chap. 12.

24. Some analysts proposed exactly the opposite course of action. Conscious of the real effects of trade deficits on production and employment, C. Fred Bergsten, for example, advocated the erection of controls on Japanese capital outflows to prevent net flows to the United States from pushing the yen down against the dollar. The Treasury, however, flatly rejected this advice. See C. Fred Bergsten, "What To Do About the U.S.–Japan Economic Conflict," *Foreign Affairs* 60 (Summer 1982): 1054–75, and "The United States Trade Deficit and the Dollar," statement before the Senate Banking Subcommittee on International Finance and Monetary Policy, 6 June 1984.

senior adviser to the Saudi Arabian Monetary Authority and now Assistant Secretary of the Treasury for International Affairs.

First, the Treasury pressured other governments to liberalize their capital markets. Japan was the most important object of these liberalization efforts and in fact had been so since 1982. In the yen-dollar agreement concluded in May 1984, the Treasury won most of what it had sought from the Japanese Ministry of Finance. Although the agreement included measures to promote both inflows and outflows of Japanese capital, the net effect was to liberate large sums of Japanese savings for American use.[25]

Second, the Treasury sought changes in US law intended to make American securities more attractive to foreign buyers. The administration persuaded the Congress in the 1984 tax bill to eliminate the 30 percent withholding tax on interest payments to foreign holders of US government and corporate bonds. Access to the Eurobond markets for US corporate and government borrowers was the proximate motive for changing the law.[26] The Treasury also received authority to determine whether such bonds could be issued to foreigners in bearer form, and it immediately granted permission for corporations to do so.

Third, the Treasury designed a new bond issue especially for foreign buyers. In September 1984 Sprinkel traveled to Tokyo, and Mulford to Europe, to market the bonds.

Foreign purchases of US government and corporate bonds surged during 1984 and the years that followed, making Sprinkel and Regan the greatest bond salesmen in history. Net foreign purchases of US Treasury securities more than doubled during 1984, from the 1983 level of $13 billion to $31 billion, and net foreign purchases of US corporate bonds rose to $16 billion from $0.6 billion.[27] During 1984–86, foreign holdings of US corporate bonds increased from $35 billion to $161 billion. Together foreign purchases of US Treasury and corporate securities comprised more than 41 percent of the increase in total liabilities to foreigners during those three years, compared to about 16 percent during 1981–83.[28] Of course, the bulk of this private capital almost certainly would have flowed to the United States even in the absence of changes in withholding,

---

25. Jeffrey A. Frankel, *The Yen/Dollar Agreement: Liberalizing Japanese Capital Markets,* POLICY ANALYSES IN INTERNATIONAL ECONOMICS 9 (Washington: Institute for International Economics, December 1984). See our analysis of the private and governmental pressures on the Treasury to negotiate the accord in Chapters 3 and 8.

26. See US Congress, Joint Committee on Taxation, *General Explanation of the Revenue Provisions of the Deficit Reduction Act of 1984,* joint committee print, 98th Cong., 2d sess., 31 December 1984, 387–98.

27. *Survey of Current Business* 67 (June 1987): 38–45, tables 1 and 2. See also Organization for Economic Cooperation and Development, *Economic Survey: United States* (Paris: OECD, November 1985), 64; Marris, *Deficits and the Dollar,* 228.

28. Calculated from *Survey of Current Business* 67 (June 1987): 38–45, tables 1 and 2.

registration, and foreign capital controls. But these data support the contention that the Regan-Sprinkel policy changes fostered greater net capital inflows on easier terms than might otherwise have taken place.

A visible drive to bring down the dollar would have been inconsistent with the administration's effort to sell dollar-denominated liabilities to foreigners. Conversely, to the extent that some investors expected a further appreciation of the dollar in the short term, and therefore foreign-exchange gains from investing in dollar assets, the refusal of the Regan Treasury to talk the dollar down facilitated capital inflows. The President and his Treasury officials derived important short-term financial benefits from the strong dollar. This may help to explain the subtle change in Regan and Sprinkel's publicly stated expectations of exchange rate trends between 1982–83 and 1984–85. It may even help explain why, with the dollar near its peak, President Reagan, in his 1985 State of the Union message, called for making the United States the "investment capital of the world."[29]

The Role of the Federal Reserve

Privately, Federal Reserve Chairman Volcker clashed with the Treasury over foreign-exchange intervention. Volcker, with the support of Anthony M. Solomon, President of the New York Federal Reserve Bank, which conducts foreign-currency operations, urged the Treasury to authorize intervention in substantial amounts during periods of unusual instability.[30] But the Fed was already under attack from members of Congress and, periodically, the administration for its extremely tight domestic monetary policy, particularly during 1981–82, and so Volcker was reluctant to confront the Treasury squarely on international monetary policy as well.

Publicly, therefore, Volcker adopted a position on intervention that tended to minimize these differences. Testifying before Congress, for example, he said that intervention could have an impact on the markets in some circumstances but that it was a "subsidiary tool" to be used with caution and was ineffective against basic monetary or fiscal policy for any sustained period of time.[31] Regan

---

29. "The State of the Union," Address Delivered Before a Joint Session of the Congress, 6 February 1985, reprinted in *Weekly Compilation of Presidential Documents* 21(6): 140.

30. For a graphic example of these private differences, see Yoichi Funabashi, *Managing the Dollar: From the Plaza to the Louvre,* 2d ed. (Washington: Institute for International Economics, 1989), 68. On the respective exchange rate authorities of the Treasury and the Federal Reserve, see our treatment in Chapter 5.

31. US Congress, House, Committee on Banking, Subcommittee on Domestic Monetary Policy, *Legislation for Alternative Targets for Monetary Policy,* hearings, 98th Cong., 1st sess., 26 April, 11 May, and 3 August 1983, 204–05, 244; Subcommittee on Economic

and Sprinkel showed reciprocal understanding: when Volcker privately urged them to intervene, they did not respond that he should instead loosen monetary policy, even when they were frustrated with the Fed's stance.

By and large, the Fed did not conduct monetary policy with a view toward stemming appreciation of the dollar.[32] The main objective of Volcker and the other Federal Reserve Board members was to suppress inflation, and appreciation of the dollar contributed to this goal. Volcker and his colleagues also wanted to prevent a recurrence of inflationary expectations during the recovery, and given loose fiscal policy they saw no alternative to maintaining real interest rates at unusually high levels even after inflation fell sharply. Preventing dollar appreciation through monetary measures alone would have meant policies so expansionary as to constitute abandonment of the primary anti-inflation campaign.

The Fed was concerned about the adverse consequences of the strong dollar: trade deficits and their impact on the economy (and the trade protectionism they generated), and the prospect of a sudden cutoff of capital inflow. But because Volcker did not want to. risk the inflationary effects of an easing of monetary policy, his only recourse was to add his voice to those arguing that the trade deficits were linked to the budget deficits and that the administration and Congress should reduce the latter.[33] In a closed economy, an independent central bank might pressure a profligate fiscal authority by refusing to "monetize" the budget deficit, thereby permitting sharp increases in interest rates. But US access to foreign capital denied the Fed even this source of leverage. Steadfast pursuit of low inflation and financial stability, in which Volcker and his Board believed deeply and from which they derived great personal authority, was their best bet given the choices.

To sum up, neglect of the exchange rate in the first Reagan administration was initially a product of domestic priorities, reinforced by a strong free-market ideology at the Treasury. Toward the end of Reagan's first term, that policy was reinforced also by an interest in marketing America's burgeoning debt overseas. The policy of exchange rate neglect was not, by all of our evidence, a response

---

Stabilization, *Federal Reserve's Second Monetary Policy Report for 1983,* hearings, 98th Cong., 1st sess., 21 and 28 July 1983, 293–94.

32. An exception was early 1985, when Volcker acknowledged that the high dollar inhibited the Fed from tightening. *Wall Street Journal,* 27 February 1985.

33. During the first Reagan term, Volcker was regularly asked whether, if the administration and Congress promised to take strong action on the budget deficit, he would commit the Fed to easing monetary policy in order to offset the dampening effect of such action on economic recovery. Volcker declined to enter such a deal. He felt such a precedent would jeopardize the Fed's independence, and he feared that the Fed might end up the only party to deliver on its promises. Instead, he made clear his expectation that if the administration and Congress took such action, an important consequence would be a lowering of interest rates and a depreciation of the dollar.

to outside lobbying by either private interests at home or officials abroad. Virtually all such direct lobbying on the exchange rate was, in fact, in the other direction, for an activist policy and depreciation.

By its own domestic measures, the first Reagan administration's economic program performed well. Inflation fell dramatically, and growth surged strongly in the first half of 1984. Avoiding the hard budget choices, maintaining domestic consumption, and borrowing from abroad proved to be politically astute in the medium run. Nevertheless, even in the year of President Reagan's overwhelming reelection victory, objections were being raised about the external impact of Reagan's "domesticism." By the end of 1984, the exchange rate had become an important public issue not only among the G-7 partners, which could be ignored, but in domestic American politics, where it would catch the attention of the second Reagan administration.

3

Political Pressure and Policy Change, 1984–1985

Criticism of exchange rate neglect and dollar overvaluation began early in the Reagan administration, but virtually no one, to our knowledge, fully anticipated either the magnitude or the duration of the misalignment that would emerge. Indeed, during most of the dollar's rise, the consensus near-term forecast was for a depreciation. But a number of economists did predict, some as early as 1981, that the mix of tight monetary and loose fiscal policy would elevate the dollar and create large trade deficits, and they called for immediate remedial action to avert or limit its impact.[1]

Burgeoning Pressure for Change

The Private Sector

The early 1980s saw political activity by some interests particularly affected by the dollar's rise. Caterpillar, Inc., a company highly dependent on foreign export markets, began raising the exchange rate issue in late 1982, with the support of the Business Roundtable Task Force on International Trade and Investment, which Caterpillar board chairman Lee L. Morgan then chaired. Morgan called the yen-dollar rate, then above 270, "the single most important trade issue facing the U.S." Senator Charles H. Percy (R-IL), from Caterpillar's home state,

---

1. C. Fred Bergsten, "The Costs of Reaganomics," *Foreign Policy* 44 (Fall 1981): 24–36; C. Fred Bergsten and John Williamson, "Exchange Rates and Trade Policy," in William R. Cline, ed., *Trade Policy in the 1980s* (Washington: Institute for International Economics, 1983), 99–120; Lawrence A. Fox and Stephen Cooney, "Protectionism Returns," *Foreign Policy* 53 (Winter 1983–84): 74–90.

Table 3.1 US merchandise trade, 1970–1988

Year	Billions of current dollars			Billions of 1982 dollars		
	Imports	Exports	Balance	Imports	Exports	Balance
1970	40.9	44.5	3.6	150.9	120.6	−30.3
1971	46.6	45.6	−1.0	166.2	119.3	−46.9
1972	56.9	51.7	−5.2	190.7	131.3	−59.4
1973	71.8	73.9	2.1	218.2	160.6	−57.6
1974	104.5	101.0	−3.5	211.8	175.8	−36.0
1975	99.0	109.6	10.6	187.9	171.5	−16.4
1976	124.3	117.5	−6.8	229.3	177.5	−51.8
1977	151.9	123.1	−28.8	259.4	178.1	−81.3
1978	176.5	144.7	−31.8	274.1	196.2	−77.9
1979	211.9	183.3	−28.6	277.9	218.2	−59.7
1980	247.5	225.1	−22.4	253.6	241.8	−11.8
1981	266.5	238.3	−28.2	258.7	238.5	−20.2
1982	249.5	214.0	−35.5	249.5	214.0	−35.5
1983	271.3	206.1	−65.2	282.2	207.6	−74.6
1984	334.3	224.1	−110.2	351.1	223.8	−127.3
1985	340.9	220.8	−120.1	367.9	231.6	−136.3
1986	367.7	225.0	−142.7	412.3	243.7	−168.6
1987	413.0	254.8	−158.2	439.0	280.1	−158.9
1988	449.7	321.6	−128.1	469.8	341.5	−128.3

Note: Export data are f.a.s. (free-alongside-ship) values; import data are US Customs values.

Sources: Survey of Current Business, various issues; Council of Economic Advisers, Economic Report of the President, February 1988.

pushed a Senate resolution to put exchange rates near the top of the agenda at the Williamsburg summit of May 1983.

Private-sector concern over the strong dollar was limited, however, by the deep recession of 1981–82, which initially masked the strong dollar's trade impact by depressing import demand. During that period political pressure on trade came primarily from firms and workers in such industries as automobiles and steel, whose problems predated the dollar's rise and were exacerbated by the overall economic slump. It was not until the Reagan recovery gained force that the US trade deficit mushroomed and the effects of the strong dollar became real and visible (table 3.1).

By early 1984 it had become clear that the United States was headed for its first 12-digit trade deficit—the largest any nation had ever experienced. Alarming as they were, the dollar figures understated the pain inflicted on Americans

Figure 3.1 Capacity utilization rates in manufacturing, United States, 1970–1989

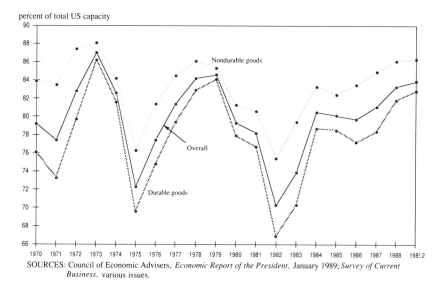

percent of total US capacity

SOURCES: Council of Economic Advisers, *Economic Report of the President*, January 1989; *Survey of Current Business*, various issues.

who were competing with foreign producers in the US market. For the rising dollar *depressed* US import prices, which were declining, on average, from 1981 through 1986. By adjusting for price changes, constant-dollar trade statistics provide a better indicator of what mattered most to US producers, namely, changes in import *volumes*. Table 3.1 shows that, for 1984, US imports in 1982 dollars were $351.1 billion (in current dollars the figure for that year was $334.3 billion); for 1985 imports in constant 1982 dollars were $367.9 billion (compared to $340.9 billion). The trade deficit, measured in 1982 dollars, reached $127.3 and $136.3 billion in 1984 and 1985, respectively.[2]

As a result of the surge in imports, US capacity utilization departed from its usual pattern during economic recoveries and actually declined in 1985 and again in 1986, finally attaining a level comparable to the previous cyclical peak only in early 1989 (figure 3.1). The growth of manufacturers' unfilled orders slowed between 1984 and 1986 (figure 3.2). Notwithstanding overall real GNP growth of 3.6 percent in 1983 and 6.8 percent in 1984, employment in manufacturing hardly rebounded at all from the recession. From a level of 20.3 million in 1980, the number of US workers employed in manufacturing fell to an average of 18.8 million in 1982 and 18.4 million in 1983, before recovering

---

2. See Chapter 7 for an elaboration of the worsening ratio of imports to production in real terms, and the impact of that trend on political activity by private groups.

Figure 3.2 Manufacturers' unfilled orders, United States, 1970–1989

billions of dollars; seasonally adjusted

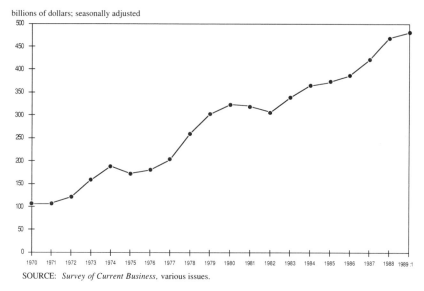

SOURCE: *Survey of Current Business*, various issues.

slightly to 19.4 million in 1984 and 19.3 million in 1985.[3] The strong dollar was not the only cause of this sluggishness, but it was widely and accurately perceived to be a primary cause.

This shift in people's economic fortunes generated a potent political response. By mid-1983 the Business Roundtable had lent its full support to Morgan's Task Force's effort to lower the dollar's value, and in February 1984 the Board of Directors of the National Association of Manufacturers was going on record explicitly against the strong dollar. But affiliation with the Republican Party and interest in Reagan's reelection in 1984 muted complaints from other quarters of the business sector until November. And the economic recovery in 1983–84 offered more than offsetting good news for many businesses—real growth in 1984 was the greatest in more than three decades, whereas inflation remained moderate at 3.9 percent.

The force of exchange rate lobbying was muted also by the variety of prescriptions offered by those advocating a lower dollar. While some called for direct intervention in foreign-exchange markets, others stressed budget deficit reduction, monetary loosening, or measures to stimulate capital outflow. If the dollar depreciation movement was multifocused in its policy targets, it was also multifocused in its political targets. Once rebuffed by the Treasury, various lobbying groups appealed to different governmental bodies—the White House,

---

3. Joint Economic Committee, *Economic Indicators*, June 1989, 14.

other executive agencies, or various audiences on Capitol Hill—and their efforts were inevitably sporadic, given the lack of a public timetable for decisions on exchange rates or international monetary policy.

By early 1985, however, the economic squeeze from the strong dollar had become serious, and many economists were arguing that much of the impact of dollar appreciation had yet to be felt in real trade performance. Furthermore, while the dollar fell that spring from its spike at the end of February, Treasury officials (and most other economists) were not willing to predict that the dollar had reached its peak and would not continue to rise.[4] The dollar did in fact rebound in the late summer. Although many private economists recognized that the dollar would depreciate in the long run, few were bold enough in the spring or summer of 1985 to declare confidently that the dollar was now on a permanent downward path.[5] President Reagan's refusal to acknowledge the strong dollar's damage to the economy and his cheering of capital inflows further undercut any confidence that the US currency would not resume its upward climb.

US industry therefore mounted a major assault on the administration's international economic policy in 1985. In the spring and summer, months before the Plaza Agreement, most of the important business and trade associations as well as many individual business leaders wrote Cabinet officials arguing that the dollar was too high and that the administration was not giving the matter sufficient attention. As described in detail in Chapter 7, they demanded meetings with the President, his chief aides, and the leaders at the Treasury.

Many groups that had not previously been heard from, such as the US Council for International Business, became active in 1985, whereas others that had long supported administration policy, such as the US Chamber of Commerce, fell silent. Much of the lobbying was strongly critical of the Treasury's hands-off policy, and all of these private groups pressed the administration to reduce the budget deficit in order to bring the dollar down. (Despite Treasury denials, it was widely acknowledged that the budget deficits were closely linked to the strong dollar. Many agreed with Feldstein's and Volcker's argument that reducing the budget deficit was the key to reducing the trade deficit.) Many of these groups also warned against embarking on trade-liberalization talks under

---

4. See, for example, the testimony of Assistant Secretary for Economic Policy Manuel H. Johnson in US Congress, House, Committee on Banking, *United States Trade and Competitiveness,* hearings, 99th Cong., 1st sess., 16 and 30 April, 14 May, 26 June, and 24 and 31 July 1985, 299–305.

5. In late 1985 and early 1986, in contrast, many economists argued confidently that the depreciation of the dollar since February 1985 had been inevitable, given the drop in real long-term interest rate differentials, and that therefore the Plaza Agreement had no substantial effect on the exchange rate.

the auspices of the General Agreement on Tariffs and Trade (GATT) without first correcting US macroeconomic and exchange rate policy.

The Congress

A prime outlet for business frustrations was Capitol Hill. Senators, Congress-men, and their staffs were deluged with demands that Congress take action itself or that it join in turning up the heat on the White House and the Treasury. During the first Reagan term, Congress had refrained from direct action to change dollar policy. Committees with jurisdiction over finance, banking, commerce, and foreign affairs had held numerous hearings on the dollar and related international financial issues, and the Senate had passed the exchange rate resolution sponsored by Senator Percy. A task force on trade, created by House Democrats, had identified the strong dollar as the main cause of the trade deficit and urged the administration to take the lead in international monetary reform.[6] Through hearings, resolutions, and symbolic advocacy, the Congress had vented frustration with the strong dollar and signaled the administration of its concern.

However, the further appreciation of the dollar through February 1985, the deadlock on budget deficit reduction that spring, and heightened industry pressure persuaded many members of Congress that routine oversight and consciousness-raising were no longer sufficient. Both Republicans and Demo-crats had hoped, for reasons of domestic management as well as international competitiveness, that the passing of the 1984 election would bring new progress in reducing the budget deficit. Those members representing tradeable-goods interests had renewed cause for alarm when it became clear in the late spring that substantial budget deficit reductions were not in sight. Members of Congress then had to give fresh consideration to second-best strategies to reduce the value of the dollar, such as exchange market intervention.[7]

Moreover, in rejecting a budget compromise crafted by Senate Republicans in the spring of 1985, the President alienated many on the Hill who were in a position to challenge the administration on trade policy. Republicans on the Senate Finance Committee, including Majority Leader Robert Dole (R-KS), had gone out on a limb by agreeing to limitations on Social Security cost-of-living adjustments (COLAs) as part of the budget deficit reduction package. Feeling betrayed by the White House, they were in no mood to do the administration

---

6. National House Democratic Caucus, *Competing for the Future: A Democratic Strategy for Trade* (Washington: National House Democratic Caucus, February 1984).

7. See, for example, US Congress, Senate, Committee on Finance, *Floating Exchange Rates' Impact on International Trading*, hearings, 99th Cong., 1st sess., 23 and 24 April 1985.

any favors when business, labor, and agricultural groups pressured them to move on protectionist trade legislation, also within their jurisdiction.

Making matters worse, the President demonstrated insensitivity to both trade policy and domestic trade politics in February 1985 by abandoning the voluntary export restraint agreement on Japanese automobiles without asking for any Japanese concession. His transfer of William E. Brock in March from the post of US Trade Representative to that of Secretary of Labor—leaving the trade post unfilled for three months—simply poured salt in the wounds of trade-minded business leaders and legislators alike.

Therefore, in early 1985, senior members of Congress responsible for trade on the Senate Finance and House Ways and Means Committees (Republicans as well as Democrats) generated a veritable explosion of trade legislation initiatives.[8] Senator John C. Danforth (R-MO) won unanimous Senate passage of a resolution endorsing trade retaliation against Japan and vaguely threatened to take up across-the-board import surcharge legislation. Just before the Bonn economic summit in May, he and Senator Lloyd Bentsen (D-TX) explicitly linked their approval of a new GATT round to inclusion of monetary issues. Danforth emphatically stated, "Resolving the exchange rate problem is the *sine qua non* of effective trade policy."[9]

With such demands unanswered, in July 1985 three respected senior Democrats—Bentsen and Representatives Dan Rostenkowski (D-IL) and Richard A. Gephardt (D-MO)—introduced a bill, the forerunner of the notorious Gephardt amendment, that would have imposed 25 percent duties on imports from countries running large trade surpluses with the United States.

Members of Congress launched a second assault through the banking committees, this time directly on exchange rate policy. Just before the August recess, Senators Bill Bradley (D-NJ), Daniel Patrick Moynihan (D-NY), and Max S. Baucus (D-MT) submitted bills making foreign-exchange intervention in specified amounts mandatory when the United States was running large current account deficits. Any of these bills would have severely reduced Treasury and Fed discretion in intervention decisions if passed. Representatives Stan Lundine (D-NY) and John J. LaFalce (D-NY) cooperated on similar legislation in the House Banking Committee, and their bill became the basis for the exchange rate provisions of the 1988 trade act.

Because Congress had no direct leverage on exchange rate policymaking, however, the stronger pressure on the administration took the form of trade

---

8. See I. M. Destler, *American Trade Politics: System Under Stress* (Washington: Institute for International Economics; New York: Twentieth Century Fund, 1986), especially chaps. 4 and 9.

9. Sen. John C. Danforth, address to the National Press Club on United States Trade Policy, Washington, 25 April 1985. See also *Wall Street Journal,* 26 April 1985.

measures. Trade restrictions were not the preferred remedy of most legislators, but they were the only remedy on which they had a handle, and the protectionist threat was the most effective club Congress had to brandish against the administration. Congress did not want to make exchange rate policy itself—indeed, informed legislators saw no practical way for Congress to do so. Rather, they wanted the administration to respond to the pressures that Congress was feeling by taking action that would affect the exchange rate. This the administration clearly had not been doing.

The Executive Branch

If legislators were frustrated, at least equally so were those Cabinet members whose constituencies were being squeezed. As the dollar appreciated in 1984, Secretary of Commerce Malcolm Baldrige, US Trade Representative Brock, and Secretary of Agriculture John R. Block argued in favor of dollar depreciation in internal administration discussions.[10] Completely excluded from exchange rate policymaking, however, they could only petition an unbending Treasury, curse the "mandarins" who kept them and others out, or scheme to get around them. Block vented his frustration with both the policy and the process when he breakfasted in June 1985 with a midwestern businessman: upon learning that his companion was going to call upon Senate Majority Leader Dole later that day, Block urged him to tell the Senator to tell the President that the strong dollar was wreaking havoc with American agriculture!

Secretary of State George P. Shultz, himself a former Treasury Secretary and businessman, expressed sympathy for business complaints regarding the strong dollar, notwithstanding his own role in the move to floating rates in 1973. The State Department had been critical of the nonintervention policy from the very beginning, arguing that it unnecessarily antagonized the Europeans and the Japanese. Although no fan of intervention himself, Shultz strongly urged the Treasury to address seriously the yen-dollar misalignment. In preparing for the Reagan-Nakasone summit of November 1983, Shultz had proposed to his Japanese counterpart, Foreign Minister Shintaro Abe, that the yen-dollar problem be raised and cited the reluctance of the Treasury and Ministry of Finance to address it.[11] The yen-dollar agreement of April 1984 was in part an outgrowth of this initiative, although as negotiated by the Treasury it tended, on balance, to weaken the yen and aggravate the US–Japan trade conflict. In the spring of 1985 Shultz tried again. In an important speech at Princeton University

---

10. Yoichi Funabashi, *Managing the Dollar: From the Plaza to the Louvre*, 2d ed. (Washington: Institute for International Economics, 1989), 70.

11. Funabashi, *Managing the Dollar*, 78–79.

he pointed to capital flows and the strong dollar as the source of trade imbalances among the United States, Japan, Europe, and the developing countries. Only macroeconomic measures to alter savings-investment balances, he argued, would be able to rectify the trade imbalances, and those should be addressed "with great energy."[12]

Thus, there had developed by mid-1985 a potent domestic coalition of business leaders, members of Congress, Cabinet members with trade and foreign policy portfolios, and think tank scholars, all pressing for strong administration action to bring the dollar down. This created a political "market," inside as well as outside the administration, that would welcome policy change on trade and exchange rates. In particular, the movement of core Reagan supporters in the large multinational companies to the trade-activist camp decisively undercut the administration's capacity to maintain the liberal trade policies it clearly favored.

Policy Change in 1985

Facing these growing pressures was a new Secretary of the Treasury, James A. Baker III, who had served as White House chief of staff during Reagan's first term. Baker and Donald Regan stunned Washington in January 1985 with the announcement that they would be switching jobs. Baker was widely respected on Capitol Hill, and so confirmation presented no problem. Nevertheless, Senators questioned him pointedly at his confirmation hearings about his views on the dollar and his plans for exchange rate and international economic policies. Business groups had already made their case to Baker at the White House as part of their efforts to move the President, and so he was well aware of their difficulties. With Regan, Baker also had attended the January Group of Five (G-5) meeting at which the finance ministers discussed strengthening foreign-exchange intervention. (The Germans in particular would press Baker to live up to the spirit of the G-5 talks when the dollar soared in February.)

The President continued to champion the strong dollar and capital inflows. Baker at first offered Congress no more than acknowledgment of the dollar problem and a promise to take a fresh look. At his confirmation hearings, Senator George J. Mitchell (D-ME) asked Baker whether the dollar was overvalued and whether he would consider intervening to lower it. Baker declined to label the dollar as overvalued, but added:

> It's obviously very, very strong. I do think there are some things that can be done to help with that situation. . . getting our fiscal deficit down so that we have less

12. George P. Shultz, "National Policies and Global Prosperity," *Current Policy Series* 684 (Washington: US Department of State, 11 April 1985).

pressure on interest rates, and, therefore, perhaps less inclination to invest in the dollar. I also think that it's in the interest of this country to encourage our trading partners to adopt [tax cuts and deregulation, so that] their economies will come back just like ours has. And that will help with the value of the dollar. . . . I should not express, nor do I have, an opinion on whether our policy of intervening only where markets are disorderly should be changed. But that's obviously something that should be looked at because some will argue that that could have a dramatic effect on the value of the dollar.[13]

Baker also noted that the strong dollar depressed inflation, and he affirmed that the January G-5 statement "was not meant to indicate a radical change in policy." However, his acknowledgment of the links among budget deficits, the dollar, and trade deficits was already a change from the Regan-Sprinkel line.

As the political crisis over administration policy deepened, the new secretary responded forcefully, first with quiet consultations with his G-5 counterparts during the summer and then by a well-publicized show of the result at the Plaza Hotel in New York in September.[14] There the G-5 finance ministers and central bank governors confirmed their agreement to attack exchange rate misalignment. With understatement typical of official exchange rate pronouncements, they declared that "fundamental" economic conditions and policy commitments among their countries had "not been reflected fully in exchange markets" and that "exchange rates should play a role in adjusting external imbalances." For this reason, they concluded, "[S]ome further orderly appreciation of the main non-dollar currencies against the dollar is desirable."[15]

This dramatic, if understated, departure from previous Treasury policy was underscored when US authorities sold dollars for yen and marks in the New York market the next day. The downward movement of the dollar, which had stalled that summer, resumed dramatically, and rapid depreciation continued until early 1987.

---

13. US Congress, Senate, Committee on Finance, *Nomination of James A. Baker III,* hearing, 99th Cong., 1st sess., 23 January 1985, 22, 65.

14. For other accounts of the change in exchange rate policy in 1985, see Robert D. Putnam and Nicholas Bayne, *Hanging Together: Cooperation and Conflict in the Seven-Power Summits,* 2d ed. (Cambridge, MA: Harvard University Press, 1987), chap. 9, especially for the relationship to the G-7 summits; Funabashi, *Managing the Dollar,* chaps. 1 and 3; Stephen D. Cohen, *The Making of United States International Economic Policy: Principles, Problems, and Proposals for Reform,* 3d ed. (New York: Praeger, 1988), chap. 10; C. Randall Henning and I. M. Destler, "From Neglect to Activism: American Politics and the 1985 Plaza Accord," *Journal of Public Policy* 8 (June 1989): 317–33; Henry R. Nau, *American Phoenix: Leadership Power in the World Economy* (Princeton, NJ: Princeton University Press, forthcoming), chap. 9.

15. US Department of the Treasury, press release, Washington, 22 September 1985. As figure 2.4 shows, the dollar had receded by roughly 10 percent from the February-March level but was rising again in the weeks immediately before the Plaza meeting.

Baker's Choices

Why did Baker move as he did? In the words of an administration insider, he had come to office with few economic convictions other than "a Texan's aversion to high interest rates and a politician's indifference to longer-range policy effects."[16] As White House chief of staff, however, Baker had carved out a formidable reputation for effectiveness. Like others of similar mold, his bent was toward action, toward addressing problems where he personally could have an impact. Reinforcing this bent was Baker's Deputy Secretary Richard G. Darman, an adroit, substantively knowledgeable policy operator who had moved with Baker from the White House.

The Treasury portfolio gave Baker a license to seek economic policy leadership, international as well as domestic. The circumstances Baker faced, moreover, made it clear that *some* significant administration action was required. The question was what specific steps to take. Most who called for action pointed to the egregious budget deficit, which was heading toward records of $212 billion in fiscal year 1985 and $221 billion in fiscal year 1986. But the Treasury Secretary, unlike his finance minister counterparts abroad, is not the central executive branch official in the budgetary sphere. Baker also faced the same reluctant President who was frustrating Senator Dole and his colleagues on Capitol Hill. A second possible course to drive the dollar down would have been to lower US interest rates, but Baker was not the key player in this game either. He could and did seek to influence Paul Volcker at the Fed, but the domestic credit markets were Volcker's sphere of action.

Baker and Darman had strong incentives, then, to focus their initial efforts on something Treasury *could* dominate, namely, what we have labeled direct exchange rate policy. This was a matter on which Treasury had the "lead" and on which it could act—privately (with Fed cooperation) through intervention in foreign-exchange markets and publicly through official statements. The exchange rate arena was also particularly susceptible to a change in declaratory policy. The new leaders could gain credit and some leverage just by saying that the dollar needed to drop. Although they could not be absolutely certain that the exchange markets would respond to either intervention or declaration with an actual depreciation of the dollar, the economic and policy conditions were favorable, and the payoff of such a response was correctly anticipated to be substantial. Prospects for foreign cooperation were also favorable: since the United States' trading partners both feared US protectionism and were critical of the laissez-faire attitude of Regan and Sprinkel, they could be expected to cooperate in bringing the dollar down. If, on the other hand, the hands-off

---

16. William A. Niskanen, *Reaganomics: An Insider's Account of the Politics and the People* (New York: Oxford University Press, 1988), 173.

policy were continued, and the dollar did not come down, the Treasury would have to fight a two-front battle to retain its autonomy in exchange rate policy: against efforts in Congress to legislate guidelines and against other agencies within the executive branch.

In addition, one important drawback of dollar depreciation, inflation, was no longer a major concern in 1985. The economic recovery had matured, yet prices were rising at moderate rates: the increase in the Consumer Price Index would be below 4 percent in 1985 for the fourth consecutive year. Meanwhile unemployment still averaged above 7 percent, and capacity utilization was actually declining. Thus, the Treasury could talk the dollar down without fear that import price increases would push inflation back up to unacceptable rates. And Baker could be more certain of Volcker's cooperation, although the Fed chief was already concerned by summer 1985 that the dollar might fall too fast and too far.

The Multilateral Dimension

Another key aspect of the Baker-Darman strategy was its multilateralism: it was developed and implemented in cooperation with other leading advanced industrial nations. This began with the Plaza Agreement's specific commitments to coordinated foreign-exchange market intervention. It would be extended to a persistent push for macroeconomic policy adjustments by the surplus countries, centering on the economic indicators exercise announced at the Tokyo economic summit in May 1986 (see Chapter 4, especially note 11). The degree of coordination actually achieved should not be overstated. Intense conflict accompanied real cooperation in exchange rates, monetary policy, and fiscal policy over the years that followed the Plaza Agreement. But whatever the outcome of the G-5 negotiations, the US approach clearly became more outward reaching in 1985.

Why did Baker and Darman move in this direction? A simpler and quicker alternative would have been to stage a press conference to announce that the dollar was overvalued and should depreciate, and that the United States would aggressively purchase foreign currencies (a good buy at rates then prevailing) until exchange rates reached more reasonable levels. Such a statement could have added that the US government would encourage the Fed to lower interest rates while it sought to reduce the budget deficit, with the need to achieve international adjustment specifically in mind. Without a doubt, such a unilateral declaration would have had a strong impact on foreign-currency markets. The new Treasury leadership could have overturned the policy of nonintervention as unilaterally as the old leadership had imposed it.

Once a change in policy was decided upon, however, Treasury leaders had several incentives to adopt a multilateral approach. First, to forestall protectionist activity in Congress, Baker and other administration officials were eager to show that foreign governments were making a contribution to solving the United States' trade problems. The view that foreign governments' trade and exchange rate policies were unfair and contributed to the US trade deficit was reinforcing business and congressional frustration and was increasing the appeal of restrictive legislation. With the Plaza Agreement and subsequent accords, the administration could argue that Japan and Europe were acting as economic allies as well as competitors.

Second, multilateral cooperation was more promising for substantive reasons: it could better help to realign the dollar and promote trade adjustment. The foreign-exchange markets are inevitably more impressed with concerted action by finance ministries and central banks than they are by unilateral actions, and the actual adjustment of the trade and current account deficits over the medium term would be facilitated by an expansion of foreign demand.

Third, the efficiency of the G-5 as a forum made the multilateral course one of relatively low cost and low risk. The G-5 uniquely comprised only those countries vital to the success of the Plaza initiative and was a forum in which sensitive negotiations could be conducted in confidence.

This fact highlights one final attraction of multilateralism to Baker and Darman in 1985. By using and strengthening the G-5, the Treasury leaders could buttress their economic policy role in Washington. Although their counterparts in other agencies might resent it, it was possible to treat the G-5 as a Treasury (or Treasury-Fed) preserve. One could act there with minimal interagency consultation. The key policy step—reversal of the policy of nonintervention in exchange markets—could be taken after minimal intragovernmental debate.[17] The Treasury Secretary could conceivably have made a unilateral declaration reversing exchange rate policy without such consultation—this was, after all, within his sphere of responsibility—but the G-5 framework enhanced the legitimacy of the action and afforded both domestic and international political protection.

---

17. The quotations in Funabashi (*Managing the Dollar*, 77, 79) are instructive on this point. "Sprinkel [then Chairman of the Council of Economic Advisers], generally speaking, didn't know what was happening." In the words of a senior administration official, "I think we informed most of the key people in the US government within 24 hours of [the Plaza], so there wasn't a lot of time to organize opposition." And the President "supported it and had no problems with it" when informed "only a few days before the Plaza meeting."

Results of the Plaza

In policy terms, the Plaza strategy was a clear success. Economists will forever debate whether the dollar would have come down anyway at about the same rate, and properly so. For Baker as a domestic and international politician, however, it sufficed that clear action had been followed by desired market movement.

When the dollar declined sharply, traded-goods producers and the Congress voiced their relief and their approbation. For the first time, the Reagan administration had shown receptive and responsive leadership in the broad international economic policy sphere. One close adviser to the President even described the Plaza as "the most successful public relations operation of the decade."[18] Later actions reinforced the administration's credibility and leadership beyond the narrow exchange rate area: on trade with an aggressive new policy announced by President Reagan in a 23 September 1985 White House speech; on international debt with the Baker Plan, unveiled at the World Bank–IMF meetings in Seoul, Korea, shortly thereafter; and on broader macroeconomic policy coordination, elaborated at the Tokyo G-7 summit meeting in May 1986.

The Plaza Agreement confirmed Baker's Washington primacy in international economic policy: he had acted on his own, with minimal intragovernmental consultation, and both economic and political markets had brought vindication. His capacity for future leadership was reinforced not only within the executive branch, but also with Paul Volcker and the Fed, with the Congress, and with his G-5 finance ministry counterparts.

But no condition is permanent, and the longer-term political success of the Treasury team rested on fulfilling certain future expectations. Baker needed to show continued immediate progress on the exchange rate front—the dollar had to keep dropping. To do so might require coordinated action on national monetary policies, where the Fed retained the lead. At the same time, Baker had to avoid a hard landing for the dollar and to work effectively with a Fed Chairman who saw this threat as more menacing than he did.

In addition, Baker and his administration colleagues had to show that exchange rate adjustment and policy coordination eventually would bring concrete results in US trade and economic performance. The inertia of the trade balance would prevent any early reversal of the deterioration, much less an actual improvement. The famous J-curve effect, according to which a depreciation actually worsens the nominal trade deficit in the short term, would continue to generate bad numbers for the trade account on top of the real trade

---

18. Quoted in Putnam and Bayne, *Hanging Together,* 205.

deficit. The greater the depreciation of the dollar, the greater the J-curve effect would be. While waiting for the nominal trade deficit to recede, Baker and the administration could highlight the international actions they were taking to bring this adjustment about. But, ultimately, the time that they had borrowed had to be redeemed with concrete results.

4

Realignment and Stabilization of the Dollar, 1985–1989

As Treasury Secretary, James Baker's primary goal was to prevent international economic crises that could interfere with steady progress and growth in the domestic economy, and to encourage, where possible, foreign government actions that would support national prosperity. He also gave high priority to preventing an outburst of trade protectionism, and his new policy of active management of the dollar was a central means to that end.

In contrast to Regan and Sprinkel's laissez-faire approach, Baker's new exchange rate policy required the cooperation of many actors over whom he had influence but not control. The Congress, the Federal Reserve, foreign governments and central banks, and not least the private markets could each jeopardize his strategy. He also confronted great uncertainties: the economic uncertainty of not knowing what precise level of external deficit was sustainable or what particular exchange rate would reduce the external deficit to that level, and the political uncertainty of not knowing how much exchange rate adjustment (and trade deficit reduction) would be required to appease the Congress and the business community on trade policy.

Within this fluid environment, Baker operated in a manner he found personally congenial, by maintaining flexibility in his bargaining and negotiating positions. He never set, to our knowledge, a specific current account goal, and he felt his way through obstacles as they arose. In doing so, he actively sought the cooperation of the Federal Reserve, the partner most important to his exchange rate policy.

The new Treasury leaders gave dollar depreciation and further stimulation of the economies of major surplus countries first priority for the year following the Plaza meeting. At the same time, Baker took a hard line on congressional trade initiatives, hoping to postpone any legislation until after the 1986 election and after the trade balance began to improve. By the end of 1986, however, he had begun shifting to the strategy of consolidation that would dominate from 1987 on: agreeing to help stabilize the dollar at now-lower rates, and working with the Congress to try to fashion a trade bill that Ronald Reagan could sign.

Managing Depreciation, 1985–1986

By the end of 1985, the dollar had broken the 200-yen level and fallen to just over 2.4 marks. Multilaterally, by the Federal Reserve's measure, it had declined 12 percent on a trade-weighted basis since the Plaza and 25 percent since its February peak. Washington seemed to breathe a collective sigh of relief. But the same exchange rate winds that blew favorably for American producers were generating storm warnings overseas. Long before year's end the consensus over the desired direction of exchange rate movement evaporated.

Little more than two weeks after the Plaza declaration, having seen the dollar drop 7 percent against the mark (to 2.65 marks to the dollar), German Bundesbank President Karl Otto Pöhl announced that the dollar had reached a level "that is acceptable to us," signaling his intention to arrest the slide.[1] Assistant Treasury Secretary David Mulford, in congressional testimony shortly thereafter, said that the German government's actions had "not satisfied" the administration; it had been the "least responsive" of the G-5 to the Plaza Agreement.[2] Pöhl responded that too much had been read into the agreement. His comments underscored Germany's ambivalence about G-5 exchange rate management.

The Japanese were considerably more cooperative. The Bank of Japan intervened aggressively in the days after the Plaza meeting, and it further supported yen appreciation by tightening monetary policy in late October, when the currency adjustment showed signs of stalling.[3] In contrast to the Germans, Japanese Prime Minister Yasuhiro Nakasone reaffirmed "efforts to see the yen appreciate" even after an 11 percent rise against the dollar.[4] Nonetheless, after the dollar fell below 180 yen in mid-March 1986, having depreciated 26 percent since the Plaza and 33 percent since February, the Japanese intervened to bring

---

1. *Wall Street Journal,* 8 and 9 October 1985.

2. *Washington Post,* 20 November 1985.

3. This move was controversial in both Japan and the United States. Fed Chairman Paul Volcker argued that monetary tightening was unnecessary because the yen was headed in the right direction anyway, and tightening could therefore precipitate too rapid a fall in the dollar and would in any case restrict rather than expand domestic demand. The policy was therefore reversed within weeks. For an explanation of the bureaucratic politics behind this Japanese monetary policy shift, see Yoichi Funabashi, *Managing the Dollar: From the Plaza to the Louvre,* 2d ed. (Washington: Institute for International Economics, 1989), 33.

At the Plaza, the finance ministers and central bank governors did not even discuss whether monetary policy would be adjusted if necessary to sustain a depreciation of the dollar. Instead, they limited their discussion to intervention responsibilities. This omission was a product, in important part, of the central bankers'' reluctance to address such matters in the presence of their finance ministry colleagues. See Funabashi, *Managing the Dollar,* 32–36.

4. *Washington Post,* 23 October 1985.

it to a halt. Baker, however, refused to acknowledge that dollar depreciation had been sufficient.

Instead, international economic diplomacy entered, in early 1986, a period of successive, Baker-sponsored dollar depreciations followed by joint monetary easing, with interest rates typically dropping by half a percentage point in each round. The mediocre growth prospects for the United States in early 1986 argued for loosening US monetary policy, and the continued real and nominal deterioration of the trade balance argued against stabilizing the dollar. But to sustain capital inflows while reducing the discount rate, the United States needed to persuade other governments to lower their interest rates as well.

Baker exploited others' fears of a weaker dollar as a bargaining device. In preparations for the January 1986 G-5 meeting in London, he threatened further depreciation of the dollar to persuade the other G-5 members to engage in joint discount rate reductions. By his own retrospective description, Baker publicly "talked down" the dollar at this time.[5] He continued this strategy for the following several months, over the vehement protests of his G-5 counterparts and central bankers. When in the summer of 1986, for example, the Bundesbank and the Bank of Japan demurred, he declared that the dollar would have to fall further unless the Germans and Japanese took measures to raise domestic demand.[6] The linkage between the dollar and foreign demand was echoed by virtually every important American economic official, including Fed Chairman Paul Volcker.[7]

Baker signaled his willingness to allow the dollar to depreciate, reinforcing the bearish attitude of the exchange markets, by suspending all intervention for the year.[8] Foreign governments were then confronted with the choice of reducing interest rates (or intervening in the foreign exchange market, which would in turn ease monetary policy) or accepting currency appreciation, which would cut future net exports. All countries had an interest in loosening monetary policy to some extent, given the economic conditions at the time, and some loosening would undoubtedly have occurred even if Baker had not threatened depreciation. But the use of the exchange rate weapon and the Fed's

---

5. US Congress, Joint Economic Committee, *The 1987 Economic Report of the President*, hearings, 100th Cong., 1st sess., 22, 23, 29, and 30 January, and 2 and 12 February 1987, 246.

6. Baker was explicit:"We would prefer not to have to rely on exchange rate adjustments alone to remedy trade imbalances, but clearly, the current U.S. trade deficit cannot be allowed to continue indefinitely. As we have indicated in the past, unless there are additional measures to promote higher growth abroad, there will need to be further exchange rate changes to reduce trade imbalances." *Washington Post*, 24 September 1986.

7. *Financial Times*, 1, 4, 19, and 22 September 1986.

8. "Foreign Exchange Operations," *Federal Reserve Bank of New York Quarterly Review*, various issues.

demonstrated willingness to ease monetary policy, probably prodded foreign central banks to loosen monetary policy somewhat earlier than they otherwise would have. The end results were significant: between January 1986 and February 1987, discount rates were lowered from 7.5 to 5.5 percent in the United States, from 5.0 to 2.5 percent in Japan, and from 4.0 to 3.0 percent in Germany.

This monetary loosening proved popular, and Baker would claim partial credit for it. Lower interest rates would also help to sustain US growth until exports could respond to dollar depreciation. But the joint loosening of monetary policy would not by itself reduce the US trade deficit, except to the extent that adjustment was likely to proceed more quickly in a global growth environment. So Baker was unwilling, in 1986, to let go of the option of nudging the dollar lower still.

The Federal Reserve and the Baker-Volcker Routine

For both monetary loosening and further depreciation, Baker needed the cooperation of the Federal Reserve. With the dollar still overvalued, the Board and the Federal Open Market Committee (FOMC) were not inclined to use monetary policy to support it. Since domestic demand was sluggish, they were not in a dilemma: both external and internal considerations pointed toward a loosening of monetary policy. But they, and Volcker most of all, were determined to avoid a free fall of the dollar and a hard landing for the economy. That meant retaining the confidence of investors worldwide in the continuing value of dollar-denominated assets, which in turn meant that monetary policy could not be eased too quickly.

There were differences within the Board as to how quickly to proceed. Those differences complicated international coordination—and coordination with the Treasury—at several points, the most celebrated of which was the "palace coup" of February 1986.[9] But to the extent that there was discord within the Board, it pulled Volcker toward Baker's position in favor of monetary ease. Those pressing for loosening were Reagan appointees, some of whom were chosen

---

9. By early February 1986, Reagan had named a majority of the seven-member Federal Reserve Board of Governors. Differing with Volcker over the importance of first securing an agreement on joint rate reductions from other central banks, the Reagan appointees overruled the Chairman and voted for a discount rate cut. After Volcker reportedly threatened to resign, a compromise was reached whereby the rate cut would be postponed for two weeks while Volcker tried to negotiate a joint interest rate reduction with the Bank of Japan and the Bundesbank. That accord was reached and implemented in March, soon enough to satisfy the easier-money members of the Board. Within months, Vice Chairman Preston Martin, one of the leaders of the coup, announced his resignation, and Volcker acceded to the subsequent discount rate cuts.

when Baker was chief of staff at the White House, a key position from which to influence the President's choices. The Fed lowered the discount rate jointly with the Bank of Japan and the Bundesbank in March, again jointly with the Bank of Japan in April, and then alone in July and August.

Regardless of the encirclement of Volcker by Reagan appointees, Baker's and Volcker's objectives were generally consistent for most of 1986. Both viewed monetary easing and a lower dollar favorably. Neither would publicly sanction exchange rate levels that would not bring substantial adjustment of the current account, and such levels were not approached in 1986. On the other hand, neither wished to fuel expectations of rapid, continuous depreciation of the dollar, lest they trigger a flight from dollar-denominated assets. The two thus walked a tightrope after the Plaza Agreement.

Baker and Volcker kept their balance through a division of labor based on their respective responsibilities (and comparative advantages). At times when depreciation threatened to get out of control, Volcker expressed his concern that the dollar not fall too quickly, although he would not state what his preferred levels were. When exchange rates stabilized, Baker refused to concede that the depreciation of the dollar had been sufficient, although he would say that he did not want to see a free fall. Thus Baker and Volcker sent what were in effect balanced, although seemingly contradictory, signals to the foreign-exchange markets. There is no evidence that they planned this "good cop, bad cop" routine in advance, and their statements reflected genuine differences in priorities, with Baker pushing the dollar down and Volcker warning about keeping the decline from racing out of control. But they succeeded in orchestrating a record depreciation of the dollar while sustaining record levels of net foreign investment in dollar-denominated securities—a formidable achievement.

Nonetheless, the Treasury leadership's ultimate success would depend on converting the promise of dollar depreciation into substantial gains on the trade front without generating a hard landing for the US economy. Foreign macro-economic cooperation would be central to this strategy. Specifically, the major surplus nations, Japan and Germany, would need to move from export-driven to domestically driven growth.

International Macroeconomic Conflict

The new Treasury leadership had taken up the cause of foreign demand stimulus in 1985, pressing the other members of the G-5 in their pre-Plaza negotiations.[10]

---

10. Changes in foreign macroeconomic policies had become part of the American international economic agenda before Baker launched his initiatives. In a passive way, it was implicit in the attitude of the Regan Treasury that if foreign governments did not like

Baker and Darman were not able at that time to obtain significant changes in macroeconomic policies, however. Instead, each country reiterated its macroeconomic policy settings, previously planned measures, and commitment to noninflationary growth, which, it was claimed, would "improve the fundamentals further." Consistent with this outcome, each finance minister denied on returning home that the Plaza Agreement implied any substantial changes in his own country's fiscal and monetary policies; the major policy adjustments would be required of the others! British Chancellor of the Exchequer Nigel Lawson and French Finance Minister Pierre Bérégovoy said that the United States had a "lot to do" with regard to policy adjustment. German Finance Minister Gerhard Stoltenberg firmly rejected calls from within his own country and abroad to advance the date of the 1988 German tax cuts, which merely compensated for fiscal drag as planned, and was supported by Bundesbank President Pöhl.

More generally, of course, foreign countries faced a choice between adjustment of their large and growing surpluses and financing the US trade deficit with investments in dollar-denominated assets. Their support at the Plaza for appreciation of their currencies against the dollar reflected only a temporary reversal of their preference for financing over adjustment, which had dominated the 1981–84 period. This shift was motivated in important part by growing US protectionism. By early 1986, however, they felt they had experienced quite enough adjustment on the exchange rate front. Putting them even more at odds with Baker on this issue was the risk of recession: both Germany and Japan had experienced quarters of zero or negative growth since the dollar decline began.

However, the macroeconomic situation also made the G-5 less resistant to Baker's urging that they take steps to expand domestic demand. Foreign governments that perceived their domestic economies to be weak were more inclined to undertake stimulative fiscal policies themselves, and less eager to press the United States to reduce *its* domestic demand. International adjustment achieved via a US recession would be a Pyrrhic victory indeed. This helped to

---

the depreciation of their currencies against the dollar, they should adopt measures to boost their own economic growth. But foreign governments seemed content with slow growth in domestic demand, particularly because their exports and overall GNP were supported by strong American demand. Between 1980 and 1985, while US average annual domestic demand exceeded GNP growth (2.5 versus 1.9 percent, respectively) the annual increase in GNP exceeded that of domestic demand in Japan (4.0 versus 2.5 percent), Germany (1.2 versus 0.3 percent) and the European Community as a whole (1.3 versus 0.9 percent).

When the dollar appreciated rapidly in late 1984 and early 1985—a rise attributed in part to the strength of the US economy relative to Europe's—some American officials began to take the view that this passive approach was not enough, and that changes in foreign macroeconomic policies should be advocated more forcefully. Volcker advised foreign governments to stimulate domestic demand by accelerating tax reductions and other measures.

neutralize what would otherwise have been a severe weakness in Baker's international bargaining position: his limited formal authority and actual influence over US fiscal policy.[11]

This was fortunate for Baker, for the US budget deficit topped $200 billion in 1985 and 1986, and prospects for reducing it were at best uncertain. In the fall of 1985 Congress took a new approach to the problem with passage of the Gramm-Rudman-Hollings Act, which established mandatory annual targets for deficit reduction. Legislators had given up on their own capacity, and that of the White House, to tackle the deficit directly through specific spending reductions and tax increases. They therefore created a *deus ex machina* to force themselves and the President to behave responsibly. But the constitutionality of the law's provisions was in doubt, and Congress could of course amend it at any time. Moreover, it was anything but clear that Congress could force the President to accede to realistic budgets by threatening crippling Pentagon cuts if he did not—Ronald Reagan was the master at this game of political "chicken," and he could credibly threaten to accede to the outcome and blame Congress for the mess that would ensue.[12]

The Domestic Payoff From the International Adjustment Effort

Baker's international negotiations gave him three things of value in Washington. Success in lowering the dollar offered the prospect of eventual easing of the

---

11. With President Reagan's opposition to a tax increase well known and congressional Democrats unreceptive to further domestic budget cuts in the absence of parallel action on revenues, Baker was left with no room for manuever between his chief executive's position and that of the Congress. So he could not carry to the G-5 bargaining table any credible proposal for a contingent US budget deficit reduction in exchange for demand stimulus abroad. Nor, apparently, did he feel that G-5 pressure on the issue would give him useful leverage with the President or the Congress.

Because Baker and Darman nonetheless sought influence over foreign macroeconomic policies, they advanced a far-reaching framework for macroeconomic coordination at the Tokyo economic summit in May 1986. The Tokyo communiqué announced the creation of a new forum of G-7 finance ministers, which would use economic indicators to guide policy adjustments in the interest of noninflationary growth. At the Venice summit of June 1987, the G-7 announced agreement on the specifics of this indicators exercise.

For a recent review see Andrew Crockett, "The Role of International Institutions in Surveillance and Policy Coordination," paper presented to the Conference on Macroeconomic Policies in an Interdependent World, Brookings Institution, Washington, 12–13 December 1988.

12. Presidential leadership, as it happened, had a different priority in 1985 and 1986: tax reform. The 1986 tax law was designed to be revenue neutral. It did, as luck would have it, help to generate a substantial one-shot reduction in the deficit for fiscal year 1987, to about $150 billion. But it took the 1987 stock market crash to focus presidential commitment on capping the deficit at these levels.

trade deficit. Enhanced multilateral macroeconomic policy surveillance offered the prospect of further expansion of foreign demand. And the global easing of monetary policy brought immediate benefits: stronger growth at home and abroad, improving the environment for trade adjustment and easing the international debt problems of the developing countries. Monetary policy in the United States would likely have been eased irrespective of international coordination; Volcker himself said as much.[13] But Baker's internationalization of the process reduced the risk of a hard landing, and his active promotion of easing at home and abroad enabled him to take partial credit for lower interest rates.

These accomplishments helped Baker maintain dominance within the administration on trade policy, with US Trade Representative Clayton Yeutter and Commerce Secretary Malcolm Baldrige and his successor C. William Verity working within a Baker-led policy coordination system. This made Baker the key interlocutor with Congress, and his unwillingness to accept *any* trade bill in 1986—even with the merchandise trade deficit at a new record and important congressional elections coming in November—prevailed over the others' preference to work with Congress to fashion a compromise. Reciprocally, the raging debate over trade policy and the very real protectionist threat from Congress greatly strengthened Baker's hand in international bargaining.

Baker also maintained the lead in Third World debt policy at a time when both the Fed and the Congress might have been disposed to take their own initiatives. All in all, he was dominating the international economic policy scene as had none of his predecessors at the Treasury since his fellow Texan John B. Connally.

Circumstances were changing, however. At home, the administration was shaken by two events of November 1986: the Democrats regained control of the Senate, and the Iran-contra scandal became public, revealing a pattern of bizarre White House policymaking. Abroad, unexpected economic strength had brought shifts in the economic priorities and the political leverage of Japan and the major European states. Baker therefore moved to a strategy of accommodation on both fronts, working with Congress on trade legislation and with the G-5 to stabilize exchange rates. Indeed, movement on the international front was under way even before the dramatic November developments.

Tentative Stabilization, 1986–1987

The basic problem Baker faced had not changed: he needed a competitive exchange rate, one that would make 12-digit US trade deficits a thing of the

---

13. Paul A. Volcker, "Statement before the Committee on Banking, Housing and Urban Affairs, U.S. Senate," press release, Federal Reserve Board of Governors, Washington, 23 July 1986.

past. At the same time, the economy needed to sustain *ex ante* capital inflows long enough for the trade balance to respond to the depreciation of the dollar. If private capital inflows were to halt—and after successive step-level devaluations of the dollar investors were growing wary of the Baker-Volcker routine—either the United States or foreign governments would have to arrange official financing.

The US economy, moreover, was doing better in 1986 than originally anticipated, registering 2.9 percent real GNP growth for the year as a whole (close to the 1985 figure of 3.0 percent). It would perform even better in 1987. Unemployment was declining and stood at 6.7 percent at the end of the year, down from 7.2 percent in 1985. It would fall further to 5.7 percent at the end of 1987 and to 5.3 percent by the end of 1988. But although consumer prices rose only modestly in 1986, benefiting from oil price declines, inflation would accelerate in 1987 to 4.4 percent on a December-to-December basis. Overall industrial capacity utilization, which had hovered around 80 percent through mid-1987, rose quickly in the second half of the year.

Most signs, therefore, indicated that the economy was running near full employment and that the larger risk was on the side of overheating. Moreover, this picture was developing *before* the widely anticipated large improvement in the real trade balance made its contribution to growth, employment, and inflation.[14] With the ultimate impact on trade of the 150-yen and 2.00-mark dollar (the levels reached in late 1986 and early 1987) still unknown and impossible to estimate with certainty, a wait-and-see stance toward further depreciation was increasingly attractive.

The Federal Reserve was acutely aware of the inflation risks posed by further dollar depreciation. Indeed, support within the Board for further loosening of monetary policy had diminished greatly by late 1986, and in early 1987 the governors began to suspect that they might have gone one discount rate cut too far. Moreover, Volcker was urging Baker to cease talking the dollar down and making deliberately ambiguous statements with that intent.

Under these circumstances, Baker's capacity to achieve further dollar depreciation was greatly diminished, and the inflationary risk of depreciation had increased. Baker therefore moved to a different tack. Beginning in autumn 1986 he acceded to a series of four agreements over a period of 15 months to stabilize exchange rates tentatively and provisionally in exchange for promises to expand foreign demand: the October 1986 Baker-Miyazawa agreement, the February 1987 Louvre Accord, the adjustment of the secret Louvre range for the yen in April 1987, and the Christmas 1987 G-7 statement.

---

14. In volume (constant-dollar) terms, the balance on goods and services deteriorated slightly between the first quarters of 1986 and 1987 (although it had dipped and then improved over the course of 1986). It would remain virtually unchanged through 1987.

These agreements were similar in several respects. First, they secretly identified ranges for exchange rates that defined intervention or consultation responsibilities on the part of the signatories. The G-7, and the G-3 in particular, were secretly experimenting with target zones. Second, the agreements included foreign macroeconomic policy promises of uncertain impact; Baker therefore hedged his commitment to specified target ranges concomitantly. Third and perhaps most important, this hedging gave the agreements an "until further notice" quality, limiting the commitment to defend secret ranges to foreseen contingencies only—and even then promising no more than best efforts within planned macroeconomic policies if private traders drove exchange rates beyond the agreed target ranges. This sort of "flexible freeze," backed by government intervention, was nonetheless sufficient to impress the markets at several points.

The Baker-Miyazawa Accord

With the third major G-7 nation, Germany, hesitant about entering any comprehensive arrangement on exchange rate and macroeconomic policy, Baker and Japanese Finance Minister Kiichi Miyazawa began discussing a bilateral accord in early September 1986. The agreement they reached was announced at the end of October. The Japanese agreed to decrease their discount rate from 3.5 to 3.0 percent, to submit a supplemental budget with additional spending to the Diet, and to proceed with tax reform. The United States made no comparable domestic policy changes but did agree to state in the communiqué that "the exchange rate realignment achieved between the yen and the dollar since the Plaza Agreement is now broadly consistent with the present underlying fundamentals." This declaration was buttressed by the threat of enforcement: the two countries "reaffirmed their willingness to cooperate on exchange market issues."[15]

For Baker, this accord served two key purposes. First, it provided proof of successful international economic management immediately before the 1986 congressional elections.[16] Second, the accord sent a signal to the Europeans that

---

15. Press release, US Department of the Treasury, 31 October 1986.

16. Funabashi (*Managing the Dollar*, 157) reports that Baker asked for Japanese help specifically with the midterm election in mind. Having helped Nakasone with public statements supporting the dollar against the yen after the Tokyo summit, and shortly before Nakasone's Liberal Democratic Party won a resounding election victory, Baker was asking the Japanese to return the favor. Baker's statements intended to buoy the dollar against the yen can be found in US Congress, Senate, Committee on Finance, *Integration of U.S. Policies on Trade, Exchange Rates, and the Accumulated Debts of Less-Developed Countries*, hearings, 99th Cong., 2d sess., 14 May 1986, 94. It remains unclear, however, why so experienced a political operator as Baker would have thought that one voter in

if they did not want to stimulate domestic demand, they could be left out in the cold—that the United States might move to cap the yen separately from the European currencies.

But Baker's dedication to stabilizing even the yen-dollar rate was fleeting. One important reason was mistrust of Miyazawa's handling of the Japanese side: the yen depreciated from the range of 152–154 to the dollar to 161 between the agreement on 26 September and its announcement on 31 October. Top Treasury officials suspected that the news had been leaked in Japan deliberately in order to lock in a lower yen rate.[17] More fundamentally, Baker wanted to preserve the option of urging the dollar still lower, if, for example, the Japanese failed to fulfill the monetary and fiscal policy part of the bargain, or if those measures proved to have little or no impact on the bilateral trade balance.

After the first of the year, Baker moved to exercise this option: the Treasury gave background press briefings signaling a willingness to see the dollar fall further.[18] The dollar experienced a "near free fall" during the month of January, by the description of some market participants. An emergency visit to Washington by Miyazawa failed to brake its slide. To this bout of depreciation, however, Volcker responded unusually sharply, arguing that the dollar had now reached a "competitive level" at which any further decline "turns from benign into danger."[19] The US financial community was also growing increasingly uneasy with the dollar depreciation policy and the financial markets began to react with alarm to drops in the dollar. For the first time since it began to promote dollar depreciation, therefore, the Treasury was seriously confronted with the possibility that the tactic could backfire by raising US interest rates. Whether owing to a massive portfolio shift out of dollar-denominated assets or to a tightening of monetary policy by the Fed to prevent such a disruption, a rapid increase in US interest rates would harm both Baker and the administration. Realizing that he was losing key allies—Volcker above all—Baker yielded at least temporarily on further depreciation and moved promptly to negotiate a multilateral currency stabilization agreement.

---

two hundred would take serious notice of a US–Japan monetary accord, partly secret in content, announced the weekend before the election.

17. For the development of the Baker-Miyazawa accord and the inside controversy over the depreciation of the yen in October, see Funabashi, *Managing the Dollar*, 156–67.

18. *New York Times*, 14 January 1987. One report quoted a Treasury official as saying that, without further stimulus to domestic demand abroad, "over time it becomes logical that there should be further currency adjustments." *Financial Times*, 15 January 1987.

19. Statements made before the Senate Banking Committee and the Joint Economic Committee, respectively. Reported in *Financial Times*, 22 January 1987; *Washington Post*, 3 February 1987. See US Congress, Joint Economic Committee, *The 1987 Economic Report of the President*, 278–338.

The Louvre Accord

The G-5 plus Canada met at the Louvre Palace in Paris in late February 1987 to call a truce on macroeconomic conflict and to try to stabilize exchange rates. (Italy, protesting its exclusion from key deliberations within the G-5, refused to join the meeting but later abided by the agreements reached there.) On the macroeconomic side, Japan lowered its discount rate again and agreed to submit a supplemental budget to stimulate domestic demand; Germany agreed to propose an increase in the planned 1988 tax cut. For its part, the United States reiterated the Gramm-Rudman targets for budget deficit reduction but presented them in terms of share of GNP: the deficit would be limited to 3.9 percent of GNP in fiscal year 1987 and 2.3 percent in fiscal year 1988. (The United States more than fulfilled this obligation for 1987 but fell well short of the ambitious 1988 goal, with deficits equivalent to 3.3 and 3.0 percent of GNP in those years, respectively.)

On the exchange rate side, the communiqué of the ministers and governors said that they:

> agreed that the substantial exchange rate changes since the Plaza Agreement will increasingly contribute to reducing external imbalances and have now brought their currencies within ranges broadly consistent with underlying economic fundamentals, given the policy commitments summarized in this statement. Further substantial exchange rate shifts among their currencies could damage growth and adjustment prospects in their countries. In current circumstances, therefore, they agreed to *cooperate closely to foster stability of exchange rates around current levels.* (emphasis added)[20]

However, as Yoichi Funabashi reports, the ministers and governors confidentially and provisionally agreed to much more specific provisions. They secretly pledged to try to stabilize the dollar, the yen, and the deutsche mark within 5 percent bands around the central rates of 153.50 yen and 1.8250 marks to the dollar. Deviation of the market rate from the central rate by 2.5 percent would trigger intervention. Deviation of 5 percent would trigger consultations over policy adjustments. Intervention would become more intense the closer the market rate moved to the 5 percent margin.[21]

The dollar appreciated in the markets in response to the accord. Within three weeks it hit the upper 2.5 percent margin against the mark, triggering dollar sales by the United States for the first time since the period following the Plaza Agreement. But the dollar fell thereafter, particularly against the yen. Baker

---

20. G-6 communiqué, press release, 22 February 1987.
21. This secret agreement is described in Funabashi, *Managing the Dollar*, 183–87.

suggested at a G-7 ministers-governors meeting in April that the yen be rebased at 146 to the dollar, and the Japanese reluctantly agreed.[22]

In 1987 US authorities supported the dollar, both verbally and with intervention, in substantial quantities for the first time since late in the Carter administration. (Except for a small amount of deutsche mark sales in May 1984, the United States had sold neither marks nor yen since April 1981. All intervention before and after the Plaza had been *against* the dollar.) Before the Louvre meeting, Baker had denied that he was still talking down the dollar.[23] Afterward he made clear his personal commitment to the agreement to "continue to cooperate closely to foster stability of exchange rates."[24] Over the course of 1987, the United States intervened to the tune of about $8.5 billion net.

However, these amounts were dwarfed by the intervention of foreign central banks to prevent the appreciation of their currencies, particularly the Japanese, as the yen continued to set new record highs against the dollar. In fact, on a net basis, private capital virtually ceased coming to the United States in 1987. Of the $154 billion US current account deficit that year, $120 billion was financed by central banks abroad.[25] Without their support, US interest rates would have had to rise a great deal to attract sufficient capital. Foreign central banks chafed under the burden of this intervention, and they repeatedly urged the United States to ensure the private financing of its deficits (that is, to raise interest rates). But the central banks were unwilling to accept the substantial further dollar drop that the absence of their intervention would have entailed.[26]

Congress was remarkably deferential to Baker's agreement to try to stabilize the dollar, notwithstanding the continuing deterioration of the nominal trade figures. Several factors were at work: an easing of industry pressures, a

---

22. Reported in Funabashi, *Managing the Dollar*, 187–90.

23. Speaking before Congress, Baker said: "The last time we were talking down the dollar was when I testified up here in the cycle of testimony at this time last year. And if you will go back and check the record, you will see that we have not said for over a year that we would not be displeased to see a further orderly, gentle decline of the dollar. So I would like to put those remarks to rest." See US Congress, Joint Economic Committee, *The 1987 Economic Report of the President*, 246.

24. James A. Baker III, remarks to the Japan Society, New York, quoted in US Treasury Department, press release, Washington, 15 April 1987. Baker said, "Let me make one point clear: A further decline of the dollar against the other main non-dollar currencies could very well be counterproductive to our goal of higher growth in those countries."

25. Bank for International Settlements, *Fifty-Eighth Annual Report* (Basel: Bank for International Settlements, 1988), 188–89.

26. Karl Otto Pöhl, "Are We Moving Towards a More Stable International Monetary Order?," speech at the American Institute for Contemporary German Studies, Washington, 7 April 1987; Gerhard Stoltenberg, 'The United States and Europe: Main Objectives for Economic Policies and International Cooperation," speech at Georgetown University, Washington, 10 April 1987.

willingness to give the dollar depreciation time to work, and the reservoir of goodwill Baker had built up on Capitol Hill. Why did the coalition of trade-exposed sectors that had sought depreciation in 1985 not oppose this move? One reason, no doubt, was that the dollar had already come down a great deal, and this had improved their competitive position substantially. Moreover, no Congressman wanted to be seen rocking the boat at a time of financial difficulty. Anxieties over inflation, fueled in part by depreciation, caused a virtual crash in the long-term bond market during the spring of 1987. To nip inflationary expectations in the bud, the Fed tightened monetary policy, which supported the dollar and hence reinforced the Louvre Accord. In any case, objections to stabilizing the dollar at a level at which no one predicted large reductions in the trade and current account balances were isolated and surprisingly weak—until the stock market crash of October.

Exchange Rate Conflict and Crash

In early August 1987, Volcker's second term as Fed Chairman came to an end, and he was replaced by Alan Greenspan. With the markets uncertain about how to read Volcker's departure, Greenspan faced an immediate credibility problem, especially regarding his determination to hold the line against inflation. To signal his firm intention to do just that, Greenspan orchestrated a discount rate increase in early September, just before his first monthly meeting at the Bank for International Settlements in Basel.

When Baker was notified that the increase would soon be announced, he strongly urged Greenspan to negotiate assurances from the Germans and Japanese that they would not raise their interest rates in tandem and thereby negate the interest differential improvements for the dollar. Greenspan decided not to do so, apparently arguing that time did not permit such negotiation and that reputational and economic considerations required the rate increase regardless of how foreign central banks decided to respond.[27] Despite differences over tactics, Baker and the administration sanctioned the discount rate increase when it was announced.

However, as Baker had warned, the Japanese followed with a half-point discount rate increase within days, and the Germans with a more modest tightening within weeks. The FOMC followed up the discount rate increase with a further tightening of monetary policy at its meeting in late September. The conspicuous omission of interest rates and monetary policy from a G-7 communiqué issued in conjunction with the World Bank–International Mon-

---

27. *New York Times,* 24 September 1987; *Wall Street Journal,* 25 September 1987; *Washington Post,* 1 October 1987.

etary Fund meetings at that same time indicated the lack of agreement within the group.[28] Those disagreements came out into the open in October when Baker strongly and repeatedly criticized the Bundesbank for its tightening. He declared that the German move violated "the spirit of our recent consultations," and that the Louvre Accord did not require the United States to participate in a ratcheting up of interest rates even if that were necessary to prevent depreciation of the dollar. Baker said that he was not seeking a lower dollar but would not advocate interest rate increases to keep it from falling if foreign central banks persisted in raising their interest rates.[29]

This proved to be the greatest mistake that Baker made as Treasury Secretary. He may have calculated that the markets would welcome assurances that US interest rates would be held down. However, open verbal warfare among the G-7 apparently undermined the markets' confidence in finance ministers' and central bankers' ability to manage economic relations. These remarks came at a time, moreover, when the markets were already anxious over inflation, fearful that exchange rate stabilization would mean greater interest rate volatility, conscious of continuing poor monthly trade statistics, and shaken by the drop of several hundred points in the Dow Jones Industrial Average from its August peak of 2700. In combination with these factors, Baker's comments contributed to the worldwide stock market crash of 19 October 1987, which brought the Dow down 508 points in one day, to 1738.

Baker immediately met with Stoltenberg and Pöhl in an effort to repair the damage and restore faith in international cooperation. On the very day of the crash, the three reaffirmed their agreement to cooperate under a "flexible application" of the Louvre Accord with the aim of "exchange rate stability around current levels."[30] (The foreign-exchange markets, interestingly, were a source of relative stability during the crash, with the dollar remaining at around 141 yen and 1.78 marks.) Although the communiqué was silent on revisions of

---

28. To the Board of Governors of the Fund and the Bank, Baker vaguely proposed a role for gold in the indicators mechanism. This was interpreted as a sop to the gold bugs within the United States during the runup to the Republican presidential primaries, in which Representative Jack F. Kemp (R-NY), a gold-standard advocate, was expected to offer formidable opposition to Vice President Bush. See, for example, Rudiger Dornbusch, "Secretary Baker Hits the Campaign Trail," *New York Times*, 7 October 1987, A31.

29. *New York Times*, 16 and 18 October 1987; *Washington Post*, 17 October 1987; *Wall Street Journal*, 19 October 1987.

30. The three-sentence statement read: "Today, Secretary of the Treasury, James A. Baker, III, Finance Minister Gerhard Stoltenberg and Bundesbank President, Karl Otto Poehl, had a very positive, private meeting in Frankfurt, Germany which had been agreed upon early last week. The parties agreed to continue economic cooperation under the Louvre Agreement and its flexible application including cooperation on exchange rate stability and monetary policies. They are consulting with their G-7 colleagues and are confident that this will enable them to foster exchange rate stability around current levels." Press release, US Department of the Treasury, Washington, 19 October 1987.

the Louvre Accord, background press briefings confirmed that they included a lowering of the dollar against the mark and a mild easing of German monetary policy, in exchange for US commitment to defend these new levels.[31] In his televised address to reassure the nation, President Reagan affirmed that "the United States remains committed to the Louvre agreement."[32]

For Baker, however, who had joined reluctantly in that agreement, the crash was a reason to lower its priority. After the markets settled down, two weeks after the crash, Baker announced that preventing a recession in the wake of the crash was a higher priority than preventing further depreciation of the dollar. He believed that the September discount rate increase was a mistake, although he had acquiesced in it at the time, and he wanted to ensure that the Fed kept "sufficient liquidity in the system." Statements by Assistant Treasury Secretary David Mulford that the currencies of the newly industrializing countries should appreciate by at least 10 to 15 percent in real terms against those of their trading partners reinforced Baker's message on the dollar.[33] These comments touched off a period of depreciation, with the dollar plunging to record lows against the yen and the mark.[34]

Baker reiterated his intention to seek foreign demand stimulus as part of a macroeconomic policy coordination package, and these goals were echoed by Lawson and Miyazawa. But what really moved to center stage was the US budget deficit. The markets riveted their attention on the budget process in Washington. Foreign heads of state pressed for deficit reduction, their finance ministers saying that it should be done even if it required that the President backpedal on his often-repeated pledge not to raise taxes. No serious new international accord could now be concluded until the United States had made progress on its own fiscal policy.

In September, Congress had revised the Gramm-Rudman-Hollings law requiring annual budget deficit cuts, correcting a constitutional flaw and substantially raising the deficit targets for fiscal years 1988 and 1989 to $144 billion and $136 million, respectively.[35] But as the new fiscal year commenced in October,

---

31. *Wall Street Journal*, 21 October 1987.

32. Reprinted in *New York Times*, 21 October 1987.

33. Press release, US Department of the Treasury, Washington, 17 November 1987, 10. See also *Financial Times*, 15 December 1987.

34. *Wall Street Journal*, 5 November 1987. White House Spokesman Marlin M. Fitzwater confirmed that Baker spoke for the administration, but said also that the administration remained committed to the Louvre Accord, international cooperation, and exchange rate stability. Baker's comment was *not* discussed with other G-7 finance ministers in advance. *Washington Post* and *Wall Street Journal*, 6 November 1987.

35. The original law, whose enforcement mechanism was declared unconstitutional by the Supreme Court, had set targets of $108 billion for fiscal 1988 and $72 billion for 1989. The actual fiscal 1987 deficit was $150 billion, above the original Gramm-Rudman-Hollings

Congress had not yet taken the specific budget actions necessary to avoid automatic spending cuts. The crash and the accompanying criticism generated pressure for a White House–congressional "budget summit," which Hill leaders had long sought but President Reagan had resisted. Reagan now acceded to the pressure. He even softened his stand against new taxes, refusing—under strong press questioning—to rule out tax increases as part of a budget agreement.

Yet Reagan's openness to new taxes seemed to diminish with each day that the financial markets showed stability. The budgetary summit eventually yielded an unprecedented two-year bipartisan budget agreement, which, however, did not contain significant tax increases. The package provided for an advertised $30 billion improvement (from the baseline projection) in fiscal 1988 and $48 billion in 1989, in order to reach the new statutory targets. Independent analysts estimated that the year-on-year reductions would be quite modest in fact, but they acknowledged that the agreement converted the temporary improvement owing to tax reform into a permanent gain.[36] Notwithstanding the modesty of this achievement and the lack of congressional enthusiasm for the package, the G-7 finance ministers went out of their way to praise it, to reassure skeptical markets.

The crash also triggered strong and vociferous domestic opposition to the process of international coordination. At a well-publicized congressional hearing just after the crash, former Chairman of the Council of Economic Advisers Martin Feldstein testified as a private citizen. He argued, "The problem contributing to the market decline was *not* the apparent collapse of international macroeconomic coordination and it was *not* the likely decline of the dollar. The problem was the false impression created by governments that continued healthy expansion requires international coordination and a stable dollar." Thus, he said, "The United States should explicitly but amicably abandon the policy of international macroeconomic coordination."[37]

Other critics of coordination were concerned for the independence of the Fed.[38] Baker had been aggressively making public pronouncements on mone-

---

target of $144 billion for that year but a major improvement over the $221 billion deficit for fiscal 1986.

36. The actual fiscal 1988 deficit rose to $155 billion, $11 billion above the target. As a percentage of GNP, however, the deficit declined from a peak of over 5 percent in fiscal 1986 to around 3 percent in 1989.

37. Martin Feldstein, "The Stock Market Decline and Economic Policy," excerpts from testimony to the House Banking Committee, 29 October 1987. Herbert Stein also argued in these hearings for further dollar depreciation. Separately, so did William A. Niskanen in "A Lower Dollar vs. Recession," op. ed., *New York Times,* 27 October 1987, A35.

38. See, for example, the congressional testimony of Milton W. Hudson, chairman of the Economic Advisory Committee of the American Bankers Association, in US Congress, House, Committee on Banking, Subcommittee on Domestic Monetary Policy, *Conduct of Monetary Policy in 1987,* hearings, 100th Cong., 2d sess., 17 and 24 March 1988.

tary policy and engaging in international discussions involving monetary policy. Although his willingness to see the dollar depreciate was perfectly consistent with the Fed's loosening of monetary policy, Baker's position could have made a tightening of monetary policy more difficult in the future. Greenspan's strong assertion of Fed independence in congressional testimony did not completely put these concerns to rest.[39]

But Baker himself was under attack: for the first time since his arrival at the Treasury, his leadership mandate was in question. Not only was he criticized for poaching on the Fed's turf and blamed for contributing to the crash, but indeed Greenspan rather than he received credit for acting decisively to limit the damage by injecting liquidity into the markets.[40] Meanwhile, Reagan elevated Beryl Sprinkel, who had lost influence over policy while chairman of the Council of Economic Advisers and had planned to resign the post,[41] to Cabinet status, strengthening his hand within the White House. The President, the White House, and other Cabinet members were now making statements on exchange rates in addition to the Treasury. Baker was also roundly criticized by Lawson and Stoltenberg and other foreign leaders.

The G-7 Bear Trap

By December, however, the Treasury was poised for a rebound, with Baker again using international exchange rate action to buttress his position in Washington. With the budget talks completed, a new G-7 declaration became possible. Arranged with the other members by telephone, a communiqué was released on 22 December. The ministers reaffirmed that "the basic objectives and economic policy directions agreed in the Louvre Accord remain[ed] valid," pledged to continue policy coordination efforts aimed at correcting external

---

39. Greenspan testified, "I know of no Federal Reserve policies which are affected by the Treasury Department." He continued, "We obviously try to coordinate with them, in the sense that we are part of the United States Government. . . . But the one thing I can assure you is that the presumption that the Treasury Department is in control of monetary policy is false." See US Congress, House, Committee on Banking, Subcommittee on Financial Institutions, *Reform of the Nation's Banking and Financial Systems,* hearings, 100th Cong., 1st sess., Part 2, 18 November and 2, 3, 9, and 10 December 1987, 21.

40. The Fed's one-sentence statement read: "The Federal Reserve, consistent with its responsibilities as the nation's Central Bank, affirmed today its readiness to serve as a source of liquidity to support the economic and financial system." *Financial Times,* 21 October 1987, 3.

41. *New York Times,* 18 September 1987. Monetarism had been largely discredited during the recovery, but Sprinkel had consistently argued against using monetary policy to stabilize the dollar, a view seemingly validated by the market crash. The new dispute about currency stablization made Sprinkel a more formidable inside proponent of floating exchange rates, and hence a greater obstacle for Baker on this issue.

imbalances, and reiterated their common interests in exchange rate stability.[42] The dollar stood at 1.63 marks and 126 yen at the time of the statement, which was interpreted to be a commitment to intervene should the dollar fall much below these levels or rise above an unspecified level that had been secretly set.[43] The immediate market reaction was skeptical. The dollar dropped to near 120 yen and 1.56 marks—record lows—in thin trading at the turn of the year.

At this point, the United States finally exhibited a more-than-tentative commitment to halting depreciation. On the first trading day of 1988, the finance ministries and central banks of the G-7 orchestrated a "bear trap" of dramatic proportions, catching those positioned in the markets to profit from further dollar decline. The amount of direct intervention was extensive, totaling at least $3 billion by one estimate during the first week of January alone, with the US contribution at $685 million. The market impact was reinforced by rumors (later denied) that the G-7 or the G-3 had a secret agreement to intervene in massive quantities. These operations brought the dollar back to the upper 120s against the yen and to 1.65–1.70 against the mark, despite the absence of changes in monetary and fiscal policies. It was an impressive display of the impact of concerted intervention. The US commitment to this dollar floor was codified when Baker declared several weeks later that the dollar was now more reasonably valued and that a decline would be "counterproductive."[44]

Dollar Rebound, 1988–1989

For the next 18 months, through July 1989, the problem was not dollar weakness but dollar strength. Beginning in late spring 1988, the currency showed surprising bullishness, penetrating what was thought to be the post-crash upper limit against the mark in the summer of 1988 and piercing the new boundary in a second major rally in spring 1989.

One early contributor to this rise was the long-awaited improvement in the US trade balance. The 1988 first-quarter nominal trade deficit declined by $5.6

---

42. The operative section on exchange rate policy read: "The ministers and governors agreed that either excessive fluctuation of exchange rates, a further decline of the dollar, or *a rise in the dollar to an extent that becomes destabilising to the adjustment process, could be counter-productive by damaging growth prospects in the world economy*. They re-emphasised their common interest in more stable exchange rates among their currencies and agreed to continue to co-operate closely in monitoring and implementing policies to strengthen underlying economic fundamentals to foster stability of exchange rates. In addition, they agreed to co-operate closely on exchange markets." (emphasis added) An annex listed the policy undertakings by each country. Press release, US Department of the Treasury, Washington, 22 December 1987.

43. *Wall Street Journal,* 23 December 1987.

44. *Financial Times,* 2 March 1988.

billion from the previous quarter (and by about as much in real terms). The deficit for the year as a whole would shrink by $30 billion, to $128 billion. That a clear reduction was under way helped to relieve anxieties in the foreign-exchange markets over adjustment and the related budget deficit, and contributed to the dollar's rise.

At least equally important was the impact of monetary policy. By spring 1988 it was clear that, contrary to almost all predictions, the economy would shrug off the effects of the October crash. The FOMC voted at the end of March to tighten monetary policy on reports of unexpected strength in the economy. That action initiated what would become a three-point increase in the federal funds rate (the interest rate paid for short-term loans between banks in the Federal Reserve System), from around 6.7 percent in early 1988 to over 9.7 percent in May 1989.

In early May 1988, in response to questions from the Senate Banking Committee, Greenspan presented the Fed's rationale for the renewed tightening: the trade deficit would decline in 1988, but monetary policy would have to restrain domestic demand in order to prevent the trade improvement from causing inflation.[45] Under these circumstances, a depreciation of the dollar would *not* contribute to trade improvement and could indeed harm it.

The Fed confronted an uneasy and sometimes critical administration in its turn toward a restrictive monetary policy. The debate that followed the crash over the stance of monetary policy and the independence of the Fed continued into 1988. During the runup to the November 1988 election, however, Baker affirmed his basic agreement with Fed policy, joining in the widespread sentiment that the Fed was expertly toeing a fine line between inflation and recession.[46]

German officials reinforced the view that the Fed had to remain firm, and Baker was making peace with them as well.[47] Despite the lack of domestic demand stimulus from Bonn, and even indications that German policy was going in the opposite direction, Baker declared his satisfaction with both German policy and current exchange rates. And in a statement with Stoltenberg in early February, he foreswore talking the dollar down.

At the Toronto economic summit in mid-June, the final such meeting in which Ronald Reagan would participate, the heads of government reviewed with nostalgia the accomplishments of the 1980s: the policy coordination process and currency realignments, but even more the achievement of substantial growth with low inflation. They also reiterated, almost verbatim, the

---

45. *Washington Post* and *Wall Street Journal*, 4 May 1988.

46. *Financial Times*, 2 March 1988.

47. *Wall Street Journal*, 8 February 1988; *Handelsblatt*, 4 May 1988.

language on exchange rate stability issued by the G-7 ministers the previous April. But the markets were unimpressed. Recognizing that the dollar was significantly above its level at the April G-7 meeting, and responding to press briefings by administration officials that suggested complacency with the appreciation to date, traders sent the dollar upward, shrugging off the effects of German interest rate increases. The German action, in turn, signaled the end of the era of joint interest rate reductions and Baker's effort to keep rates down.

The Rally of 1988: An Election-Year Conspiracy?

To many observers, Baker had now embarked on a strategy of "skating through" the several months remaining until the US presidential election. In fact, the appreciation of the dollar fueled rumors of an international conspiracy to buoy the dollar and help elect George Bush as the nation's 41st President.[48] When asked, Baker called these charges "ridiculous" and countered that foreign central banks cooperated with the administration because it was in their own interest to do so.[49] Indeed, robust growth in the United States, tightening of monetary policy, and improved trade balances offered good reasons for the market to be bullish on the dollar.

Nonetheless, even if the G-7 did not orchestrate it, Baker had several incentives to accept a moderate dollar rise in mid-1988 despite its potential for retarding adjustment in the medium term. First, given its recent experience, the Treasury probably did not want a sudden halt to appreciation, which might spark a drop in the dollar and, in consequence, instability in the market. This was just what had happened in the months following the Louvre Accord. Second, Baker may well have been feeling the lingering effects of the early postcrash criticism of his strategy of international coordination and exchange rate stabilization. Third, dollar appreciation was insurance against possible

---

48. David Hale, "U.S. Economic Outlook and Monetary Policy," testimony before the Senate Committee on Banking, Housing, and Urban Affairs, *Federal Reserve's Second Monetary Policy Report for 1988,* 12 and 13 July 1988, 33–58; Jeffrey E. Garten, "How Bonn, Tokyo Slyly Help Bush," *New York Times,* 21 July 1988; *Washington Post,* 22 July 1988; Irwin M. Stelzer, "The Election Dollar," *The American Spectator,* September 1988, 28–33. In responding to questions posed at the above hearings of the Senate Banking Committee, Alan Greenspan denied knowledge of any conspiracy (130).

49. *Washington Post,* 22 July 1988. It was certainly in the interest of the other G-7 governments to encourage private-sector financing of the US deficits. Foreign leaders were conscious of the risks to their economies of a rapid adjustment of the US trade deficit. Moreover, with US fiscal policy on hold until the election, mid-1988 would have been a poor time to employ financial threats to pressure the administration to take determined budget action. Any attempt to do so in the election season would certainly have backfired against the trade and investment interests of the United States' economic partners.

instability in American stock and bond markets during the election campaign. Fourth, improved trade performance had temporarily removed the exchange rate from the dispute between the executive and legislative branches over trade legislation. Although Capitol Hill maintained an interest in exchange rate policy, it became a lighter potential counterweight to the Sprinkel nonintervention view. In sum, the immediate economic effects of dollar appreciation were positive and came at a time when the trade balance was showing clear improvement. No important short-run consideration argued for a determined effort to limit the dollar's rise.

So the Secretary avoided statements about the dollar's rise such as both he and the other G-7 officials had made at earlier times: that these levels were "destabilizing to the adjustment process" or "counterproductive." The markets continued to perceive the Treasury to be complacent about the renewed rise of the dollar and its intervention to be merely symbolic. In the six weeks after the Toronto summit, the dollar reached 1.90 marks and 135 yen: this level was more than 10 percent above its trough at the beginning of the year, on a trade-weighted basis.[50] In response, the United States sold about $3 billion in the foreign-exchange markets, the most since the immediate post-Plaza intervention almost three years earlier. But the American effort was not billed as heavy or concerted.

The Treasury was fully aware that the markets *believed* that the G-7 would support the dollar through the election, and it did not act to discourage that impression. So, if the "international conspiracy" theory is not necessary to explain the dollar bubble of 1988, at least Treasury exchange rate policy did not resist the rise and probably contributed to it.[51]

After the Fed raised the discount rate to 6.5 percent in August 1988, the markets drove the dollar up to 1.92 marks. Now the Treasury joined its foreign counterparts in visibly concerted intervention, although in small quantities.[52] In late August, European central banks, led by the Bundesbank, raised their

50. "Treasury and Federal Reserve Foreign Exchange Operations," *Federal Reserve Bank of New York Quarterly Review* (Summer 1988): 90–95.

51. Willett and Wihlborg argue that simply placing a credible floor under the dollar caused it to appreciate, by truncating the normal distribution of exchange rate forecasts by market participants. See Thomas D. Willett and Clas Wihlborg, "International Capital Flows, the Dollar, and U.S. Financial Policies," paper presented to the American Enterprise Institute Conference on Monetary Policy in an Era of Change, Washington, 16–17 November 1988, 31–32.

52. This level was the upper limit of the range originally agreed upon at the Louvre. However, that range was thought to have been lowered during the bilateral consultations following the stock market crash. In January 1989, the United States led a concerted intervention against the dollar when it appreciated above 1.82–1.83 marks, a level closer to what was thought to be the postcrash upper limit.

interest rates (the second round in five weeks). This marked the dollar's peak in 1988 and the beginning of a three-month decline.[53]

The Rally of 1989

The markets greeted the election of George Bush by accelerating the dollar depreciation that had begun shortly before. Traders voiced fears, spurred by Bush's "read my lips" commitment against new taxes, that the new administration and Congress would be unable to mount a serious attack on the US budget deficit. Foreign leaders' advice that decisive action should be taken on the budget in the first several months of the new administration—even if it required tax increases—heightened the sense of impending international conflict over US fiscal policy.[54]

In response, Bush promised to address the budget issue immediately upon inauguration and moved quickly to announce his appointments: Baker would become Secretary of State; Nicholas Brady, who had replaced Baker at the Treasury in September 1988, would stay on there; and Richard Darman, who had left government in April 1987, would have direct responsibility for budget negotiations as Director of the Office of Management and Budget.

Well before year's end, the markets stabilized. Then in early 1989, reacting to robust US growth combined with sharp price increases, the Federal Reserve further tightened monetary policy. This it did notwithstanding either the upward pressure thereby placed on the dollar or the public statements by the administration that the Fed was exaggerating the risk of inflation. With a lag, the Fed's tightening was matched in Germany and Japan, but their currencies also suffered from the political weakness of both Chancellor Helmut Kohl and Prime Minister Noboru Takeshita and their respective ruling parties. Contrary to the expectations of late 1988, therefore, the dollar rose persistently. In May and June it shattered its upper limit against the yen (140) and the mark (1.90–1.92), rising above 150 and 2.00, respectively, to a two-and-a-half year high.

These market developments confounded the analysts who had detected a slowing of the US economy in the monthly statistics and had forecasted renewed deterioration in the US trade account at these exchange rates.[55] In fact, the sharp improvement had run its course, the trade balance having shown no clear trend

---

53. By the end of the year, the central banks had accomplished, without disastrous results, the tightening that they had attempted before the crash.

54. See *Wall Street Journal,* 11 November 1988.

55. William R. Cline, *American Trade Adjustment: The Global Impact,* POLICY ANALYSES IN INTERNATIONAL ECONOMICS 26 (Washington: Institute for International Economics, 1989); International Monetary Fund, *World Economic Outlook,* April 1989, 16–19.

since the spring of 1988. Furthermore, with interest rate differentials little changed, many experts argued that the dollar surge of 1989, like that of 1984–85, was a speculative bubble, detached from the fundamentals.[56]

The Treasury intervened to check the dollar's rise, first at the 1.82–1.84 level and then in the mid-1.90s. The piercing of the 2.00-mark and 140-yen levels in May provoked a statement from the White House reaffirming the desirability of stable rates and the commitment to G-7 coordination.[57] However, consensus among the G-7 had broken down: not only would the Bundesbank and the Bank of Japan not raise interest rates in tandem with the Fed (the monetary coordination problem of September 1987 had become reversed!), but the Bundesbank was conspicuously absent from concerted intervention operations. Despite a German current account surplus of $48.5 billion in 1988, which continued to rise in 1989, Bundesbank President Pöhl publicly stated that the low mark posed no problems for the German economy.

The G-7 coordination process had broken down very visibly, yet the leading member undertook no correspondingly visible effort to repair it. In the absence of real coordination, the verbal support that the Treasury now offered for the G-7 process had a platitudinous ring. Therefore, when the Bundesbank finally intervened in the exchange markets and then raised interest rates in June, the credibility of the coordination process was not notably enhanced, even though the dollar now began to recede.

By early June the US economy was visibly slowing, with recession beginning to supplant inflation as the primary threat. By the time of the Paris economic summit in July, the dollar had fallen to around 140 yen and 1.9 marks. In their communiqué from Paris, the seven leaders spoke positively of their efforts "under the Plaza and Louvre agreements" aimed "at fostering stability of exchange rates consistent with. . . economic fundamentals."

Secretary Brady declared in a postsummit interview, however, that the dollar was not actually discussed at the summit. Nor, with the dollar at these levels, did Brady see any urgent need for the heads of government to address exchange rate or coordination issues. "Why change the throttle settings when we've had seven years of economic progress?" he asked.[58] Brady maintained that the April G-7 position on exchange rates was still in effect.[59] But the dollar had broken through widely perceived target ranges since that meeting, and although it

---

56. See, for example, the views of Martin Feldstein, quoted in *Washington Post*, 16 May 1989, D1.

57. *New York Times*, 23 May 1989.

58. Transcript of the *MacNeil-Lehrer Newshour*, WNET, New York, 17 July 1989.

59. Testimony by Nicholas F. Brady before the Joint Economic Committee on the Paris Economic Summit, 19 July 1989.

receded thereafter, the G-7 failed to muster a coordinated response. The markets therefore continued to wonder where the exchange rate regime was headed.

The Treasury's Reports to Congress

In the summer of 1988, even as improvement in the trade balance was stalling, Congress finally enacted—and the President signed—the Omnibus Trade and Competitiveness Act. The new law was a product of the trade deficits fostered by the strong dollar, and it included, as discussed at length in Chapter 6, a subtitle on "Exchange Rates and International Economic Policy Coordination." This required that the Treasury report semiannually on "international economic policy, including exchange rate policy" to the Senate and House banking committees. The list of topics to be covered gave heavy emphasis to the relationship between currency markets, on the one hand, and current account and trade balances, on the other.

Issuing the first report in October 1988, on the eve of the national elections, the Treasury gave an optimistic assessment of global growth, inflation, and current account adjustment prospects. The department agreed that further US adjustment was "necessary and desirable" but relied mostly on the promises of G-7 policy coordination for policy changes that could reduce the external deficit in the future.[60] It argued that the dollar (then at 126.50 yen and 1.80 marks) need not fall to continue the adjustment process, and it reiterated the September commitment of the G-7 to exchange rate stability. The report did not, however, discuss the secret target ranges, nor did it specify what a "sustainable" current account surplus was, as several Congressmen had requested.

In its April 1989 update, the Treasury was less sanguine about the correction of the trade deficit; its brief treatment of the subject was headed, "External Adjustment at More Measured Pace." But it offered no new recommendations for reducing the deficit further.[61]

The Treasury thus addressed, in these reports, some of the exchange rate issues surrounding the double rally of 1988–89. In its discussion of active measures, however, the prime focus was not on the G-5 or the G-7, but on the newly industrializing countries (NICs) of East Asia. Both reports were dominated by the declaration that the currencies of Korea and Taiwan should

---

60. US Department of the Treasury, "Report to the Congress on International Economic and Exchange Rate Policy," Washington, 15 October 1988, 27–28. Among other things, the report officially codified the change in the Treasury's view of the effectiveness of foreign-exchange intervention.

61. US Department of the Treasury, "Report to the Congress on International Economic and Exchange Rate Policy," Washington, April 1989.

appreciate substantially against the dollar. This was a response to the requirement in the omnibus trade act that the Treasury formally designate countries
that "manipulate" their currencies and negotiate realignments; it had also been
an important focus of US exchange rate policy since late 1986, as the East Asian
NICs had pegged their currencies to the dollar while the yen appreciated. The
reporting process gave the Treasury added leverage over those two countries;
the Korean and Taiwanese authorities allowed the won and the New Taiwan
dollar to appreciate significantly at the time of both the October and the April
reports. In 1988, however, Korea and Taiwan accounted for only 3.9 and 5.7
percent, respectively, of US imports and 2.5 and 2.3 percent of US exports. But
together they filled nearly half of the pages of the April 1989 Treasury report.
Treatment of the broader movement of the dollar was, in contrast, brief and
perfunctory.

Lessons of 1985–1988

Exchange rate policy in 1985–88 differed sharply from that in 1981–84 in both
substance and process. In contrast to its predecessor, the Baker-Darman
Treasury developed a view as to what the exchange rate ought to be (over the
short term), or at least in what direction it should go, and sought to communicate this view to the markets through deliberate statements. In the most
fundamental departure from the Regan-Sprinkel laissez-faire philosophy, US
policy has, since early 1987, targeted the dollar within provisional ranges agreed
upon multilaterally with the other G-7 countries.

In support of exchange rate objectives, Baker approved intervention in the
markets. Moreover, unlike in the 1981–84 period, the intervention and capital-
market policies of other countries became an important instrument of US
exchange rate policy. And at key points the Treasury coordinated its action with
the intervention of other G-7 governments.

Although he raised the *sensitivity* of the Treasury to broad economic considerations in pursuing international adjustment, Secretary Baker discouraged
greater *openness* of the policy process. Simply being more responsive to trade
concerns in exchange rate policy determination did not make the process more
participatory; Baker in fact vigilantly guarded Treasury's formal authority in this
area from encroachment by other agencies, as Treasury Secretaries generally do.
He used the interagency Economic Policy Council, which he chaired, to address
trade policy, but he kept exchange rate matters within his own small circle.

Because the Baker Treasury had redressed the main grievances of Congress
and private groups regarding exchange rate policy, the interest of outside actors
tended to wane (see Chapters 6 and 7). Perhaps by design, and certainly in
result, the Treasury (together with the Fed) preserved its claim to dominating

the actual process of exchange rate policymaking by doing what these outside actors demanded in terms of substance.

However, pursuit of an active exchange rate policy required more consultation with other government officials. Consultation with the Chairman of the Fed was essential. Consultation with the Secretary of State was important in securing support for the initial shift to activism. During depreciation and stabilization, the Treasury reached beyond Washington to foreign officials. Baker and Darman proposed and established a formal consultative mechanism within the G-7 to monitor macroeconomic and balance of payments developments and to coordinate macroeconomic and exchange rate policy when performance deviated from agreed-upon objectives.

Moreover, exchange rate policy was opened up by statute in 1988, the Treasury's resistance notwithstanding. The exchange rate reporting requirement of the 1988 trade act, a permanent change, now subjects Treasury policy to public purview every six months. Whether the report achieves its objective of increasing the accountability of the Treasury to the Congress on exchange rate matters depends on how the provisions are implemented, and in particular on how aggressively legislators employ their new leverage. But the prerogative of Congress to oversee exchange rate policy is clearly incorporated into law.

Exchange rate policy during 1985–88 exhibited both long- and short-run orientations. The short-term horizon tended to dominate the Treasury's public statements. The decisions of Baker, Darman, and Mulford to talk the dollar down, stabilize it, or accede to appreciation were, like the negotiations leading to the Plaza Agreement, made in an environment of often-conflicting pressures and preferences of foreign governments and central banks, Congress, private actors, and the Federal Reserve. Treasury leadership had to grope and feel its way through these domestic and international political obstacles. Hence US exchange rate policy during this period twisted and turned to adapt to the latest changes in macroeconomic and trade variables, and to short-term political considerations such as the 1986 and 1988 elections.

The Baker Treasury did espouse a vague long-term objective: to reduce the US current account deficit to sustainable levels while maintaining US and world growth and avoiding inflation. Baker and Darman developed the G-7 process of enhanced multilateral surveillance in order to promote the long-term restructuring of the US and foreign economies, and they worked to institutionalize these procedures so that they might outlast the tenure of their creators.

However, the long-term orientation of US exchange rate policy was unsatisfactory in most other respects. There was no official estimate of what a "sustainable" current account deficit was, nor of whether that target could be achieved at the exchange rates set after the Louvre Accord. To the contrary, all official indications were that a sustainable current account deficit could not be forecast on the basis of current policies and exchange rates.[62] And although there were intermittent efforts thereafter to facilitate further step-level depreciations, these did not prove effective.

Exchange rate policy from 1985 to 1989 was co-determined by the need to reduce the trade deficit and the requirements of domestic economic prosperity. In 1985 and 1986, these goals were in harmony: the economy still had excess capacity, and unemployment was still above its nonaccelerating-inflation rate. The risks therefore seemed to be in the direction of a recession. So monetary ease and dollar depreciation could help reduce the trade deficit and buoy domestic growth. But by 1987 the economy was reaching fuller, if not full, employment and capacity utilization, and inflation and inflationary expectations were rising. The exchange rate weapon could not be wielded under these new conditions without risk to the domestic economy, a fact illustrated initially by the results of the Louvre stabilization and post-Louvre monetary tightening and dramatically confirmed by the October 1987 stock market crash. International adjustment through deliberate exchange rate changes was temporarily shelved, and a floor was placed under the dollar. The Treasury countenanced the perverse twin dollar rallies of 1988–89 because the short-term consequences for market confidence and anticipated inflation (both domestic factors) were given greater weight than the long-term consequences for trade adjustment.

Any Treasury team would have been subject to such political and economic forces, and the result—in most instances—would have been similar policy responses. But in the face of these fundamentals, the Baker-Darman management of policy was unusually skilled and politically successful. Some commentators wryly dubbed their accomplishments "magic,"[63] as the exchange rate mysteriously moved in support of the political fortunes of Reagan and Bush. The dollar depreciation of 1985–86 initiated an export boom and thereafter a reduction in the trade deficit, first in real and then in nominal terms, which buoyed the economy in the election year 1988. Internal and external economic prosperity contributed enormously to the success of the Bush election campaign, also managed by Baker. (For the third presidential election in a row, the economy favored the Republican candidate.) The improved trade performance also helped the administration to eliminate the most egregiously protectionist aspects of the omnibus trade legislation as it worked its way through Congress, and to secure approval of the US–Canada Free Trade Agreement in 1988 as well.

---

62. See US Department of the Treasury, "Report on Exchange Rates and International Economic Policy," 15 October 1988. For recent (discouraging) projections of the US current account balance through 1992, assuming continuation of current policies, see Cline, *American Trade Adjustment*, 15.

63. Funabashi, *Managing the Dollar*, 85.

When the depreciation of the dollar appeared to become a problem for the financial markets, Baker moved successfully to halt it, with the help of foreign governments and central banks, although not without episodes of volatility and enormous central bank intervention, as net private capital inflow to the United States essentially ceased in 1987. The appreciation of the dollar in 1988 temporarily relieved nagging concerns about financial instability, a hard landing, and inflation. It appeared so well timed for the electoral prospects of George Bush that the conspiracy theory enjoyed widespread credibility.

Much of Baker's magic in exchange rate management was, as with all magicians, illusion. Baker had dissociated himself from failure and associated himself with success throughout his political life, and at the Treasury he remained adept at perceiving the handwriting on the wall—at the Fed or in the exchange market—and moving with the trend: in 1985 and 1986, when the dollar probably would have declined at least somewhat without his talking it down; in early 1987 when Fed tightening would have supported the dollar regardless of the Louvre Accord; and after the stock market crash when Fed loosening would have lowered the dollar on its own.

Yet much of Baker's successful management was not illusion but reality. Few analysts predicted that the dollar would fall as fast as it did between the Plaza and the Louvre, and no one predicted that a realignment could be accomplished so rapidly without triggering the much-feared hard landing. By the time Baker left the Treasury in August 1988, the exchange markets were riveted on statements of the G-7 and the prospects for international coordination.

Baker's tenure at the Treasury is a dramatic illustration of how officials with both international and domestic responsibilities can enhance their influence by using powers in each arena to their benefit in the other. We know of few others who have played this game so adeptly.[64] In talking down the dollar and pressing allies for an expansion of domestic demand, Baker was fighting for the popular domestic causes of continued growth and reducing the trade deficit. At the same time, foreign governments perceived Baker as a bulwark against growing protectionism within the United States. Powerful interlocutors at both his domestic and international bargaining tables were therefore willing to give Baker things he could use at the other table. Baker thereby became the linchpin of a multinational deal that initiated adjustment and maintained continued financial flows to the United States until visible reductions in the trade deficit

---

64. Helmut Schmidt raised himself to the status of world statesman and most popular German Chancellor since Konrad Adenauer by riding this virtuous domestic-international spiral. One example of his use of this strategy is revealed in Robert D. Putnam and C. Randall Henning, "The Bonn Summit of 1978: A Case Study in Coordination," in Richard N. Cooper, Barry Eichengreen, Gerald Holtham, Putnam, and Henning, *Can Nations Agree? Issues in International Economic Cooperation* (Washington: Brookings Institution, 1989), 12–140.

could reassure investors. That Baker had formal authority over neither monetary, nor fiscal, nor trade policy made his central role all the more remarkable.

On a grimmer note, the second Reagan term saw continued failure on the fiscal front. International payments and exchange rate considerations were no more incorporated into budget policymaking during 1985–89 than they had been during 1981–84. President Reagan reportedly gave the dollar and international pressure slight consideration when signing the Gramm-Rudman-Hollings compromise in September 1987, and somewhat more emphasis in his immediate response to the October crash.[65] But the postcrash environment was exceptional.

Baker and Darman do not appear to have sought with any consistency to *use* international pressure or international economic arguments to gain domestic budgetary leverage. To the contrary, they seem to have maintained intra-administration dominance of exchange rate policy and the forums of macro-economic coordination by steering clear of the key substantive issue—the budget deficit—that would have given the process serious content.

Epilogue: The Early Bush Administration

In stark contrast to his predecessor, George Bush had to confront the exchange rate issue almost immediately after his decisive election victory. With the dollar falling and anxieties about future administration policies growing, Bush sent out mixed signals. His first reaction was complacent: "Once in a while I think about those things, but not much." His more considered response, in his second press conference as President-elect on 14 November, was to declare his commitment to "exchange rate stability," but not "to peg the dollar to any existing currency." Bush clearly aimed to reassure the markets: He would act on the budget deficit, "a matter of grave urgency." And the existing policy, "built around policy coordination and exchange rate stability," he declared, "will be the policy of the George Bush administration."[66]

During that same postelection period, Secretary Brady dismissed the notion that the depreciation of the dollar reflected the markets' verdict on the

---

65. The President's statement on the day after the crash, intended to reassure the markets, linked the Louvre Accord and US budget deficit reduction in the same sentence. After citing the agreement among Baker, Stoltenberg, and Pöhl to coordinate policies to provide for noninflationary growth and stable exchange rates, he said, "The United States remains committed to the Louvre agreement, and today I signed the preliminary sequester order under the Gramm-Rudman-Hollings law. However, I think it is preferable, if possible, that the executive and legislative branches reach agreement on a budget deficit reduction package. . . . " Reprinted in *New York Times*, 21 October 1987.

66. *Washington Post*, 14 and 15 November 1988.

prospective fiscal policies of the Bush administration. Observing that the exchange markets fluctuate and that the dollar was again at the level of January 1988 (121–123 yen and 1.73–1.75 marks), Brady echoed Bush's initial remarks, saying, "I don't really worry about it very much."[67]

Taken at face value, such words might have signaled a return to the pattern of exchange rate neglect characteristic of new administrations, Reagan's in particular. But there was no dramatic break with Baker's policies. Aside from these initial comments there was rhetorical continuity and some intervention. The large, persistent trade imbalances and the potential for financial instability made exchange rate neglect risky both economically and politically. Nonetheless, other issues would take priority in the administration's first six months, particularly the savings and loan crisis at home and the debt crisis in the Third World, which consumed most of the Treasury's energies in international forums.

Brady buttressed his capacity on the international front by retaining his chief exchange rate experts, promoting David Mulford to the newly created position of Under Secretary for International Affairs,[68] and naming Charles H. Dallara to replace Mulford as Assistant Secretary. The Brady Treasury also convened the G-7 in Washington twice in the first three months after the inauguration. Both meetings were called mainly for the purpose of launching the Secretary's new debt plan, however, and neither advanced the cause of policy coordination. The first meeting, in February, issued no communiqué, at Brady's insistence—a break from the past. The second, on the other hand, indicated a G-7 preference for a gentle fall of the dollar by adding the qualifier that an *excessive* depreciation would be counterproductive.[69] At neither meeting could the United States offer significant action on the budget; during this very period, in fact, Darman was negotiating a budget agreement with congressional leaders that would duck the painful questions, particularly taxation.

By late spring, however, the dollar had risen well outside the secret target ranges to which the G-7 was committed, and its credibility was badly shaken. The Treasury confronted the policy choice of whether to disband or restore the target ranges and, if the latter, whether to mount a new effort to reunify the G-7

---

67. *Wall Street Journal*, 21 November 1988, C13.

68. Baker had left vacant the venerable position of Under Secretary for Monetary Affairs, previously filled by Robert V. Roosa, Paul A. Volcker, Anthony M. Solomon, and Beryl W. Sprinkel.

69. The communiqué read: "The Ministers and Governors agreed that a rise of the dollar which undermined adjustment efforts, or an excessive decline, would be counterproductive, and reiterated their commitment to cooperate closely on exchange markets." Statement of the Group of Seven, press release, Washington, 2 April 1989.

in its commitment to the old target ranges or to revise them.[70] The Treasury chose to intervene in moderate quantities and to reiterate statements of commitment in a moderate tone, but declined to take stronger action. Coupled with monetary policy changes that were essentially cooperative but that took place outside of any framework of deliberate coordination, the Treasury's response raised the specter of a policy retreat—if not to the laissez-faire exchange rate policies of the first Reagan administration, then at least away from the highly activist approach taken by the second.

As of late July 1989, furthermore, the exchange rate was clearly far less of a priority than it had been during the Baker-Darman heyday. In part this reflected the dollar's lower value: the misalignment was far less egregious than in 1985. It also reflected the necessary commitment of energies to other urgent matters: the financial plight of the savings and loans and the Latin debtors had been too long neglected. But above all, the Brady Treasury's relative inattention to exchange rates reflected an incapacity to face up to the central problem of US international economic policy: the continuing huge imbalance on current account, the contribution of the budget deficit to this imbalance, and the need for a bold, integrated policy approach aimed squarely at its resolution. Without such an approach, the gains from targeting the exchange rate would be limited.

As this book goes to press, the Bush administration is little more than half a year old, and so a definitive judgment would be premature, to say the least. But the new administration has, at minimum, lost the chance to tackle the deficit problem at a particularly propitious time: its initial months in power. It has brought talent to the task, but not yet serious policy commitment. The good relations that Darman has developed with House and Senate budget leaders seem to have been achieved through a spring 1989 budget package that causes little immediate pain to anyone, and hence does little about the problem it ostensibly addresses. There is no evidence, moreover, that Secretary Brady, the cabinet member best placed to recognize the external-internal connections, has used international economic arguments to underscore the need for bold action on the budget deficit (and even tax increases if necessary) in administration discussions.

Hence the United States approaches the 1990s with the same egregious domestic imbalance that lies at the root of its trade and current account imbalance. Future exchange rate policymakers will suffer in consequence. But they will have company.

---

70. Conflicting accounts emerged of internal dissent over whether to jettison target ranges in favor of a more "flexible" exchange rate policy. See Peter T. Kilborn, "New Strategy on the Dollar," *New York Times*, 22 May 1989, D1; Hobart Rowen, "The Dollar Confounding Experts, Central Banks, Continues to Rise," *Washington Post*, 23 May 1989, A1.

Part II

Actors, Institutions, and Processes

5

The Treasury–Federal Reserve Nexus

The Treasury Department stands above all others in government in determining exchange rate policy. In the jargon of Washington bureaucratic politics, the Treasury has "clear primacy" in this policy area. But as the preceding chapters have described, Treasury Secretary James Baker did not embark on his new, activist policy of dollar depreciation in 1985 alone with his G-7 allies. Before taking this major step, he consulted with Federal Reserve Chairman Paul Volcker. And in early 1987, when a rapid dollar decline induced an upturn in US interest rates and Volcker became dissatisfied with the strategy of talking the dollar down, Baker and Deputy Secretary Richard Darman desisted and negotiated the Louvre Accord with the G-7 partners to seek stabilization instead. Neither the Plaza Agreement nor the Louvre Accord was the Fed's creation; both were negotiated primarily by the Treasury Secretary. But Volcker was party to both, and the options available to Baker were strongly influenced by the disposition of the central bank, and of the markets as well.

Clearly the Treasury must act in concert with the Fed; together they form the heart of the closed policymaking system. The Federal Reserve controls many of the funds available for intervention, the machinery of foreign-currency operations, and, most importantly, domestic monetary policy. It also maintains closer ties than does the Treasury to the Bundesbank, the Bank of Japan, and other key central banks. Thus, Baker knew that he was unlikely to be successful if the Fed did not support his exchange rate policies. Similarly, Volcker needed the Treasury's active involvement to reduce exchange rate volatility and the risks of financial instability and a hard landing. And although it was not his specific responsibility, Volcker was interested in stemming protectionism on Capitol Hill. The mutual dependency of the Treasury and the Federal Reserve is the subject of this chapter.

The relationship between the Treasury and the Fed is substantially different from that in most other major advanced countries, where the central bank is subject to direction or strong guidance by the finance ministry, which is thus predominant both *de jure* and *de facto* in exchange rate policy. But because the Fed is autonomous in domestic monetary policy, which in turn affects exchange rates, the Treasury must consult intensively with it on matters relating to currency management.[1] The law defines the exchange rate authorities of the Treasury and the Fed only ambiguously; those authorities have been clarified through bargaining and decades of cooperation (and conflict) in practice.

Whether the unique Treasury-Fed power-sharing arrangement is optimal for exchange rate management is not at all clear. We have noted in earlier chapters that the Fed and the Treasury have generally operated autonomously with respect to important private economic interests and the Congress, and have at times given these interests short shrift. We have also observed that exchange rate policy changes more often and more quickly than do underlying US interests. What policy strengths and shortcomings originate from the power-sharing arrangement between the Treasury and the Fed? Has their bargaining yielded good policy? Or has policy taken second place to the working out of institutional compromises? Does the legal ambiguity contribute to insensitivity to the interests of outside actors, particularly in the traded-goods sectors, as officials in each bureaucracy, fearing that their prerogatives could be challenged, become preoccupied with the concerns of the other? Does the bifurcation of exchange rate responsibility contribute to the closure of the policymaking system?

At least as important, does the basic division of labor make sense? Should the Treasury continue to make decisions on foreign-exchange intervention while the Fed retains independent control over monetary policy? Should the Treasury have greater authority over international than over domestic monetary policy? In an environment of high capital mobility, the barriers between the domestic money market and the foreign-currency market have been eroded. The exchange rate impact of the Treasury's purchase of dollars through intervention can be offset by the Fed's supply of dollars through open market operations. Although wielding nominal power over exchange rates, is the Treasury not actually impotent to affect them except temporarily, unless it is able to persuade the Fed to change monetary policy? If so, should the Treasury be given the authority to instruct the Fed to support its exchange rate

---

1. The relationship between the German finance ministry and the Bundesbank, the other formally independent G-7 central bank, is also somewhat more equal and less clearly defined than most. There are nonetheless important contrasts with the Treasury-Fed relationship: the Bundesbank has full authority over foreign-exchange intervention under the floating exchange rate system and owns all of Germany's international reserves. Under the European Monetary System, the Bundesbank has provisionally accepted the obligation—made to other central banks, not the German finance ministry—to intervene at the margins. To the extent that it wants to abide by that freely entered-into obligation, as it has for ten years, the Bundesbank is dependent on the finance ministry to negotiate parity changes when necessary to avoid running a more expansionary monetary policy than it desires.

objectives with domestic monetary policy? Alternatively, should full exchange rate authority be vested in the Fed?[2]

To explore these questions, we outline the relationship between the Fed and the Treasury as treated in US law and as it has evolved in practice. We review the essential elements of Treasury-Fed interaction during the 1980s, in order to assess the benefits and the shortcomings of present institutional arrangements at the core of the policymaking system.

Shared Power and Responsibilities

Negotiations between the Treasury and the Fed over exchange rate authority are given wide latitude by the ambiguous statutory treatment of the prerogatives and responsibilities of each in exchange rate management. US law often leaves the roles of executive agencies with overlapping jurisdictions unclear. But the legal basis of the division of responsibility between the Treasury and the Fed with respect to exchange rates is unusually obscure. This ambiguity leaves more room for, and creates greater necessity for, negotiations among the experienced professionals within each bureaucracy.

A series of negotiated agreements and tradition have defined current practices with respect to foreign-exchange intervention, public declarations, and international negotiations.[3] These arrangements have not always worked well. But every official directly involved in exchange rate policymaking to whom we have spoken at either the Treasury or the Fed strongly insists that conflicts can be worked out between the two without resort to outside arbitration from the Congress.[4] No dispute has yet arisen that has driven either bureaucracy to seek an alliance with outside actors. Both prefer to negotiate within nebulous legal

---

2. We are examining here not whether the targeting of monetary policy toward the exchange rate is desirable, but the assignment of responsibility for decisions on how to target monetary policy. We believe that the dollar should be an important target of monetary policy, however, within the broad substantive framework spelled out in Chapter 8.

3. For another examination of this relationship between the Treasury and the Federal Reserve, related to events in the 1970s, see Stephen D. Cohen and Ronald I. Meltzer, *U.S. International Economic Policy in Action* (New York: Praeger, 1982), 38–45.

4. We are aware of two cases during the 1970s in which members of Congress offered to clarify the relationship legislatively by giving explicit authority to the Treasury for exchange rate management. Under two different administrations, the Treasury declined this authority. One case is recorded in the public testimony of former Secretary William E. Simon in US Congress, House, Committee on Banking, Currency and Housing, Subcommittee on International Trade, Investment and Monetary Policy, *To Provide for Amendment of the Bretton Woods Agreements Act*, hearings, 94th Cong., 2d sess., 1 and 3 June 1976, 43–44.

guidance rather than risk loss of control over the outcome through congressional involvement in defining responsibilities.

Intervention and the Law

The legal right of both the Fed and the Treasury to buy or sell foreign currencies is undisputed. The Treasury is explicitly authorized by the Gold Reserve Act of 1934 to intervene in the foreign-exchange market to stabilize the dollar. That legislation created the Exchange Stabilization Fund (ESF) for that purpose and placed it under the "exclusive control" of the Secretary of the Treasury, subject to the approval of the President. That control is specifically not subject to review by any other officer of the government.[5]

Statutes do not explicitly grant the same authority to the Federal Reserve, but a series of legal opinions and years of practice have also established the Federal Reserve's authority to intervene. Finding insufficient funds in the ESF in the early 1960s to defend the dollar and the nation's gold stock under the Bretton Woods regime, the Treasury sought to create Federal Reserve swap arrangements with other central banks for foreign-exchange intervention, to avoid having to request a supplementary ESF allocation from Congress.[6] To permit this plan to go forward, opinions of the general counsels of the Federal Reserve and the Treasury, as well as the Attorney General, recognized the Fed's legal authority to intervene.[7] Any doubts stemming from the lack of explicit statutory authorization have been extinguished by almost three decades of practice.

Can either the Treasury or the Fed block intervention by the other? Here the law is more ambiguous, even if in practice the Treasury has decided when intervention would take place and in what amounts. No statute explicitly gives the Treasury *exclusive* authority over all foreign-exchange operations (only those

---

5. Gold Reserve Act of 1934, reproduced in *Statutes at Large,* vol. xlviii, part I, 73rd Cong., 2d sess., 24, 25, and 30 January 1934, 337–44. The House Banking Committee argued in 1985 that, after the switch to flexible exchange rates, amendments to the act had removed the mandate to use the ESF for stabilization of the dollar. See US Congress, House, Committee on Banking, *Competitive Exchange Rate Act of 1985,* report, 99th Cong., 1st sess., 20 December 1985, 16–17. The Treasury's use of these funds for dollar stabilization has not been challenged, however, and these amendments have not constrained the Treasury in practice.

6. F. Lisle Widman, *Making International Monetary Policy* (Washington: International Law Institute, Georgetown International Law Center, 1982), 123.

7. See Howard H. Hackley, Memorandum to the Federal Open Market Committee on legal aspects of a proposed plan for Federal Reserve operations in foreign currencies, 22 November 1961; Robert H. Knight, Memorandum to the Secretary of the Treasury, 6 January 1962, reproduced in US Congress, House, Committee on Banking, *Report on the General Agreements to Borrow,* 1962, 87th Cong., 2d sess., 353–66.

from the ESF) or the ability to direct the Fed to intervene in the market with its own funds. No law states that the Treasury is in charge of exchange rate policy or the exchange rate. And the Fed is sensitive to legislation that would explicitly or implicitly confer such authority on the Treasury. This may have been a motive when, for example, in 1985 a Fed official advised a House banking subcommittee that the Fed should report on exchange rates separately from the Treasury rather than only being consulted by the Secretary before issuing his report. (See Chapters 4 and 6. That this was the formal position of the Fed has been strongly denied, however, by a senior official.)

The Treasury has nonetheless maintained its legal right to block Fed intervention on the grounds that the Secretary is the chief financial officer of the US government, the US representative to international financial organizations such as the International Monetary Fund and the World Bank, and the chairman of the National Advisory Council, and on the basis of the President's constitutional role in foreign policy.[8] The Fed maintains that none of these legal arguments supersedes the authority it derives from the Federal Reserve Act, as interpreted, to conduct intervention; that law makes no mention of review outside of the Fed. However, the Fed has never put this legal argument to the test by intervening in the market against an express directive of the Treasury. After the shooting of President Reagan in April 1981, for example, the Fed intervened without the Treasury's prior approval but not over its opposition. In the interpretation of this unresolved legal question, therefore, the weight of practice tends to favor the Treasury. Challenging the Treasury is a step the Fed would take only in extreme circumstances and only when it calculated considerable political support for its action in the Congress.

Could the Treasury force the Fed to intervene against its will? Here enters an important distinction between *who* conducts intervention and *from whose account* the intervention funds come. The Treasury does not have legal standing to instruct the Fed to intervene on the Fed's own account. But because the Federal Reserve Bank of New York acts as the agent for the Treasury as well as for the Federal Open Market Committee (FOMC) in foreign-currency operations, the Treasury can instruct the New York Fed to intervene on the Treasury's own account. Breaking the agency agreement, although violating no explicit law, would be a breach of contract. More important, such a decision would have ramifications for Fed-Treasury relations beyond the immediate exchange rate area, as the New York Fed also acts as the Treasury's agent in placement of

---

8. These reasons have been repeated by Treasury officials in congressional testimony over the years. See the testimony of William Simon, cited above, and of Beryl W. Sprinkel in US Congress, Joint Economic Committee, *International Economic Policy*, hearing, 97th Cong., 1st sess., 4 May 1981, 11, 18.

government debt. A decision by the Fed not to honor the agency agreement might well encourage the Treasury to shop around for another agent!

The law thus defines a crucial part of the environment in which the Treasury and the Fed have negotiated and renegotiated their respective roles over time and the basis of their cooperation. In summary, the law grants both organizations the right to intervene in the markets, but the Treasury argues that it is first among equals and has the right both to prevent the Fed from intervening and to instruct the Fed to intervene on the Treasury's account. The Fed has challenged neither assertion by action.

Treasury-Fed Intervention in Practice

Although the law gives each bureaucracy the right to intervene without the permission of the other, in practice virtually no intervention takes place without mutual consent. Participants describe intervention decision making as a "mutual veto system" (a somewhat confusing phrase, because what is meant is that *either* party can block action). However, the system operates in a context in which the Treasury has the upper hand.

Since the resumption of intervention activities in the early 1960s, the Fed has assured the Treasury that it would not intervene without its approval, but has never recognized the Treasury's right to veto Fed intervention as a matter of law. The 1962 FOMC guidelines on intervention instructed the Fed Chairman to "keep the Secretary of the Treasury fully advised and to consult on such policy matters as may relate to the Secretary's responsibilities."[9] This carefully phrased sentence was interpreted by Treasury officials to mean that the Fed would never intervene without the Secretary's approval.[10] This understanding was reportedly reinforced after the switch to floating exchange rates in the early 1970s by a letter from then-Chairman Arthur F. Burns to then–Treasury Secretary George Shultz, which has never been made public. During 1972–74, in fact, the Treasury blocked the Fed from intervening on several occasions.[11]

---

9. "Authorization Regarding Open Market Transactions in Foreign Currencies," in *Forty Ninth Annual Report of the Board of Governors of the Federal Reserve System, 1962.* Approved by the Federal Open Market Committee on 13 February 1962 (Washington: Federal Reserve, 1963), 60.

10. Widman, *Making International Monetary Policy,* 124.

11. See, for example, Robert Solomon, *The International Monetary System, 1945–1976: An Insider's View,* 2d ed. (New York: Harper & Row, 1982), 338; Charles A. Coombs, *The Arena of International Finance* (New York: Wiley, 1976), 227, 232, 234. Volcker, then Treasury Under Secretary for Monetary Affairs, assured the House Banking Committee that there was no possibility that the Fed would intervene without the Treasury's consent. See US Congress, House, Committee on Banking, Subcommittee on International

The Treasury and the Fed also informally agreed, in the late 1970s, that when intervention was necessary they would provide roughly equal amounts of funds. The Fed insisted on this arrangement to ensure that the Treasury would have the financial incentive to back the exchange rate policy it was asking the Fed to support. Although the rule is not strictly adhered to, the 50–50 split characterized intervention during 1985–88.

The Treasury and the Fed have created a well-defined apparatus for coordinating foreign-exchange intervention. The process does not always work smoothly, but it has worked by and large. It is reinforced by several procedures. The first is the roughly equal financial participation in foreign-exchange operations just described. Second, all intervention, whether on the account of the Fed or from the ESF, is conducted through the same officer at the New York Fed. Third, officials at the Treasury, at the Federal Reserve Board in Washington, and at the New York Fed confer frequently and regularly whenever the markets are open, and yet more often when the markets are unstable. Fourth, the norm of cooperation is strong, enhanced by the interchange of personnel between the Fed and the Treasury over their professional lifetimes.

Finally, the threat of intervention by Congress is an important discipline ensuring coordination. The banking committees have frequently raised questions about the degree of coordination between the Treasury and the Fed.[12] During hearings after the collapse of the Bretton Woods regime, both the Treasury and the Fed assured the Congress that they would cooperate. In one such hearing Chairman Burns promised that he would immediately notify Congress if the Treasury and the Fed failed to resolve differences over intervention.[13] Members of the banking committees have also explicitly asked, on occasion, whether the responsibility for intervention should be redivided between the two bureaucracies.[14] Prevention of congressional meddling in

---

Finance, *To Amend the Par Value Modification Act of 1972*, hearings, 93rd Cong., 1st sess., 6, 7, 13, 14, and 21 March 1973, 99–100.

12. See, for example, US Congress, House, Committee on Banking, Subcommittee on International Finance, *To Amend the Par Value Modification Act of 1972*, 99–100, 372–73; House, Committee on Banking, *To Provide for Amendment of the Bretton Woods Agreements Act*, 1976, 44; Joint Economic Committee, *International Economic Policy*, 1981, 18.

13. US Congress, Joint Economic Committee, *How Well Are Fluctuating Exchange Rates Working?* hearings, 93rd Cong., 1st sess., 20, 21, 26, and 27 June 1973, 189.

14. A controversy over the use of ESF funds and the switch to floating rates called into question the usefulness of the ESF in the mid-1970s. Representative Sam M. Gibbons (D-FL) asked whether the ESF should be simply dissolved in favor of the Federal Reserve carrying out all intervention. See US Congress, House, Committee on the Budget, Task Force on Tax Expenditures and Off-Budget Agencies, *Exchange Stabilization Fund*, hearing, 94th Cong., 2d sess., 18 February 1976. Witnesses, including Paul Volcker, then President of the Federal Reserve Bank of New York, argued that the ESF should be retained. It was retained, but its administrative expenses were thereafter placed on budget and subjected to an audit by the General Accounting Office.

arrangements that have proved mutually satisfactory is a powerful incentive for both bureaucracies to cooperate.

In practice, both the Fed Chairman and the Treasury Secretary make public statements and conduct international negotiations that involve exchange rate policy. At times, statements of the Chairman can have at least as great an impact on exchange markets as those of the Secretary. While deferring to the Secretary to make declarations as to what is "the exchange rate policy of the United States," the Chairman is free to make statements about the need for stability in the markets and what exchange rate levels would be desirable, and to imply whether monetary policy might be adjusted in response to movements in the rate. The Chairman discusses monetary policy coordination with the presidents of foreign central banks, with a view toward stabilizing exchange rates. As the Chairman must be included in any serious international negotiations by the Secretary, the Chairman is a member of the G-7. The Secretary, however, is the acknowledged leader in committing the United States to any international accord.

Impact on Federal Reserve Autonomy

Because of international financial market liberalization and increased capital mobility there is today a much stronger link between monetary policy and the exchange rate than earlier in the postwar period. Consequently there is a greater need not only for the coordination of exchange rate intervention policy but also for the coordination of that policy with the Fed's domestic monetary policy. This in turn creates inevitable conflicts between the autonomy of the Fed in the domestic sphere—also a negotiated rather than a legal matter—and the Treasury's lead on exchange rate policy.

Neither bureaucracy is completely insensitive to the primary wishes of the other in this conflict: the Treasury shares the Fed's interest in price stability, and the Fed is likewise interested in exchange rate stabilization. Moreover, the two bureaucracies tend to be allies within broader US governmental debates in the importance they give to anti-inflation and exchange rate goals versus, for example, output and employment objectives. Nonetheless, the potential for conflict over the extent to which monetary policy should take exchange rate considerations into account is high in periods of activist exchange rate policy.

Because the Secretary of the Treasury has broad economic responsibilities domestically and internationally, the Fed must give due weight to the Secretary's international commitments in the exchange rate field or run the risk of being perceived as outside the government (rather than as part of the government but not subject to the administration). But neither can the Secretary underestimate the importance of the Fed's domestic monetary policy, which can undercut the Treasury's credibility in international bargaining. The result is a delicate game between powerful bureaucracies.

As a former participant in this game has described it, the outcome of conflict is determined by the relative political position of the Chairman and the Secretary. But that position is itself a product of, among other things, general economic conditions. When the economy is in recession and inflation is falling, the Secretary will be in a stronger position than when growth is robust and the financial markets and the public are looking to the Fed to squelch inflation. Large trade imbalances tend to favor the Treasury, on the other hand. The Treasury can also improve its bargaining position vis-à-vis the Fed through the advice it provides on presidential appointments to the Fed's Board of Governors.

Interbureaucracy Conflict and Cooperation in the 1980s

During the first Reagan administration, the main point of contention between the Treasury and the Fed was whether to take an interest in exchange rate volatility. The Fed repeatedly urged the Treasury to intervene in the foreign-exchange markets in order to stabilize the dollar. At first, in 1981 and 1982, the Fed from time to time recommended selling dollars for foreign currency. It pressed less frequently to go into the market during 1983 and 1984, now recognizing Regan and Sprinkel's tenacity in their nonintervention policy. Virtually all of the intervention authorized by the Regan Treasury was instigated by the Fed.

Nonetheless, despite their advocacy, Volcker and the Fed were clearly not keen on intervention and did not see it as a solution to the problem of the dollar's misalignment. Volcker consistently said that intervention could play a constructive subsidiary role but could not substitute for action on the fundamentals. The US budget deficit, in contrast, was fundamental, and it was the principal cause of the growing trade deficit through the foreign borrowing it promoted. Furthermore, as the dollar soared and the twin deficits grew, Volcker flatly contradicted President Reagan, who in his 1985 State of the Union address called for continued capital inflow. Volcker stated:

> Economic analysis and common sense coincide in telling us that the budgetary and trade deficits of the magnitude we are running are not sustainable indefinitely in a framework of growth and prosperity. They imply a dependence on foreign borrowing by the United States that, left unchecked, will sooner or later undermine the confidence in our economy essential to a strong currency and to prospects for lower interest rates. . . . We cannot logically take actions to reduce our trade deficit and at the same time welcome the associated capital inflows from abroad. The trade deficit and our capital inflow are two sides of the same coin. . . . In essence, a lasting

solution to the problem of our external imbalance rests on simultaneously restoring internal financial equilibrium.[15]

Although these clashing pronouncements revealed deep differences between the President and the Fed, they did not engender a serious conflict, as the Fed is remote from fiscal policymaking.

In general, the Reagan administration shared the Fed's prime objective of reducing inflation. Nonetheless, during Reagan's first two years in office, administration officials—supply-siders and monetarists alike—criticized the Fed's domestic policies. Volcker was consequently less eager than he might have been to press intervention on the Treasury, and this had the effect of opening a "second front." The President, however, never urged Volcker to adopt an easier monetary policy.[16] For their part, Regan and Sprinkel never pushed monetary loosening on the Fed to counter the strong dollar, even when they were critical of Fed policy on domestic grounds. The passive exchange rate policy of the Treasury required virtually nothing in the way of cooperation from the Fed.

Baker's shift to an activist policy, however, did. Volcker would have to sign onto the G-5 Plaza communiqué, along with his central bank counterparts, and he would have to acquiesce in further monetary loosening. Volcker consented to Baker and Darman's declaratory policy, although he amended the communiqué to emphasize that an *orderly* depreciation of the dollar was sought, and he consented to foreign-exchange intervention. He participated in the alternate talking down and stabilizing of the dollar we have labeled the Baker-Volcker routine. Volcker shared Baker's purpose in heading off protectionism in Congress; he likewise shared Treasury's intent to pressure the surplus countries to expand domestic demand.

When Baker pressured the G-5 central banks for easier monetary policy, the Fed acquiesced. Not only did petroleum and general price trends favor the Treasury position, as did the need for trade adjustment, but Reagan appointees to the Fed Board wielded increasing power. Treasury pressure for easy money reinforced the Fed's predisposition to loosen, which had prevailed since the third quarter of 1984 (and perhaps had gone one discount rate cut too far). Without dominating the Fed, Treasury policy certainly contributed to a political

---

15. US Congress, Senate, Committee on Foreign Relations, *The United States in a Global Economy*, hearings, 99th Cong., 1st sess., 27 and 28 February and 6 March 1985, 5–6.

16. See, for example, William Greider, *Secrets of the Temple: How the Federal Reserve Runs the Country* (New York: Simon and Schuster, 1988); Martin Anderson, *Revolution* (San Diego: Harcourt Brace Jovanovich, 1988); William A. Niskanen, *Reaganomics: An Insider's Account of the Politics and the People* (New York: Oxford University Press, 1988).

and economic environment in which the Fed was pressed to loosen monetary policy and found it beneficial to do so.[17]

There was a limit, however, to the Fed's acquiescence in both direct and indirect exchange rate policy. In late 1986 and early 1987, when inflation fears were compounded by fear of a hard landing, Volcker and the Fed diverged from the Treasury. Volcker publicly stated his objection to continued depreciation. And with long-term interest rates turning upward in response to the recent dollar decline, the Treasury likely anticipated that the Fed would accept further market-driven rate increases or even tighten monetary policy to prevent a further slide. That divergence was decisive: the Treasury surrendered the exchange rate weapon—temporarily—and tried to extract countervailing concessions from the G-7 partners in the Louvre Accord. Baker and Darman agreed to stabilize exchange rates, provisionally, despite the fact that the rates then prevailing could not bring substantial US trade adjustment, let alone trade balance, and despite the lack of assurance either of strong Japanese and German programs to stimulate demand or of having reached the primary political goal of squelching trade protectionism.

The independence of Fed policy was underscored during the rebound of the dollar in 1988 and 1989. Even when the Treasury's preference for domestic monetary ease coincided with a preference for restraining the appreciation of the dollar, the Fed's position prevailed. No fundamental adjustments of monetary policy were invoked to preserve the credibility of the target ranges, and small adjustments, such as in June 1989, were infrequent. The inflation and growth environment, as well as the political atmosphere, are thus essential to explaining the outcome of Fed-Treasury disputes over exchange rate and associated monetary policy.

Assessment of Present Arrangements

The present division of responsibilities between the Treasury and the Fed has both major shortcomings and major benefits, as our review of the 1980s has illustrated. We conclude that exchange rate policy has not always been well served by these arrangements, but that they provide a solid structure on which to build. They do not suggest a need for radical reforms.

Because present arrangements constitute a mutual veto system, there is a bias toward inaction with respect to intervention. If either party refuses to act, the

---

17. Henry R. Nau, in contrast, argues that Baker dominated the Fed through the Plaza strategy, with the result that monetary policy became imprudently expansionary. See Henry R. Nau, *American Phoenix: Leadership Power in the World Economy* (Princeton, NJ: Princeton University Press, forthcoming), chap. 9.

other cannot force it to do so. Although both the Fed and the Treasury maintain the legal right each to intervene without the approval of the other, that right is not exercised in practice. Simply because two bureaucracies must agree, intervention is less frequent, smaller, and tardier than it would be if one were given full responsibility. (The same does not hold for public statements, which can still be effective when one party speaks and the other does not, although these too are certainly more effective when both speak in unison. When Treasury and Fed contradict one another, however, the trend of the dollar tends to be accentuated.)

A second problem with present arrangements is that the Fed can be intimidated on exchange rate policy by threats to its autonomy in domestic monetary policy. The Fed perceives frequent threats to its independent operation of monetary policy, and deflecting such attacks is its highest bureaucratic priority.[18] It fears that systematic exchange rate stabilization would constrain its domestic monetary autonomy. But even at times when it prefers to intervene and sterilize, the Fed is not likely to press its case to the fullest when it anticipates that the administration will demand a corresponding shift in domestic monetary policy, as probably happened in 1981–82.

Finally, any power-sharing arrangement is particularly dependent upon constructive personal relations between the leaders of the two organizations. It is not easy to generalize about what produces the desired sort of relationship, but several factors seem important. One is compatible professional experience: cooperation will be easier, for example, if both the Treasury Secretary and the Fed Chairman have prior experience in international finance, or if at least one has worked within the other's bureaucracy (as Volcker did at the Treasury). Another facilitating factor is a pragmatic bent, or at least an absence of strong ideological precommitments. A third is similar, or at least compatible, policy goals and political allegiances. None of these factors operates absolutely: the Treasury-Fed relationship benefited from Volcker's experience but certainly surmounted Baker's financial inexperience. The point is that successful co-determination of exchange rate policy under present arrangements does depend on an effective relationship between independent senior actors, which cannot always be counted upon.

Set against these three important shortcomings of present arrangements are several important advantages. First, functional linkages to other policy areas are an important benefit of vesting exchange rate policy leadership in the Treasury, which either has direct control over these other policies or, as a lead voice within

---

18. For works emphasizing the position of the Fed in domestic monetary policy see, for example, William Greider, *Secrets of the Temple;* John T. Woolley, *Monetary Politics: The Federal Reserve and the Politics of Monetary Policy* (New York: Cambridge University Press, 1984).

the administration, at least has more influence over them than does the Federal Reserve. We have argued that exchange rate and external considerations should be given greater weight in the process of making fiscal policy than they have in the past. Although the Treasury Secretary does not have the influence or control over the US budget that his foreign counterparts have over theirs, the Secretary does have authority over tax policy and is always in form, and frequently in fact, the senior maker of US economic policy short of the President. The Treasury Secretary is thus better placed than other Cabinet officers to connect different policy strands and to adjudicate conflicts between external and internal economic considerations.

The Treasury is also better placed than the Fed to facilitate coordination between the architects of trade and exchange rate policy. That connection was important to the exchange rate policy reversal of 1985, and particularly to the political use of dollar depreciation to forestall and dilute trade protectionism. The Treasury's lead on exchange rate policy is also consistent with its authority to impose or withdraw capital controls, administer taxes on international financial transactions, and borrow or extend official loans abroad, and of course it is consistent with its representation of the United States in the International Monetary Fund and the multilateral development banks.

This international role underscores a second strength of present arrangements, for if Treasury leadership facilitates policy coordination at home, it does likewise abroad: with *foreign* fiscal, structural, and regulatory policies. International conflict over and coordination of these policies is a highly political matter, involving trade-offs and bargains often agreed upon only at the highest level, at the G-7 economic summit meetings. In these negotiations, the United States has often offered to help stabilize exchange rates in exchange for changes in foreign policies. Were this commitment not the administration's to make, potential bargains might not be struck in the future. Meanwhile, the near parity of the Fed provides a useful check on overuse of the exchange rate weapon.

Third, US policy toward the international monetary system and questions of its reform is also highly political, and domestic deliberations in this area should be conducted by authorities with explicitly political (as opposed to technocratic) responsibilities. The dialogue between the executive branch and the Congress is better conducted through the political authority of the Secretary of the Treasury and the President than through the Chairman of the Fed; this becomes particularly important as Congress's interest in exchange rates rises. For similar reasons, linkages and trade-offs between exchange rate and international financial policy on the one hand and foreign and national security policy on the other are better drawn by the Treasury and the President.

Fourth, effective coordination between the Treasury and the Fed, which would be desirable under any redivision of responsibilities, is strongly encouraged by the present arrangement. Indeed, the possibility that the President or the

Congress will intervene in Treasury-Fed conflicts over exchange rates is a powerful incentive for the two to work hard at achieving consensus and workable compromise. Shifting authority toward one or the other, or even statutory clarification of present arrangements, might reduce this incentive for collaboration.

Finally, splitting responsibility for exchange rate policy between the Treasury Secretary and the Chairman of the Fed makes it possible for them, under certain circumstances, to better manage market expectations than either could acting alone. The holders of these positions often have been frustrated by their inability to communicate their own intentions and perceptions to the market.[19] Indeed, any official who has given interviews to journalists on technical subjects such as international finance knows it is often difficult to convey subtle or nuanced views to the markets through the public media. As reported and then interpreted, officials' views are often (although by no means always) greatly simplified. Important qualifications can be dropped. Stated preferences for a depreciation of the dollar as long as it is orderly and gradual are likely to be met with sharp short-term market movements. A single official, constrained by an inability to communicate more than one simple message to the market at a time, could alternately express desire for movement and then for stabilization, but could not do so without quickly losing credibility. *Two* officials with acknowledged exchange rate responsibility, on the other hand, can do so, as the Baker-Volcker routine demonstrated.

Should we retain the present separation of exchange rate from monetary policy authority? Most of our arguments in favor of the present system have stressed the importance of current Treasury authority. That authority could be strengthened by granting the Secretary the power to block the Fed from sterilizing the effects of intervention on the money supply. To make this effective would require giving the Treasury full authority over monetary policy. This radical suggestion is the subject of extensive research elsewhere and involves issues of domestic monetary control that go considerably beyond the scope of the present study. We are certainly not inclined to endorse it here.

Ending the separation by giving the Fed rather than the Treasury full authority over the exchange rate is a less radical proposal and would parallel the Bundesbank's authority over the relationship between the mark and currencies outside of the European Monetary System. It would give the Fed complete discretion in deciding whether to target monetary policy toward the domestic

---

19. Secretary W. Michael Blumenthal's widely perceived talking down of the dollar in 1977 is a case in point. See Cohen and Meltzer, *U.S. International Economic Policy in Action*, 18–23, 33, 59–60; Robert D. Putnam and C. Randall Henning, "The Bonn Summit of 1978: A Case Study in Coordination," in Richard N. Cooper, Barry Eichengreen, Gerald Holtham, Putnam, and Henning, *Can Nations Agree? Issues in International Economic Cooperation* (Washington: Brookings Institution, 1989), 48–50.

price level or toward the exchange rate. It would also remove the Treasury from the Fed's deliberations with other central banks over foreign-currency operations.

However, this proposal would also weaken important Washington policy linkages: between the exchange rate on the one hand and trade and fiscal policies on the other. There is an urgent need, as we have stressed, to strengthen these linkages. During the 1980s, fiscal policy was more poorly coordinated with exchange rate policy than was monetary policy.

Because there remains a significant role for direct exchange rate policy, as argued in Chapter 1, and because Treasury-Fed collaboration can be effective, there is no urgent need for complete organizational integration of exchange rate and monetary policymaking. Furthermore, coordination between international and domestic monetary policy can be improved through measures that stop short of such integration. We prefer the strategy of enhancing cooperation between the Treasury and the Fed on matters surrounding the *execution* of exchange rate policy while offering to other agencies, the Congress, and affected economic interests a stronger voice in the determination of exchange rate policy *goals*. Before elaborating on these recommendations in Chapter 8, we turn to an examination of the roles of Congress and of private economic interests in the exchange rate policy process.

6

The Role of Congress

As it does for trade, the Constitution gives Congress broad authority over the national currency. Authority specifically over exchange rates derived originally from the power of Congress to establish the gold value of the dollar and thus its value in terms of all other currencies linked to gold. That power in turn flowed from Article I, section 8, of the Constitution, which grants Congress the power "To coin money, regulate the value thereof, and of foreign coin. . . "[1] Under the Bretton Woods regime, therefore, the external value of the dollar was determined by statute. The Bretton Woods Agreements Act, section 5, specifically forbade proposals or agreements to change the par value of the dollar, among other things, without congressional authorization in law.

Yet neither Constitution nor statute prevented President Richard M. Nixon from acting, without congressional participation, to close the gold window—to suspend convertibility of the dollar into gold—in August 1971 and to devalue the dollar shortly thereafter. Nixon's move ended the Bretton Woods regime and removed one important source of congressional leverage.[2] Once the link to gold was severed and exchange rates were made flexible in 1973, Congress lost that formal handle on exchange rate policy. In fact, well before Nixon jettisoned Bretton Woods the impracticality of direct congressional exchange rate management had become generally accepted; management of exchange rates

---

1. The last phrase was intended by the framers to prevent states from undermining the federal power of coinage through their valuation of foreign coin in *domestic* circulation at that time. The phrase has not been interpreted as a broader grant of authority over the value of the US currency in terms of foreign currency. For interpretations of this clause in the early years, see Philip B. Kurland and Ralph Lerner, eds., *The Founders' Constitution*, vol. III (Chicago: University of Chicago Press, 1987), 1–12.

2. Congress was worried about the drain of gold from the United States in the 1960s and for that reason questioned the valuation of the dollar under Bretton Woods. President Nixon's actions were therefore consistent with congressional concerns, and Congress did not oppose his decision. Nonetheless, Congress sanctioned these moves, and the switch to floating exchange rates, only after the fact. For explanations of the fall of Bretton Woods and the roles of bureaucratic actors, see Joanne Gowa, *Closing the Gold Window: Domestic Politics and the End of Bretton Woods* (Ithaca, NY: Cornell University Press, 1983); John S. Odell, *U.S. International Monetary Policy: Markets, Power, and Ideas as Sources of Change* (Princeton, NJ: Princeton University Press, 1982).

requires quick responses to market conditions for which only an executive agency is suited. Hence Congress has delegated broad operational and policy responsibility to the Treasury and the Federal Reserve.

However, Congress retains the power to oversee exchange rate policy and to threaten legislation to constrain executive flexibility. It can also limit executive discretion by raising the visibility of the exchange rate in public debate, and it can influence exchange rate policy through links to policy areas where it has greater practical influence, such as trade policy. Although lacking a practical handle on exchange rate policy under the flexible exchange regime of the 1980s, Congress can engage in exchange rate policy entrepreneurship through the use of these incentives and levers. After an initial delay, it became very effective in doing so.

Congressional Roles in the 1980s

Activity by members of Congress to influence exchange rate policy took four principal forms during the 1980s. The first was *routine oversight:* keeping regular watch on Treasury and Fed activity through regularly scheduled hearings and reports. The second was *issue development and consciousness raising,* achieved both through simply reacting to business pressures and through acting as issue entrepreneurs. The third form was proposed *legislation targeting the prime symptom* of exchange rate misalignment, namely, burgeoning imports and stagnating exports. The fourth was proposed *legislation that targeted exchange rate policymaking directly.* Of these, the threat of trade legislation proved the most potent means of influencing the administration's exchange rate posture, but the fourth, direct exchange rate legislation, is of greatest interest to those seeking to link policymaking on the dollar to broader US economic policy interests.

Routine Oversight

The Treasury is obliged by law to report to the banking committees of Congress on the agreements entered into and transactions undertaken on the part of the Exchange Stabilization Fund (ESF). Those reports are submitted at the end of each month as well as annually and are confidential. The committees receive this information while it is relatively current, whereas the general public is informed only quarterly through reports of the Federal Reserve Bank of New York, which themselves are delayed by more than a month. The Treasury's reporting is limited, however, to ESF transactions and does not include intervention on the account of the Fed.

Congress also oversees Treasury-Fed cooperation through standing assurances that the two bureaucracies will cooperate in foreign-exchange matters and that Congress will be immediately informed should the process break down. Both of these mechanisms are passive and do not easily offer Congress opportunities to weigh in on policymaking.

Hearings and investigations provide an avenue for members of Congress to assert their substantive concerns about exchange rate policy. The exchange rate is often considered in public hearings of many different committees on many different subjects. The finance, foreign relations, and commerce committees of both houses frequently raise the issue, as does the Joint Economic Committee.

The banking committees, with primary legislative jurisdiction in this area, are the most likely to hold hearings specifically on the exchange rate. The Secretary of the Treasury, his senior deputies, and the Chairman of the Fed testify regularly before these committees on exchange rates and international financial matters. Indeed, the Secretary has used congressional hearings as a platform from which to make public declarations about a desired level or direction of change of the dollar. These hearings have developed into a principal channel through which the general public learns the content of that policy and officials' intentions. Short-term movements in the markets are often attributed to congressional testimony. Hearings are also an opportunity for members of Congress to sound out other senior members of the administration with responsibilities in trade, industry, agriculture, and labor, for example, on their views of the Treasury's policy.

These mechanisms proved inadequate for Congress in the 1980s. Congress responded by legislating changes in routine procedures to strengthen reporting requirements beyond the monthly ESF reports and occasional hearings (discussed later in this chapter). But en route to this outcome, members of Congress, in tandem with producer interests, used their committees and spoke out on the House and Senate floors to raise the visibility of the exchange rate issue and prepare the way for policy change.

Issue Development and Consciousness Raising

Over the course of the 1980s Congress held more hearings that raised the exchange rate issue than in any previous decade. It was a topic in more than 130 hearings and was given in-depth treatment in at least one-third of these.[3] At first, members were merely skeptical of the nonintervention policy of Regan and

---

3. As measured by the number of hearings indexed under this heading by the Congressional Information Service and by the authors' qualitative assessment of the exchange rate's treatment in them.

Sprinkel. That skepticism grew into outright opposition as the dollar soared, the trade balance plunged, and particular sectors were badly damaged.

Congress played an important role vis-à-vis the private sector and the community of academic economists with views on exchange rate management. Congress passively reflected and conveyed the views of private interests to the administration. But its role was also an active one of managing the input of private interests, stimulating private pressure on the administration, lobbying the administration on behalf of those interests, and raising public consciousness about the importance of the exchange rate during the nonintervention period.

Channeling Producer Discontent

First, through hearings, conferences, and special studies Congress provided a platform for those private interests hurt by the strong dollar during 1981–85 and those private economists who were predicting that it would have a disastrous impact on the trade balance. Providing a Washington megaphone for aggrieved producers and labor unions on these issues was a constituency service. With little capacity for direct impact on exchange rate policy, and not yet sufficiently motivated to threaten drastic action, Congress could in this way forward complaints to the Treasury and vent the frustrations of its business and labor constituents. Legislators could be content in this relatively passive role as long as economic damage from the strong dollar was limited to particular sectors and private groups had not been broadly mobilized on the issue.[4]

It was generally the strong views of a significant minority that made their way through these congressional proceedings into the public and the administration eye. The manufacturing and agriculture sectors were heard in the early and mid-1980s, and the financial sector was heard in 1987 and 1988. However, these interests were not an exact reflection of the concerns of the public at large. Congress sorted among the various interests and chose which views would be heard through committee proceedings. Hearings were often convened to make a specific intellectual or political case: for action in the exchange rate area during the period of neglect, and later, against the raising of US interest rates to defend the dollar.

---

4. Once the second Reagan administration had responded to private concerns with support for dollar depreciation in 1985, Congress played less of a role in simply faithfully forwarding these concerns. The number of corporate officials testifying on the exchange rate issue in hearings declined dramatically after that year. As the Treasury moved toward exchange rate stabilization, new concerns that this would destabilize domestic interest rates and financial markets were voiced through Congress after the stock market crash of October 1987.

Second, while still holding to the role of channel for private advocacy, members of Congress could assist private groups in their efforts to lobby the administration and the Treasury directly on the exchange rate issue. Republican members were particularly important in this regard. For example, House Minority Leader Robert H. Michel (R-IL) and Senator Charles Percy helped Lee Morgan of Caterpillar obtain initial meetings with the President and the Secretary of the Treasury. This function of Congress was more important during 1981–85 when producer discontent was rising than it was after the Plaza Agreement brought hope of a trade correction.

Issue Entrepreneurship

Congressional activity crossed the line, frequently and increasingly, from channeling private concerns to advocating policy in members' own names and mobilizing private interests in support of legislators' positions. To buttress the position that something needed to be done about the strong dollar during the first Reagan administration, members of Congress encouraged private actors to speak out, in hearings and elsewhere. Members also encouraged private-sector support of congressional initiatives offered as an alternative to trade remedies, such as the exchange rate provisions of the trade bill. Members and their staffs were not always satisfied with the support they received for their initiatives. Before the 1984 election, in particular, many of the most important corporate officers were reluctant to criticize the administration's policies publicly. But Congress did have an impact at the margin on the overall level and timing of interest-group activity on exchange rates.

Congress was the focal point for raising the consciousness of the public at large about the exchange rate. Much of the deliberation within Congress was a genuine effort to reach (and communicate) greater understanding of the technical issues surrounding the exchange rate: its effect on trade balances and the domestic economy, its link to capital flows and the budget deficit, and the ability of the Treasury and the Fed to govern the exchange rate through foreign-exchange intervention and domestic monetary policy. The public and private input of the economics profession was particularly important in this regard, since congressional hearings were a particularly attractive target of opportunity for economists who dissented from administration policies. While educating themselves, legislators could at the same time impress upon organized interests and the general public the critical importance of the strong dollar to the trade debacle. This activity aimed directly at rebutting statements of the President and senior Treasury officials that there was no relationship between the budget deficit and the strong dollar or that the strong dollar was good for America.[5]

Trade Legislation

As dollar misalignment persisted together with administration inaction, congressional entrepreneurship spilled over into advocacy of specific legislation. Members proposed measures to restrict imports either in particular industries like steel or across the board (import surcharge proposals), or in (threatened) retaliation against other nations' barriers to US exports (Senator John Danforth's proposals).

When the strong dollar triggered a flood of imports, a rise in protectionist bills was a predictable result.[6] This did not mean Congress was explicitly using trade bills only to gain leverage over exchange rates—many members genuinely sought protection for their constituents. Others wished to pry open foreign markets. When the relationship between trade and exchange rates was perceived, moreover, trade legislation was frequently thought to be a way of offsetting, or insulating sectors from, the effects of the strong dollar, rather than a way of placing pressure on the administration to change its nonintervention policy.

In 1985, however, senior members of Congress drew a strong linkage between the two. Before the Bonn economic summit in May, where the administration would press the Europeans to initiate a new round of GATT negotiations, Senators Danforth (a Republican) and Lloyd Bentsen (a Democrat) explicitly linked their approval of the initiative to inclusion of monetary issues. Danforth was emphatic:

> No trade agreements, however sound, no trade laws, however well enforced, will give Americans a fair chance to compete in the international marketplace if an overvalued dollar has the same effect as a 25–50 percent tariff. To say this is not to belittle trade agreements. Rather it is to state the absolute necessity of dealing

---

5. At least one poll indicates that Congress lost this public relations contest with the "Great Communicator." Taken when the dollar was near its peak, a *New York Times*–CBS poll reported that 60 percent of respondents thought that the strong dollar was "good for U.S. trade" while only 25 percent thought that it was bad! Among those respondents who cared about trade, the perverse gap was only slightly less skewed. *New York Times*, 9 June 1985. We would not infer, however, that Congress had little or no effect on public beliefs, particularly in the circles more concerned with trade policy.

6. The increase in the *number* of such bills was clearly discernable, although it was somewhat less dramatic than contemporary press reports suggested. See I. M. Destler, *American Trade Politics: System Under Stress* (Washington: Institute for International Economics; New York: Twentieth Century Fund, 1986), 75, especially fn. 24.

effectively with the exchange rate issue. One way or another, the problem must be solved. . . .

Congress should insist on clear plans for rectifying the exchange-rate problem and for enforcing our rights under existing [trade] agreements as conditions for granting the president fast track authority for implementing a new negotiating round.[7]

Senator Bentsen spoke for a 13-member group of Democratic Senators, whose views reverberated positively among House Democrats.[8]

The movement within Congress for a wholesale revamping of US trade policy that was not explicitly linked to exchange rate policy had at least as powerful an impact on the administration. The evidence that Congress was increasingly disposed to legislate on trade, the evidence that import restrictions were growing in popularity, the interest of many House Democrats in trade's partisan potential, and the determination of Senate Republicans to equal the Democrats in trade toughness—all "got the administration's attention," as Bentsen put it after the Plaza.

Thus, partly by inadvertence but partly by design, members of Congress, lacking comparably effective sources of influence over the administration, used their comparative advantage in trade policymaking in their conflict with the administration over international economic policy in general and exchange rate policy in particular. Most members did not want sweeping trade barriers, but it was clearly within their power to impose them. The administration could not ignore this prospect.

Congressional threats to take drastic trade action served to prod the administration to play a role that had evolved for it over decades: that of managing the exchange rate and running interference for the Congress on product-specific trade policy.[9] Just as Congress did not want to make product-specific trade policy, so it did not want to make exchange rate policy itself. Rather, legislators

---

7. John C. Danforth, address to the National Press Club on United States Trade Policy, Washington, 25 April 1985.

8. "The New Global Economy: First Steps in a United States Trade Strategy," Preliminary Report of the Senate Democratic Working Group on Trade Policy, April 1985, 28. On the House side, Democrats had been developing their trade policy program since 1983. In an early 1984 report, the Democratic Caucus cited the strong dollar as a primary cause of the trade problem and advocated currency management, suggesting that a target zone system be considered. See National House Democratic Caucus, Task Force on Trade, *Competing for the Future: A Democratic Strategy for Trade* (Washington: National House Democratic Caucus, February 1984), 7–9. The link was hammered home in a report released on 17 October 1985: *A Democratic Program for Trade* (Washington: National House Democratic Caucus, Task Force on Trade, 1985).

9. For an elaboration of the argument that Congress has systematically sought to divest itself of product-specific trade policymaking, while retaining the authority to set broad guidelines and the ability to make "protectionist noise" to satisfy constituent producer interests, see Destler, *American Trade Politics*, especially chaps. 2 and 4.

wanted the administration when setting exchange rate policy to respond to the private pressure being applied to the Congress, which the administration had manifestly not been doing. Much of this pressure, after all, had been originally directed toward the Treasury and met firm resistance there. Private interests then turned to Congress for help.

For congressional leverage on trade policy to be effective in persuading the administration to change its exchange rate policy, two conditions were necessary. The administration had to prefer open trade policies more than it believed the Congress did, and the administration had to calculate that a depreciation of the dollar would eventually ease pressure in Congress for protectionist trade legislation. Fortunately, both conditions held in the mid-1980s.

Given the continuing demands of industries for specific trade relief, why did dollar decline eventually mute congressional protectionism? One reason is that there were counterpressures to protection, from exporters and from firms that market foreign products or use them as inputs.[10] Members of Congress caught between protectionist and antiprotectionist pressures could circumvent the dilemma by pressing for a depreciation of the dollar, since its negative impact on import-dependent groups could not be blamed on Congress. Second, the decline of the dollar that began in 1985 offered members the prospect and later the reality of reduced pressure from traded-goods producers as those producers' real trade situations improved. Third, most members of Congress remain philosophically predisposed toward fair and open trade.[11] Protectionism as a doctrine has declined steadily in popularity from the 1930s on, and although many members are inclined to attack what they see as unfair foreign trade practices, very few see official import barriers as desirable in themselves. Legislators tend to hold fewer preconceived attitudes toward government intervention in foreign-exchange markets and, when forced to choose, will usually opt for intervention in the market for currencies rather than in the market for goods. (This is one way in which ideas have been powerful in international economic policymaking.) Accordingly, many members who opposed trade restrictions policy could agree that the United States should depreciate the dollar. Exchange rate change therefore became a consensus position within the Congress, whether pressed through direct or indirect legislative assaults on administration policy.

When the Congress forced it to choose, the Reagan administration also preferred a regulated exchange market over regulated traded-goods markets. It was the lesser of two evils. The congressional assault on trade policy struck at the heart of the Reagan coalition, which included the multinational corpora-

---

10. I. M. Destler and John S. Odell, *Anti-Protection: Changing Forces in United States Trade Politics*, POLICY ANALYSES IN INTERNATIONAL ECONOMICS 21 (Washington: Institute for International Economics, September 1987).

11. This point draws upon extensive interview evidence but not scientific surveys.

tions that would be most harmed by protection and foreign retaliation. Given bipartisan support for trade action, the movement also threatened to split Republicans politically as well as give the Democratic Party a popular cause. These considerations were more compelling than congressional pressure on the trade issue alone.

That pressure had another fundamental impact on exchange rate policy: it greatly strengthened James Baker's hand in negotiations over currencies and macroeconomic policy with trade partners in the G-7 during 1985–86 and the newly industrializing countries (NICs) in 1987–89.[12]

Direct Legislation on Exchange Rates

Last and clearly not least were congressional efforts to legislate directly on exchange rates. As some members moved from skepticism to outright opposition to the nonintervention policy, Congress began to develop legislative proposals to direct the Treasury, restrict its discretion, and render it more accountable to the relevant committees.[13]

Congress had fired several warning shots over the Treasury's bow by mid-1985. As early as May 1983, the Senate passed unanimously a resolution sponsored by Senator Percy strongly urging the President to seek an international consensus on policy coordination and to initiate talks to achieve "better alinement [sic]" of exchange rates, the yen-dollar rate in particular, at the Williamsburg economic summit.[14] Although the resolution did not induce the

---

12. The Louvre Accord, on the other hand, was not the product of changing congressional pressure. The urgency of the trade issue in the Congress declined between 1985 and 1987, but the resolve to proceed with legislation did not wither, and there had not yet been a reduction in the protectionism of trade proposals. The Treasury apparently took the view that further depreciation of the dollar would do little to discourage trade protection, at the margin, and posed substantial risks to financial stability. Dollar stabilization encountered little opposition in Congress on trade policy grounds in 1987.

13. For another account of the development of legislation in the exchange rate and trade areas, see Barbara A. Fliess, "Mastering Economic Interdependence: Trade, Dollar, Debt and Policy Integration in the United States," Working Paper No. 8, Seminar on the Foreign Policy Process, School of Public Affairs, University of Maryland, July 1988.

14. Senate Resolution (S.Res.) 135, 98th Cong., 1st sess., submitted 6 May 1983. The resolution was passed on 25 May, three days before the summit began. It was not submitted for a vote in the House. The heads of government did indeed agree at Williamsburg to language that seemed to strengthen their commitment to international coordination and exchange rate management. They declared, among other things, "While retaining our freedom to operate independently, we are willing to undertake coordinated intervention in exchange markets in instances where it is agreed that such intervention would be helpful." However, this softly worded commitment seemed to address the problem of exchange rate volatility more than misalignment, and it resulted in little change in practice. One year later, a hearing was granted in the House on a resolution

administration to change its policy at that time, it added to the impetus behind the negotiations to liberalize Japanese capital markets to which the Treasury agreed four months later.

In May 1985, the Senate passed a resolution sponsored by Senator Bill Bradley (D-NJ) that called on the Treasury and the Fed to cooperate with the Group of Five to lower the dollar. The Senate acknowledged that budget deficit reduction was the preferred means to achieve depreciation, but the President had foreclosed this possibility that spring by scuttling the Republican-supported budget deficit reduction package. Exasperated Senators therefore pressed for such "steps as are necessary" to lower the dollar, including intervention.[15]

Amid the congressional ferment over trade policy in the summer of 1985, members of Congress began to refashion their resolutions on exchange rate policy for incorporation into statute. In addition to imposing an import surcharge on target countries, the Bentsen-Gephardt-Rostenkowski bill, submitted in mid-July, would have required the Secretary of the Treasury to develop a plan for a multilateral effort both to reduce exchange rate volatility and instill "moderation" in the dollar's rate and to specify the institutional modalities for implementation and a schedule for negotiations to secure foreign agreement.[16]

Before the August recess, Senators Bradley, Daniel Moynihan, and Max Baucus submitted their own exchange rate legislation. Senator Bradley's proposal would have created a "Strategic Capital Reserve" akin to the ESF, which the Treasury would be required to use to purchase at least $3 billion in

---

(H.J. Res. 585) directing the President and the Federal Reserve to lower the dollar in cooperation with foreign central banks and to expressly repudiate the nonintervention policy. See US Congress, House, Committee on Banking, Subcommittee on Domestic Monetary Policy, *To Assure a Reasonable and Stable Exchange Rate for the Dollar*, hearing, 98th Cong., 2d sess., 9 August 1984, 3–6. This resolution was not passed by the House.

15. The resolution read: "[If fiscal adjustments cannot be made,] the only remaining timely option for lowering the dollar is intervention in foreign exchange markets by the Treasury or the Federal Reserve." *Congressional Record*, 99th Cong., 1st sess., 15 May 1985, S6154.

16. H.R. 3035, 99th Cong., 1st sess., sec. 103, submitted 18 July 1985. Reproduced in US Congress, House, Committee on Ways and Means, Subcommittee on Trade, *Trade Emergency and Export Promotion Act*, hearing, 99th Cong., 1st sess., 17 September 1985, 15. The overvalued dollar was at the center of Rostenkowski's rationale:

People are beating down the doors of Congress because government has no clear plan to shore up our international competitiveness; no plan to reduce the overvalued dollar to allow U.S. exports to compete abroad and domestic goods to compete with imports at home; no plan to minimize the impact of rapidly increasing imports that this high dollar now causes; and no plan to systematically eliminate unfair practices of barriers abroad.

Quoted in Stephen D. Cohen, *The Making of United States International Economic Policy: Principles, Problems, and Proposals for Reform*, 3d ed. (New York: Praeger, 1988), 210.

foreign currency each quarter when the previous four quarters' current account deficit exceeded 1.5 percent of GNP and the dollar was at least 15 percent above the level required to balance the current account. The Federal Reserve was specifically instructed not to sterilize the effects of this intervention on the money supply. The Moynihan-Baucus proposal directed the Treasury and the Fed to purchase foreign currencies to create a foreign-currency reserve. The common element of both proposals was mandatory intervention, which all three Senators argued was necessary given the administration's record to date.[17]

Secretary Baker was responding to this movement as well as to pressure on trade policy when he decided in mid-August to proceed with the Plaza announcement. The Treasury strongly opposed all of Congress's efforts to restrict its discretion in exchange rate and intervention policy. When Bradley queried Baker and Richard Darman at a chance meeting on the day of the Plaza announcement, Darman quipped, "You can take your bill out of the hopper."[18] The Treasury argued that the Plaza Agreement obviated exchange rate legislation on the grounds that it was now pushing against an open door.[19]

However, members of Congress were not convinced that the Plaza Agreement represented a decisive change of policy, especially because the extent of the policy reversal was being downplayed by Baker at the time, and because the Regan Treasury had retreated from cooperative-sounding international statements several times before.[20] They continued efforts to legislate exchange rate

---

17. US Congress, House, Committee on Banking, Subcommittee on International Finance, Trade and Monetary Policy, *Exchange Rate Misalignment*, hearing, 99th Cong., 1st sess., 23 October 1985.

18. *Wall Street Journal*, 9 October 1985. We agree with Senator Bradley's own assessment: "It's clear that they were responding to the possibility that Congress might mandate such a move."

19. See the testimony of Assistant Secretary Mulford in US Congress, Senate, Committee on Banking, *Exchange Rate Misalignment*, 41–73; US Congress, House, Committee on Banking, Subcommittee on International Finance, Trade and Monetary Policy, *The Strategic Capital Reserve Act of 1985*, hearings, 99th Cong., 1st sess., 14 and 19 November 1985, 90–112.

20. Speaking to David Mulford during hearings on exchange rate legislation, Representative LaFalce reasoned that Congress should not be satisfied only with the Plaza accord:

[U]ncertainty exists given the changes that have taken place in the administration, the changes that could take place tomorrow. You might be replaced tomorrow and we would have a switch of Don Regan and Jim Baker once again; Beryl Sprinkel could come back to Treasury and you could go to the Council of Economic Advisers. And, to tell you the truth, because personnel changes have had so much to do with policy changes, I seriously believe that Congress ought to attempt to work more aggressively, either through legislation or through oversight or a combination of the two, with the administration on processes as well as product.

See US Congress, House, Committee on Banking, Subcommittee on International Finance, Trade and Monetary Policy, *The Strategic Capital Reserve Act of 1985*, 104. The

policy in the House as well. There, in the Banking Subcommittee on International Finance, Representative Stan Lundine (D-NY) proposed Bradley's plan, which became the basis of a compromise with the senior Congressmen: John J. LaFalce (D-NY), Stephen L. Neal (D-NC), and Walter E. Fauntroy (D-DC). By the end of 1985, a total of seven different bills in both houses, actively supported by many different members, contained sections on exchange rate policy.

What is more, support for this legislation came from both sides of the aisle. The House Republican alternative to the Democrats' trade bill contained a section mandating an international monetary conference to follow through on the Plaza and consider systemic reform.[21] A number of Republicans on the House Banking Committee indicated sympathy for exchange rate legislation. Their position meant that the administration could not ignore these legislative developments. Bipartisan activity was underscored by the joint efforts of two widely mentioned prospects for the presidential nominations of their respective parties, Senator Bradley and conservative supply-sider Representative Jack Kemp (R-NY). In November they sponsored a well-publicized "congressional summit" on exchange rates and international monetary reform in which both Baker and Darman agreed to participate.[22]

Congressional enthusiasm for legislation in this area did not extend to mandatory intervention, particularly if unsterilized as in the Bradley proposal, or to withholding GATT round authorization, as recommended as well by Representative Lundine. Expert testimony before the House Banking subcommittee reinforced this skepticism and backed the move toward compromise.[23] Representative LaFalce brokered a consensus bill which excluded these proposals but retained the following five main provisions: a "competitive exchange rate" would be an explicit goal of US policy; the President would seek an international conference on exchange rate reform; a strategic capital reserve

---

House Democratic Trade Task Force also argued that the Plaza initiative was "too little and too late." See *A Democratic Program for Trade,* 17 October 1985, 1.

21. Proposed "Trade Partnership Act of 1985," H.R. 3522, 99th Cong., 1st sess., submitted 8 October 1985.

22. Bradley and Kemp did not push a common proposal, and they disagreed on the role gold might play in a reformed international monetary system, but they did agree that systemic reform should be considered and that Congress had a role to play in urging the administration forward. Secretary Baker assured the conference that the Plaza meeting was "not a one-shot effort, but one part of enhanced cooperation." He nevertheless discouraged hasty action toward formal reform. See *Washington Post,* 12 November 1985.

23. C. Fred Bergsten urged a shift of focus from mandatory intervention targets to current account and exchange rate targets with periodic reports by the Secretary and the Fed Chairman setting forth these targets and the means for their implementation. See Bergsten, "Correcting the Dollar and Reforming the International Monetary System," statement before the Subcommittee on International Finance, Trade and Monetary Policy, 19 November 1985, especially 8–13.

would be established within the existing ESF; the Treasury Secretary would report to Congress on exchange rates semiannually; and the recommendations of the International Monetary Fund in bilateral consultations with the Treasury, as provided under Article 4 of the Fund, would be disclosed.[24] This version, which became the most thoroughly elaborated and successful such proposal in the Ninety-ninth Congress, passed the full Banking Committee by a solid margin in December 1985. Action on the floor of the House was delayed pending the development, early in the next session, of the omnibus trade bill, into which the Banking Committee exchange rate provisions were incorporated.

Meanwhile, as the omnibus trade bill worked its way through its various stages over 1986–88, language pertaining to exchange rates was also reported out of the House Ways and Means Committee and the Senate Banking and Finance Committees. The Senate provisions were not as forceful as those of the House, as they gave the Treasury greater flexibility in negotiations and in reporting on exchange rate policy. Senators Bradley, Moynihan, and Baucus became less inclined to give these provisions priority, as none sat on the Banking Committee and in the post-Plaza environment there was no immediate need to require Treasury intervention. However, the fact that all four committees were active ensured that significant exchange rate provisions would be included in the final bill.

Seeking to replace the Gephardt amendment with something that would command broad support, Ways and Means Committee Chairman Dan Rostenkowski (D-IL) inserted in the pending bill a provision developed by the committee staff for an "exchange rate equalization tariff." Directed at those NICs that maintained undervalued currencies—the same targets as the Gephardt provision—this section would have required the Treasury Secretary to open exchange rate negotiations with these countries and authorized imposition of a tariff equivalent to their undervaluation if the negotiations did not succeed in raising the value of those currencies.

The committees reconciled these alternative exchange rate provisions in the conference committee on the trade bill in early 1988. The final compromise closely resembled the House Banking Committee's requirements for reporting and international negotiations. As enacted, the Omnibus Trade and Competitiveness Act of 1988 contained a subtitle labeled the "Exchange Rates and International Economic Policy Coordination Act of 1988." It backed away from earlier language requiring the Secretary of the Treasury to state, in public, what a competitive exchange rate for the United States would be. But it did declare that "a more stable exchange rate for the dollar at a level consistent with a more appropriate and sustainable balance in the United States current account should

---

24. US Congress, House, Committee on Banking, *Competitive Exchange Rate Act of 1985*, report, 99th Cong., 1st sess., 20 December 1985.

be a major focus of national economic policy." To advance this goal, it mandated multilateral negotiations on policy coordination and reform of the exchange rate system, and it required the Treasury to identify countries that "manipulated" their currencies for trade advantage and to initiate bilateral negotiations with them to correct unfair rates. The law also required regular Treasury reporting to the Senate and House Banking Committees. The law is specific as to the contents of the report, which must include:

- An assessment of the impact of the exchange rate on the current account and trade balance, overall economic performance, competitive position, and indebtedness of the United States.

- Recommendations for policy changes necessary to achieve a "more appropriate and sustainable" current account balance.

- Reporting of the results of bilateral negotiations with countries that manipulated their currencies.

- Analyses of exchange-market developments and their causes, including capital flows, and of intervention, among other things.[25]

Throughout this period, the Treasury vigorously opposed legislation directly affecting exchange rates, and the administration was able to get provisions mandating specific policy actions removed. Yet the congressional initiatives still had substantial impact. Legislative proposals can of course be a form of grandstanding to special constituencies, but these proposals appear, for the most part, to have been serious efforts by policy-minded members of Congress to ease the trade—and trade policy—bind. They were less visible and less important than proposals to impose trade barriers, but they nonetheless made a difference: they pressed the administration to take key actions during the legislative process, and they established procedures for stronger accountability in the law that was enacted.

Congressional focus on the yen-dollar rate preceded the Treasury's decision to proceed with the negotiations on Japanese capital-market liberalization. A flurry of congressional threats to restrict Treasury discretion preceded and accompanied the Plaza decision. Congressional proposals targeting the NICs accompanied Treasury pressure on Taiwan and Korea to halt the real depreciation of their currencies and revalue them. And the Omnibus Trade and

---

25. The Omnibus Trade and Competitiveness Act of 1988, Public Law 100–418, Title III, Section 3005. This section is reprinted in *Congressional Record*, 100th Cong., 2d sess., 20 April 1988, vol. 134, no. 51, H1949.

Competitiveness Act imposed new reporting requirements, ensuring a continuing spotlight on exchange rate relationships.

The Treasury's Exchange Rate Reports

The Treasury chose to use the reporting process to apply public pressure on Korea and Taiwan to further appreciate their currencies against the dollar. Congress applauded this focus in the reports presented to the banking committees in October 1988 and April 1989. The success of this strategy won praises from the Treasury for the reporting process, ironically. Secretary Brady called it "an enormously useful vehicle." Assistant Secretary Mulford, who had argued vehemently against the stronger versions of the provision, praised it as well and stressed the importance of cooperation with the Congress.[26]

However, as reviewed in Chapter 4, the reports gave only perfunctory treatment to the far more important question of the dollar's multilateral effective value, which had been rising. The Treasury refused to address what level of current account deficit might be "sustainable," except to imply that current levels were unacceptable, and it offered no serious recommendations to reinvigorate adjustment, which it acknowledged was slowing.

The legislation provides for hearings, at which the Secretary is required to testify, precisely to ensure that the Treasury does not evade fundamental questions. But Congress was not successful in extracting clear statements of policy and intent in the first two such hearings. The Senate Banking Committee held a well-attended hearing on the April 1989 report, at which Brady and Mulford testified personally. Senators clearly communicated their interest and concern, but the Secretary was excused from answering questions, and committee members did not challenge Mulford's optimistic projections for the trade balance. Despite the efforts of some members, Chairman Donald W. Riegle (D-MI) in particular, the questions did not effectively challenge the Treasury's complacency about the sustainability of the trade deficit, nor was there any follow-up by the House Banking Committee. Members allowed themselves to be distracted by the Treasury's targeting of Korea and Taiwan,[27] and leadership

---

26. The Treasury experienced the same conversion as did the Fed with respect to the Humphrey-Hawkins requirements to report monetary growth targets. Initially hostile to these provisions, senior officials at the Fed now regard them as useful channels through which to communicate its intent to the public and the markets.

27. In 1987, such targeting had been appropriate, but by 1989 substantial appreciation of the won and the New Taiwan dollar had rendered this emphasis misplaced on substantive grounds. See C. Fred Bergsten, "Currency Manipulation? The Case of Korea," and John Williamson, "Exchange Rate Policy in Hong Kong, Korea and Taiwan," testimony before the Subcommittee on Trade of the Senate Finance Committee, 12 May 1989.

changes within both committees contributed to the Treasury's ability to set the agenda. If the reporting process is to meet its stated objective of rendering the Treasury more accountable to the Congress on exchange rate matters, the oversight process cannot be diverted from questions about the dollar's overall value. It remains to be seen whether this innovation in the exchange rate policy process meets this objective.

Conclusion: Congress Plays a Constructive Role

Because Congress is sensitive to a broad array of economic interests, it served the valuable function of linking the diverse areas of international economic policy—trade, debt, and exchange rates—in the mid-1980s.[28] The first Reagan administration was unwilling to integrate trade and international monetary policy. Given its unusual fiscal and monetary policy mix, its nonintervention on exchange rates undercut its professed and sincere policy of open trade and resulted in more specific concessions to protectionist pressures than in any administration since Herbert Hoover's. Although many tried, no official in the first Reagan administration was successful in highlighting the contradiction and persuading White House and Treasury leaders to choose between "free" currency markets and free trade.

In contrast, important members of Congress and their staffs were alert, well before 1985, to the danger that appreciation of the dollar posed to support for the liberal trade regime and American adherence to the GATT. When leaders who recognized this link arrived at the Treasury, the congressional trade policy threat helped them mobilize support for (or acquiescence in) policy change among others in the administration, including Secretary of State Shultz and, not least, the President himself.

Congress also played an integrative role in relation to interest groups pressing for protectionism. Working with their administration counterparts, congressional leaders and Hill-based international economic policy specialists tended to act as a corrective lens, refracting and rechanneling this pressure toward more constructive purposes than market closure. Compared to private lobbyists, members of Congress were somewhat more inclined to focus on the root causes of the trade problem, as opposed to its symptoms. Many in fact recognized that trade protection would do little to redress the imbalance of trade whereas exchange rate changes could, given time.

---

28. For a contrasting view on the role of Congress in policy integration, see Fliess, "Mastering Economic Interdependence."

There remained, however, the most important single source of the trade deficit, namely, the budget deficit. Notwithstanding strong efforts by individual Senators and Congressmen, Congress as a whole proved to be no better than the executive at integrating fiscal and foreign economic policy in practice. The intellectual link was recognized in virtually all of the resolutions and legislation on exchange rate policy. In 1987 Representatives Fernand J. St. Germain (D-RI), Sam M. Gibbons (D-FL), Don J. Pease (D-OH), and Don Bonker (D-WA) sponsored a pre-Venice summit resolution urging the President to reduce the US budget deficit by 1.5 percent of GNP over two years in exchange for stimulative policies from summit partners. This was never enacted, but Congress did attach to the 1988 trade act a reporting provision, advanced by Representative Pease, requiring that the link between the budget and trade deficits be specifically analyzed by the Office of Management and Budget and by the budget committees of the House and Senate, in their annual budget assessments.[29] However, Congress needed presidential leadership, or at least cooperation, in order to reduce the budget deficit.

This underscores a broader limitation: Congress is not a good place to accomplish the actual integration of policy. Jurisdiction over trade and exchange rate matters, for example, is split between the trade and the banking committees. There has therefore been a tendency for the latter to be insulated from the "real" effects of exchange rate developments, whereas the former, which feel the full brunt of protectionist lobbying, only have authority to act on trade.[30]

The executive branch is far better suited to forcing integration in practice. Executive leaders are better positioned to develop a strategic view linking various strands of policy concern and to address conflicts among policy objectives. They are also better able to anticipate the exchange rate consequences of present policies and act preemptively. When executive leaders fail to integrate—as occurs all too frequently in the real world—the consequences can be severe. At such times, congressional activity highlighting policy linkages and pressing for action, even at a general and technically unsophisticated level, is a wholly appropriate and indeed necessary second-best alternative.

Yet it took four years for Congress to mount a determined challenge to Reagan administration policy. What explains the delay? First, although sensitive to a broad range of views, Congress cannot forge a consensus among experts. When

---

29. After consultation with the Council of Economic Advisers and the Congressional Budget Office, respectively. See "Federal Budget Competitiveness Impact Statement," Omnibus Trade and Competitiveness Act of 1988, Title V, Subtitle D.

30. Even after 1985, interest groups were not directly pressuring the banking committees to advance exchange rate legislation. Such legislation was driven by members themselves, who saw an opportunity to place their stamp on the trade debate and offer an alternative that could command broad support, and by their staffs. Once proposed, the legislation was supported by interest groups (see Chapter 7).

international monetary experts disagreed on the desirability and feasibility of direct exchange rate policy, Congress was stymied until a substantial movement in favor of dollar activism emerged. Second, Congress could not anticipate the parade of private interests to its door in response to an overvalued currency. Despite the efforts of some entrepreneurial members, before Congress as a whole was to force the administration's hand it had to feel that broad pressure. Why that pressure was slow in building, and its impact when it did build, are subjects of the next chapter.

7
Private Groups and Interests

Whereas Congress and the executive agencies have formal links to the closed system, weak though they may be, private actors are wholly outside the established policymaking process. Businesses, banks and financial institutions, labor unions, and other interested private organizations, although crucially affected by the value of the dollar, have no formal mechanisms or procedures through which to weigh in on exchange rate policy. Many of them sought nonetheless to influence policy during the 1980s through direct lobbying of the administration and Congress and through campaigns to tip public discussion in their favor. We focus in this chapter on their political (as opposed to their market) activity, which elevated the dollar to the status of a major political issue.[1]

Both individual firms and trade associations were active. They lobbied both the central exchange rate actors, the Treasury and the Fed, and those outside the inner circle, the other executive agencies and the Congress. They began to advocate exchange rate policy change in 1982, became particularly vocal and active in 1984 and 1985, and have continued to advocate exchange rate objectives, although less vociferously, during the period of realignment and stabilization.[2]

---

1. Market activity, as manifested in exchange rate movements, is often the *object* of exchange rate policy, and thus affects Treasury behavior regularly. But private market action is taken to execute needed transactions, not for the purpose of affecting the exchange rate's level or volatility. In this chapter, we are interested in how private actors use political resources to influence government policies that affect the exchange rate.

2. From the establishment of the Bretton Woods regime until the 1980s there were virtually no private pressures directly on exchange rate policy. For analyses of policymaking in earlier periods see John S. Odell, *U.S. International Monetary Policy: Markets, Power, and Ideas as Sources of Change* (Princeton, NJ: Princeton University Press, 1982); Joanne Gowa, *Closing the Gold Window: Domestic Politics and the End of Bretton Woods* (Ithaca, NY: Cornell University Press, 1983); Stephen D. Cohen and Ronald I. Meltzer, "U.S. Foreign Exchange Rate Policymaking, 1977–78," in Cohen and Meltzer, *United States International Economic Policy in Action: Diversity of Decision Making* (New York: Praeger, 1982), chap. 2; Stephen D. Krasner, "United States Commercial and Monetary Policy: Unravelling the Paradox of External Strength and Internal Weakness," in Peter J. Katzenstein, ed., *Between Power and Plenty: Foreign Economic Policies of Advanced Industrial States* (Madison, WI:

Private groups pressed in only one direction, for policy changes to lower the dollar, during most of the period under review. Their activity, far from meeting opposition from conflicting interests, confronted mainly apathy among potential private allies, especially during the early 1980s. Some groups had an interest in government *non*interference in the foreign-exchange markets, but no group, to our knowledge, lobbied in support of the strong dollar in the early and mid-1980s, even though many importing and retail companies clearly benefited. Only after the dollar had substantially depreciated did the administration begin to face conflicting pressures from private groups, and even then the new critics of Baker's policy favored a more passive Treasury approach rather than a specific exchange rate objective.

Such political activity was new to the exchange rate policy arena, and it had a major impact on that policy's course and content. It was not the only force acting on exchange rate policymakers, but it was important in its own right and was a catalyst for much, though not all, of the pressure from Congress and other executive agencies on the primary policymakers.

Virtually every lobbying group acknowledged that monetary and fiscal policy were the root causes of the strong dollar and the first place to turn for its correction. No serious group overlooked this fact; none argued that there was a simple causal relationship between direct intervention or declaratory policy and the level of the dollar. All saw action on the fundamentals as the prime remedy. But as the dollar soared and the costs to industry multiplied, a growing number of private voices argued that no potential remedy should be spurned. Even if the Reagan administration proved unable or unwilling to adopt "first-best" policies, it should still, they argued, reverse the Regan-Sprinkel nonintervention posture on exchange rates. Many others remained skeptical of intervention and Treasury declarations and argued that budget deficit reduction and changes in monetary or trade policy were the only remedies, without which direct efforts to influence exchange markets would be of little avail. But even these skeptics responded predominantly to the strong dollar and explicitly cited it as *the* proximate cause of their competitiveness disadvantage.

We begin by surveying private pressures for government action that would affect the exchange rate. Then we examine the pressures on the government to take a hands-off policy. Finally, we assess the impact of these pressures on policy and offer concluding observations about private involvement in the exchange rate process, leading to our recommendation in Chapter 8 that a private-sector advisory committee on exchange rates be created.

University of Wisconsin Press, 1978), 51–87; Janet Kelly, "International Monetary Systems and National Security," in Klaus Knorr and Frank Trager, eds., *Economic Issues and National Security* (Lawrence, KS: Regents Press of Kansas, 1977).

Pressures for Activist Policy: The "Real" Sectors

As recounted in Chapter 3, protests against the rising dollar began in the early 1980s. For the most part, however, export-dependent multinationals did not involve themselves deeply in the issue until 1984 and 1985. What drove them, by all evidence, was a sudden, severe deterioriation in their real trade balances, one that seemed likely to worsen unless government took strong action.

As is universally recognized, the dollar value of US imports shot up from $249.5 billion in 1982 to $334.3 billion in 1984 and $340.9 billion in 1985 (table 3.1), and the nominal trade deficit shot up, for the same years, from $35.5 billion to $110.2 and $120.1 billion. Yet the real impact on traded-goods producers was even more severe, because the strong dollar depressed the relative price of imported (and, indirectly, exported) products. A better measure of economy-wide trade pain, therefore, is the ratio of the volume of merchandise imports to that of total US goods production. This ratio (obtained by dividing the constant-dollar value of imports by the constant-dollar value of goods production) stayed flat at about 19 percent in 1980–82 but then jumped to 21 percent in 1983, 23 percent in 1984, 24 percent in 1985, and 26 percent in 1986 (table 7.1). The rise in manufacturing imports as a share of real manufacturing output was even greater. This ratio (again measured in constant dollars) rose from 19.7 percent in 1980 to 32.0 percent in 1985, while the comparable ratio for manufactured exports declined from 25.5 percent to 17.7 percent during those five years (table 7.2). In 1986, the import ratio for manufactures registered 34.1 percent, while that for exports sank to 17.2 percent.

These real import ratios were much higher than any in US postwar experience. More important, the change was unprecedented in its rapidity. Import pressure affected the overall position of American companies, as capacity utilization declined and unfilled orders stagnated (see figures 3.1 and 3.2). The strong dollar was not the only cause of the sluggishness of the industrial sector, but it was widely, and accurately, perceived to be a primary if not the leading cause.[3]

---

3. For studies linking the strong dollar, trade competitiveness, and the condition of the manufacturing sector see Lionel H. Olmer, *U.S. Manufacturing at a Crossroads: Surviving and Prospering in a More Competitive Global Economy* (Washington: US Deparment of Commerce, 14 June 1985); Paul R. Krugman and George Hatsopoulos, "The Problem of U.S. Competitiveness in Manufacturing," *New England Economic Review* (January/February 1987) 18–29; Rudiger Dornbusch, James Poterba, and Lawrence Summers, *The Case for Manufacturing in America's Future* (Rochester, NY: Eastman Kodak, 1988); William H. Branson and James P. Love, "U.S. Manufacturing and the Real Exchange Rate," in Richard C. Marston, ed., *Misalignment of Exchange Rates: Effects on Trade and Industry* (Chicago: University of Chicago Press, 1988), 241–74.

Table 7.1   US merchandise trade, output, and spending, by volume, 1970–1988

Year	Total US output of goods (billions of 1982 dollars)	Merchandise imports as percent of output	Merchandise exports as percent of output	Total US spending on goods (billions of 1982 dollars)	Merchandise imports as percent of spending
1970	1,030.0	14.7	11.7	1,060.3	14.2
1971	1,037.6	16.0	11.5	1,084.5	15.3
1972	1,093.8	17.4	12.0	1,153.2	16.5
1973	1,175.0	18.6	13.7	1,232.6	17.7
1974	1,159.2	18.3	15.2	1,195.2	17.7
1975	1,125.0	16.7	15.2	1,141.4	16.5
1976	1,194.7	19.2	14.9	1,246.5	18.4
1977	1,256.2	20.6	14.2	1,337.5	19.4
1978	1,329.1	20.6	14.8	1,407.0	19.5
1979	1,354.6	20.5	16.1	1,414.3	19.6
1980	1,344.2	18.9	18.0	1,356.0	18.7
1981	1,386.0	18.7	17.2	1,406.2	18.4
1982	1,319.1	18.9	16.2	1,354.6	18.4
1983	1,367.0	20.6	15.2	1,441.6	19.6
1984	1,509.2	23.3	14.8	1,636.5	21.5
1985	1,553.6	23.7	14.9	1,689.9	21.8
1986	1,599.0	25.8	15.2	1,767.6	23.3
1987	1,663.3	26.4	16.8	1,822.2	24.1
1988	1,762.3	26.7	19.4	1,890.6	24.8

Export data are given in f.a.s. (free-alongside-ship) terms; import data are US Customs values.

Sources: Survey of Current Business, various issues; Council of Economic Advisers, *Economic Report of the President,* February 1988. See table 3.1 for import and export volumes (1982 dollars).

The manufacturing work force never experienced the economic recovery of the mid-1980s; employment virtually stagnated at the lows reached in the trough of the 1982 recession. Relative to the total work force, therefore, manufacturing employment declined from 23.4 percent in 1979 (its absolute peak) to 20.9 percent in 1982 and 19.8 percent in 1985.[4]

---

4. Council of Economic Advisers, *Economic Report of the President,* January 1989, table B-43, 356–57. This trend continued despite the correction of the dollar, with manufacturing employment falling to 18.3 percent of the work force by the end of 1988. The absolute number of manufacturing workers rebounded modestly, from an average of 19.3

Table 7.2 US manufacturing trade and output, by volume, 1970–1988

Year	Total US mfg. output (billions of 1982 dollars)	Manufactured imports (billions of 1982 dollars)	Imports as percent of output	Manufactured exports (billions of 1982 dollars)	Exports as percent of output	Mfg. trade balance[a] as percent of output
1970	506.8	77.5	15.3	84.51	16.7	1.4
1971	515.5	84.6	16.4	84.99	16.5	0.1
1972	561.2	98.2	17.5	92.79	16.5	−1.0
1973	621.3	101.9	16.4	112.82	18.2	1.8
1974	591.6	97.2	16.4	134.18	22.7	6.2
1975	547.5	81.0	14.8	129.02	23.6	8.8
1976	600.6	101.7	16.9	131.11	21.8	4.9
1977	645.0	113.5	17.6	130.12	20.2	2.6
1978	683.4	132.5	19.4	143.10	20.9	1.5
1979	697.1	133.8	19.2	150.27	21.6	2.4
1980	665.4	131.4	19.7	169.80	25.5	5.8
1981	676.1	145.3	21.5	162.57	24.0	2.6
1982	634.6	144.0	22.7	139.70	22.0	−0.7
1983	675.5	168.2	24.9	130.19	19.3	−5.6
1984	757.9	221.5	29.2	139.55	18.4	−10.8
1985	786.8	251.6	32.0	139.49	17.7	−14.2
1986	804.6	274.3	34.1	138.16	17.2	−16.9
1987	839.5	285.4	34.0	154.48	18.4	−15.6
1988	—	295.9	—	183.76	—	—

a. Manufactured exports minus manufactured imports.

Sources: Council of Economic Advisers, *Economic Report of the President,* February 1988 and January 1989, tables B11 and B105 (imports are US Customs values 1970–73, 1981–88; f.a.s. values 1974–80); Organization for Economic Cooperation and Development (OECD), *Historical Statistics of Foreign Trade 1965–1980,* 16; OECD, *Monthly Statistics of Foreign Trade,* various issues; Bureau of the Census, *Highlights of US Export and Import Trade,* various issues.

Similarly, the agricultural sector remained in recession through most of the decade, not only because of weak commodity prices and discriminatory foreign import and export practices but as a result of the strong dollar as well. Between 1981 and 1985, the surplus on agricultural trade shrunk from $26.5 billion to $9.0 billion, principally reflecting a rapid decline in exports from $43.3 billion

million in 1985 to 19.7 million in December 1988, yet never matched its 1979 peak of 21.0 million. Employment suffered in part because of strong productivity growth in this sector.

to \$29.0 billion over that period (and into 1986). Domestic agricultural production stagnated through the middle and into the late 1980s.[5]

By 1984 and 1985 a broad range of US producers already knew, from their own bottom lines, what these statistics would later demonstrate: that the strong dollar posed a general, rather than a concentrated, competitiveness problem. What was worse, economists predicted that substantial further damage from the continued appreciation during those years was still in the pipeline.[6] Worse yet for corporate officers, labor leaders, and the agricultural community, neither private economists nor the Treasury could provide assurance that the appreciation had ended, that the late February 1985 level of the dollar represented a peak from which it would steadily decline without government action. Thus, a broader consensus on the need for action coalesced, and the message sent to the administration became more uniform, stronger, and therefore more effective.

The goods-producing sectors of the economy were not particularly concerned about the high *volatility* of the dollar, and they did not petition the Treasury to dampen short-term fluctuations. Their central concern was the sustained *misalignment* of the currency, against which no inexpensive hedging strategies could be applied. Major corporations could hedge against the adverse impact of such misalignments by diversifying their production and sourcing across countries. But even those that had so diversified suffered lower profits in dollar terms when their foreign subsidiaries' earnings were translated onto the consolidated financial statements. Moreover, geographic diversification is expensive and thus unavailable to small and medium-sized corporations. And no hedging devices were available to shield US workers and farmers from unemployment in their industries.

It was, as already noted, business interests that were most active against the strong dollar, and most effective. But labor and agriculture were engaged also. We turn briefly to these groups before treating more extensively the broad business campaign.

Labor

Major industrial unions like the United Auto Workers and the United Steelworkers were losing jobs and members to import competition well before the

---

5. Measured in nominal terms. Agricultural production expanded in real terms beginning in 1985. Council of Economic Advisers, *Economic Report of the President,* January 1989, tables B-8 and B-9, 318–19.

6. Stephen Marris projected that the exchange rates prevailing in the period from October 1984 to March 1985 would have generated a \$300 billion current account deficit by 1990. See Stephen Marris, *Deficits and the Dollar: The World Economy at Risk,* rev. ed., POLICY ANALYSES IN INTERNATIONAL ECONOMICS 14 (Washington: Institute for International Economics, 1987), table 3.2.

dollar misalignment of the 1980s. But the squeeze on manufacturing employment resulting from the strong dollar made a difficult situation worse, helping to reduce overall membership in AFL-CIO unions from 13.6 million in 1979 to 11.3 million in 1985.[7] Driven by its industrial unions, the AFL-CIO thus took a serious interest in the exchange rate for the first time during the 1980s.

The AFL-CIO Executive Council declared early in 1984 that the "overvaluation of the dollar greatly contributed" to the trade deficit.[8] Its chief economist, Rudolph A. Oswald, criticized the administration's laissez-faire policy and advocated foreign-exchange intervention to correct it.[9] When asked for its view, in mid-1985, on whether a new round of trade negotiations should be launched in the GATT (discussed below), the AFL-CIO was emphatic:

> . . . the Administration's proposal for a new round of multilateral trade negotiations should not be allowed to take the place of needed efforts to deal with specific domestic trade problems and should not substitute for specific action correcting the imbalance in exchange rates. . . . there must be a major effort to readjust currency values to more realistic levels and to bring some measure of stability to the exchange rate system.[10]

However, even though the AFL-CIO was solidly in the exchange rate activist camp, most of its lobbying energy went toward trade and industrial policy rather than exchange rate remedies. When the AFL-CIO Executive Council issued its strong 1984 statement (no sooner than did the broad-based trade associations representing management), union leaders argued that a correction of the dollar would not solve the US competitiveness problem in the absence of these changes in trade and industrial policy.

Nor did the automobile, steel, and textiles unions give priority to exchange rate solutions. Instead, the United Auto Workers gave foremost billing to domestic-content legislation in 1982–83, and all three unions backed voluntary restraint agreements for their products. Although quantitative restraints did not fully insulate domestic producers from the strong dollar, as the cases of automobiles and textiles demonstrate, they did dampen the adverse effects. Moreover, once established, restraint agreements diverted the political energies

---

7. Bureau of the Census, *Statistical Abstract of the United States,* 107th ed. (Washington: US Department of Commerce, 1987), table 691.

8. AFL-CIO, "Statement by the AFL-CIO Executive Council on International Trade and Investment," Bal Harbour, FL, 20 February 1984.

9. US Congress, House, Committee on Ways and Means, Subcommittee on International Trade, *U.S. Trade Deficit,* hearings, 98th Cong., 2d sess., 28 and 29 March and 10, 12, 15, and 25 April 1984, 366–77.

10. AFL-CIO, "Statement by the AFL-CIO Executive Council on Trade," Washington, 8 May 1985, reproduced in Advisory Committee for Trade Negotiations, *Chairmen's Report on a New Round of Multilateral Trade Negotiations* (Bal Harbour, FL: AFL-CIO, 15 May 1985).

of the protected industries away from exchange rates and macroeconomic policy and toward the terms of the agreements themselves.

Finally, Republican control of the White House and, through 1986, the Senate impeded labor's ability to influence exchange rate policy. Labor leaders saw the White House as generally hostile, and lobbying the administration as a waste of political resources. Labor's main allies were in the Congress, the Democratic House in particular. And House Democrats, as described in Chapter 6, had more leverage over trade than over exchange rates.

Agriculture

Price competition is particularly important in agricultural trade with its relative lack of product differentiation, and so the strong dollar affected exports of this sector as quickly as any other. Farm lobbies cited the strong dollar as a source of difficulty in position statements and in meetings with administration officials and members of Congress. But since the budget deficit was central to the dollar problem, and many farm groups were already pressing the government for more generous commodity support programs, the agriculture community was in a weak position to demand a reversal of exchange rate policy. Moreover, the omnibus farm legislation was up for renewal in 1985. So, although they maintained that a change of exchange rate policy would be desirable, farm groups saved their main energy for programs that could benefit them more directly.

Their focus on other issues did not mean that agriculture and labor had no impact on exchange rate policy: even if they did not have a direct impact on the Treasury, they certainly contributed to growing sentiment in the Congress and among the general public against the strong dollar and thus to the political "market" for policy change. But the political activity of the core Republican constituency, the business community, was the most influential with administration officials whose hands were on the levers of exchange rate policy.

Business

Clamoring for Policy Change, 1982–1985

Business interests pressed the Reagan administration and Congress both on their own as individual companies and as groups, pooling their resources through advocacy organizations. Among the individual companies, Caterpillar, Inc., led by Lee L. Morgan, was the first and perhaps best-known exchange rate activist.

Morgan was soon joined by a host of others who shared, if not his sense of emergency regarding the undervaluation of the Japanese yen, at least his view that the exchange rate was a growing problem that the government should acknowledge and act decisively to correct. Those included Philip Caldwell of Ford, David M. Roderick of US Steel, Edson W. Spencer of Honeywell, Robert W. Galvin of Motorola, and Ruben F. Mettler of TRW.

As the dollar continued to appreciate through 1983 and 1984, a second wave of companies were spurred into exchange rate activism. Edmund T. Pratt, Jr., of Pfizer, who led the private-sector advisory group to the new round of multilateral trade negotiations (MTN), told the administration that the exchange rate problem should be addressed before embarking on those negotiations.[11] IBM and Xerox, initially on the sidelines, shifted position and advocated change in the international monetary system.

Corporations, like labor, had a range of policy concerns, and the dollar never equaled in priority for them such bottom-line matters as tax policy. There remained important companies, such as Exxon, that refused to criticize the administration's exchange rate policy. But a deluge of corporate criticism came down on the government in 1985. Lee A. Iacocca of Chrysler denounced American complacency on the high dollar, particularly vis-à-vis the yen.[12] Colby H. Chandler of Eastman Kodak called for a new dollar policy in a meeting with the President in spring 1985. Roger B. Smith of General Motors wrote Secretary Baker in mid-1985 stressing the need for dollar depreciation.

These and other business interests worked simultaneously through organized groups. The National Association of Manufacturers (NAM), at the persistent behest of Lawrence A. Fox, Vice President for International Economic Affairs, was among the first of the associations to identify the dollar as a major problem for business. Beginning in 1982, Fox and other NAM officials worked to build a coalition of association members for policy change and to present their case to the Treasury, other agencies, and the Congress.

Initially, the exchange rate was not sufficiently salient to motivate corporations to develop a joint position. But by early 1984 enough NAM members had been hurt by the appreciating dollar that its Board of Directors unanimously advocated "an explicit U.S. exchange rate policy supportive of U.S. trade performance."[13] That policy was to include international policy coordination, "a greater degree of structure" in the exchange rate system, and special attention to the international role of the yen—all with the purpose of realigning the

---

11. See *Chairmen's Report on a New Round of Multilateral Trade Negotiations,* 15 May 1985.

12. Yoichi Funabashi, *Managing the Dollar: From the Plaza to the Louvre,* 2d ed. (Washington: Institute for International Economics, 1989), 73.

13. NAM, "Resolution on the Exchange Rate for the U.S. Dollar," Washington, 10 February 1984.

dollar—and the United States taking the lead in international monetary reform.[14] However, the NAM board declined to endorse any particular reform proposals such as target zones.

When the Treasury's laissez-faire policy persisted, the NAM sent one of the strongest statements on the issue by any private organization to Secretary Baker. In a position paper personally presented to him in July 1985, NAM leaders were direct:

> The U.S. Government has failed so far to come to grips with the misalignment of the dollar and its serious adverse impact on the overall U.S. economy. . . . [W]e must undertake steps immediately in cooperation with the central banks and finance ministries of other countries to help assure that the dollar is heading in the right direction. . . while improving the operation of the present floating exchange rate "non-system.". . .We believe that the President should clearly and openly indicate that the United States has a trade problem that goes beyond the context of specific market access limitations affecting U.S. exports. . . . The Secretary of the Treasury should acknowledge the national interest in achieving realignment of the dollar with other major currencies. . . Congressional testimony this spring by two assistant secretaries of the Treasury that the dollar may not be overvalued obviously causes us concern and tends to confuse the Congress. . . . [15]

In addition, the NAM warned that dollar overvaluation could doom a new multilateral trade round. While declaring its own support, the association cautioned that "politically . . . it is difficult to imagine that effort succeeding if there is not parallel progress in reforming the international exchange rate system."[16]

Lee Morgan of Caterpillar carried on his crusade through the Task Force on International Trade and Investment of the Business Roundtable. In contrast to the NAM effort, which was initiated by the association's staff and later endorsed by the company membership, the Business Roundtable comprised the chief executive officers of the major US multinational companies, and so its campaign was company-driven. Morgan developed a coalition against the strong dollar and held numerous meetings with administration officials to press for policy change. Frustrated at the outset by a polite but unresponsive Treasury, Caterpillar and the Task Force sought to encircle the Treasury with advocates of policy change.

Morgan and the Business Roundtable enjoyed extraordinary access to senior Washington policymakers. From late 1982 through early 1985, he and his Task

---

14. Those reforms should reflect "changes in the economic fundamentals [among countries] which determine competitiveness." The board also called for changes in fiscal and monetary policies to lower the dollar while still meeting macroeconomic objectives.

15. NAM, "The U.S. Dollar Exchange Rate Problem: NAM Position Paper," Washington, 16 July 1985.

16. Letter from NAM President Alexander B. Trowbridge to Edmund T. Pratt, Jr., 16 April 1985, 2.

Force held at least a dozen meetings with top administration officials, individually or in groups, including at least two with the President, five with Treasury Secretary Regan, and two with the Vice President. At all these meetings the group argued for policy action to reverse the dollar's rise. Morgan authored at least as many letters, some directed to five or six Cabinet members, specifically raising the exchange rate issue.

Morgan's first major meeting was with Treasury Secretary Regan, Secretary of State Shultz, Commerce Secretary Baldrige, Council of Economic Advisers Chairman Feldstein, US Trade Representative Brock, Attorney General Edwin Meese, and Joseph Wright (a deputy to David Stockman at the Office of Management and Budget) at the White House on 27 October 1982. At that meeting, Regan apparently argued that the dollar (which would soon reach its high point of 278 against the yen in November) would come down eventually, and he asked Morgan and the other business leaders what solutions they would propose. Morgan replied that developing solutions was a responsibility the administration could not legitimately abdicate.[17]

As the Treasury remained unmoved, Morgan and the Task Force recast their arguments in terms of economic fundamentals and, in the case of the yen-dollar rate, in opposition to Japanese restrictions on capital inflow and domestic financial market regulation that kept the yen down. Morgan sponsored a report that laid out a plan for Japanese capital-market liberalization and articulated US objectives for the accord that was later negotiated with Tokyo and implemented.[18] But the short-run impact on the dollar was, if anything, to accelerate its appreciation (see Chapter 2).

The Business Roundtable as a whole issued a comprehensive policy statement on the trade deficit in January 1985. The full group argued that reducing the trade deficit was urgent and that reducing the budget deficit—and specifically entitlements—would be the best way to achieve it. The Roundtable indicated that both foreign-exchange intervention and capital controls might be appropriate, provided foreign governments cooperated. But intervention and controls without budget deficit reduction would be counterproductive, as would an

---

17. Letter from Lee L. Morgan to meeting participants, 4 November 1982. Morgan wrote:
. . . we are concerned about the attitude of some people that this yen/dollar problem is one that will take care of itself if we give it time. To be blunt, that's just not a satisfactory response to a serious problem. We don't have time to deal with fundamental economic forces. . . . I believe more needs to be done. We—the businessmen—can help input ideas, but we believe the responsibility clearly lies with you—our government—to develop policy options to address both the short- and long-term problems of American competitiveness, with special reference to the yen valuation.

18. David C. Murchison and Ezra Solomon, "The Misalignment of the United States Dollar and the Japanese Yen: The Problem and Its Solution," 19 September 1983 (unpublished).

import surcharge under any circumstances. The Roundtable argued that the consideration of such drastic and harmful measures dramatized the "crisis in U.S. export competitiveness" and the urgent need for action.[19]

In early 1985, Morgan passed the chairmanship of the Task Force to Edson W. Spencer of Honeywell, who continued to urge a change of exchange rate policy on the administration. In a letter to the President in April, Spencer argued that the major cause of the growing trade deficit was the high value of the dollar and that the administration and Congress should immediately act to cut the budget deficit in order to bring it down. He also called for a review of the international exchange rate system.[20] The Task Force endorsed a new round of trade negotiations but said that parallel discussion of the "persistent disequilibrium of the current exchange rate system" was, among other things, important to ensure its success.[21] Under Spencer and Honeywell, the Task Force stressed direct exchange rate policy less than under Morgan. But the need to get the dollar down remained at the center of the lobbying effort. In a private meeting with Baker in early August, Spencer warned that the trade and dollar problem was undermining business support for the administration and that Honeywell would work with the Congress on trade legislation.

Some business associations that were not active early in the Reagan administration became more active late in the first term. The US Council for International Business, representing large multinational companies and banks, formed a working group on exchange rates in 1984. In June 1985 the Council recommended to Secretary Baker that the exchange rate be made "an explicit and primary concern for monetary and fiscal policymakers."[22] The Council favored the initiation of a new trade round but added that the high dollar made 1985 a poor time for it, and recommended parallel discussion of the world finance and investment system to address macroeconomic and structural problems causing exchange rate misalignment.[23]

In early 1985, US Trade Representative William Brock initiated a comprehensive effort to sound out the business community on the desirability of a new MTN round. Presented in May, the final report sent Brock and the Reagan administration a clear and unexpectedly strong message:

19. Business Roundtable, "The Trade Deficit—Its Causes, Consequences and Cures," January 1985.

20. Letter from Edson W. Spencer to Ronald Reagan, 10 April 1985.

21. Business Roundtable Task Force on International Trade and Investment, "Getting from Here to There: Preparation for a New Round of Multilateral Trade Negotiations," April 1985, i.

22. US Council for International Business, *Annual Report 1985*, 4.

23. US Council for International Business, "Statement on a New Round of Multilateral Trade Negotiations: Recommended U.S. Business Objectives," Washington, 18 April 1985, 1–2.

[Because the broader economic and financial environment is the fundamental cause of the trade crisis], a new MTN cannot become the sole, or even the most significant, U.S. trade policy objective during the negotiating period. Yet, that is exactly what the private sector fears could happen. The great majority of groups surveyed strongly recommend that negotiations on exchange rates and financial issues take place simultaneously with a new round of trade negotiations. But above all, in pursuing a new round of multilateral trade negotiations, the private sector believes that the U.S. must begin immediately to address federal budget deficits and to coordinate U.S. monetary and fiscal policy with U.S. trade policy.[24]

As mentioned above, the AFL-CIO, the Business Roundtable Task Force, the NAM, and the US Council for International Business, among others, also took this general view.

In 1984 and 1985 the US Chamber of Commerce was also petitioned by some of its members and by the other business representative associations to adopt a position on exchange rate policy. For the Chamber, however, with the most diverse membership of all the business associations, the exchange rate was a more divisive issue. Consequently, it declined to adopt a public posture. Without the Chamber on board the dollar-depreciation bandwagon, the business community lacked complete unity on the issue. As events were to show, however, absolute unity was not necessary to be effective.

Cheering Depreciation, 1985–1986

Secretary Baker responded to these pressures, among others, with the Plaza Agreement in September 1985. It quickly became the reference point for further lobbying activity. Virtually all business groups applauded the change and urged that the Treasury continue to pursue the new policy vigorously. The Business Roundtable Task Force was quick to support Baker's move and advocated, on the basis of a report prepared by a special working group, international monetary negotiations "to establish a durable framework of agreements to restore better balance in trade and financial relationships."[25] Shortly thereafter, the full Business Roundtable applauded the Plaza initiative, supported the use of concerted foreign-exchange intervention to realign the dollar, and proposed international monetary reform and adjustment of the fundamentals.[26] The US Council for International Business elaborated its position and called for enhanced

---

24. *Chairmen's Report on a New Round of Multilateral Trade Negotiations*, 2. This combined the views of the policy advisory committees on investment, services, labor, industry, and defense with those of the Advisory Committee for Trade Negotiations.

25. "Strengthening United States Trade Laws: Recommendations of the Business Roundtable Task Force on International Trade and Investment," 21 October 1985.

26. Business Roundtable, "Background Statement on International Monetary Policy," 7 January 1986.

policy coordination in the G-5, continued concerted intervention, and integration of exchange rate and balance of payments considerations into monetary and fiscal policy formation.[27]

Despite their acclaim for the Plaza Agreement, business groups differed with the Treasury over the merits of the exchange rate provisions of the trade bill as they were then being developed in the House Banking Committee (see Chapter 6). The NAM favored the measures and urged its membership to encourage legislators to support them.[28] So did the Business Roundtable and the US Council for International Business.[29] In their consensus position on the omnibus trade legislation, the coalition of these and other important business associations supported maintenance of exchange rates "appropriate to U.S. balance of payments and trade interests" and the semiannual reporting requirement, while opposing the exchange rate equalization tariff.[30] Business was not the motive force behind this proposal, but once it was put forward by legislators, business support was virtually unanimous.

Accepting Stabilization, 1987–1988

As the period of managed depreciation was coming to a close, the NAM issued a generally supportive statement labeling the G-7 initiative "a major technical success." But the NAM declared that "a further appreciation of the major industrial country currencies will be necessary to improve the U.S. trade balance." It also called for action to raise the value of the non–G-7 currencies.[31] In particular, the NAM called for "vigorous bilateral negotiations" on currency alignment with Taiwan, Korea, and Hong Kong and reconsideration of currency relationships with Canada and the Latin American countries. When Baker decided to stabilize the dollar at the Louvre, the NAM reiterated the need for

---

27. US Council for International Business, "Statement on Exchange Rates and International Economic Policy Coordination," 11 March 1986.

28. NAM, "Issue Brief: The Dollar Exchange Rate and U.S. Trade," Washington, 18 March 1986. The NAM did propose that the requirement in the Committee's version that the Treasury publicly state desirable levels for the exchange rate be dropped.

29. Business Roundtable, "Statement on International Monetary Policy," April 1986; US Council for International Business, "Statement on Exchange Rates and International Economic Policy Coordination," 11 March 1986.

30. The Business Coalition on Trade, "Positions on H.R. 3, The Trade and International Economic Policy Reform Act of 1987," Washington, 7 October 1987. The members of this coalition were the Business Roundtable, the National Association of Manufacturers, the US Chamber of Commerce, the US Council for International Business, the Emergency Committee for American Trade, and the National Foreign Trade Council.

31. NAM, "NAM International Monetary Affairs Task Force Interim Report," Washington, 27 January 1987.

policy coordination, with faster growth in Germany and Japan, and the exploration of reform of the exchange rate system based on the *de facto* target zone experience.[32] With the dollar at 140–150 yen and 1.80 marks, many companies thought that depreciation had been arrested prematurely, before the beneficial effects on US trade had emerged, and they urged that Baker not resist market tendencies to push the dollar down.[33] In December 1987, after the stock market crash, NAM President Alexander B. Trowbridge wrote Secretary Baker declaring that "the further fall in the dollar. . . from the Louvre levels was appropriate." The letter backed continued efforts at international economic cooperation and reform of the monetary system and signaled "the need for new currency reference ranges and economic policy coordination among the major industrial countries."[34]

Yet there was a greater difference of opinion among manufacturing constituencies in 1987 than there had been in 1985. And as export orders boomed and inflationary expectations surged, lobbying for further dollar depreciation virtually evaporated. Reflecting in part the sentiment of the New York financial community, the US Council, just after the Louvre, issued a statement warning against allowing dollar depreciation to go too far. In March 1988 its working group on exchange rates declared that the time was ripe for stabilizing exchange rates and that the next administration should initiate international monetary reform.[35]

Sympathy for Flexible Rates: The Financial Sector

Relative to the sectors dealing in tradeable goods, the US financial community was not so active on exchange rate issues in the 1980s. Although generally skeptical of the feasibility of government control of the foreign-exchange markets, the most influential commercial and investment bankers neither actively opposed nor supported those corporate officials from the real sector who

---

32. NAM, "Competing in the Global Economy: A Strategy for International Competitiveness," Washington, April 1987, 9.

33. For example, these conclusions were reached at a meeting organized by the Institute for International Economics in July 1987 on the question, "Has the Dollar Fallen Enough?" Supported by representatives from 10 major multinational companies, as well as several academic experts, these views were subsequently communicated directly to Secretary Baker. See also the following report, sponsored by Eastman Kodak: Rudiger Dornbusch, James Poterba, and Lawrence Summers, *The Case for Manufacturing in America's Future* (Rochester, NY: Eastman Kodak, 1988).

34. Letter from Alexander B. Trowbridge to James A. Baker III, 10 December 1987.

35. US Council for International Business, "Report of the Exchange Rate Working Group," New York, 10 March 1988.

called for a depreciation of the dollar in 1982–85. The internationally engaged banks had an interest in a higher dollar, but they did not actually lobby for it. And even though the banking community has a strong interest in exchange rate flexibility, currency stabilization was never so likely as to warrant overt, preemptive political activity.

Like American business and industry, the financial community is very diverse, comprising money-center commercial banks, investment banks, institutional investors, and financial exchanges, among other institutions. In the best position to communicate their views and needs to the Treasury and the Federal Reserve are the largest money-center banks and the key investment banks. The financial community tends to be driven to political action on issues that affect the quality of its loan portfolios, barriers to market entry at home and abroad, and the general health of the economy, on which their own long-term health depends. The banking sector did not perceive these fundamental interests to be threatened by exchange rate policy, for the most part, over the course of the 1980s.

Appreciation of the dollar downgraded the portfolio quality of some regional banks tied to traded-goods industries and agriculture. But the US economy overall performed well from the banks' perspective, leaving the domestic portfolios of the most influential banks intact. True, the strong dollar complicated the servicing of the large debts of Third World countries, but it had offsetting benefits here as well. Banks did provide much of the impetus for the yen-dollar agreement in 1983–84, but that reflected their interest in access to the Japanese financial services markets rather than the level of the dollar. Thus, although they were politically active in many policy areas during the 1980s— international debt and international and domestic financial market liberalization, for example—the banks were rarely active on exchange rate issues per se.

This was particularly true when the issue was the relative *strength* of the dollar. Given the complexity and multinational character of these key financial institutions, the *level* of the dollar has crosscutting effects on bank interests. Those banks (or divisions within banks) that depend heavily on business with US–based producers suffer when a strong dollar undercuts those producers. On the other hand, a strong dollar is associated with low domestic inflation, confidence in economic policy, and, above all, confidence in US financial assets.[36] The net result is that the upper-level management of many large commercial banks tends to be agnostic with respect to the level of the exchange

---

36. The exchange rate also affects the interests of American financial institutions through its impact on their capital positions relative to foreign competitors. When the dollar rises, the net worth of US banks, and therefore their capacity to expand, acquire other banks, and take risks, increases. This effect, however, depends on banks' management of their exposure to currency fluctuation, and it does not appear to have weighed on the minds of most American financiers when expressing their views to the government on exchange rate matters.

rate, but a strong dollar has broad appeal in the financial community more generally. Thus, the rare occasions when bankers are alarmed by movements in the dollar's value are those when the problem is dollar weakness, not dollar strength.

The appreciation of the dollar in the early and mid-1980s did not worry the large money-center US banks. Virtually no strong voices emerged in the financial community in favor of foreign-exchange intervention or loosening monetary policy to stem the appreciation of the dollar during the first Reagan administration. The policy shift in 1985 brought neither support nor opposition from this quarter. Nearly all agreed that the budget deficit should be reduced, but unlike the corporate community the financial community had not been moved to action on this issue on account of the strong dollar. But when, as described in Chapter 4, Baker and Darman's talking down of the dollar seemed to threaten a hard landing in early 1987, many bankers privately voiced strong objections to this strategy, for many of the same reasons that prompted Paul Volcker to urge Baker to desist. Bankers were also concerned that dollar depreciation would aggravate US inflation, and their opposition to currency depreciation became more persuasive as inflation rose.

Banks do have a strong preference on the separate, more systemic question of fixed versus flexible exchange rates. Exchange rate flexibility has made foreign-exchange trading one of the fastest-growing and most profitable banking activities during the 1980s. Foreign-exchange revenues of the 16 most active American banks increased from $279 million in 1977 to $2.3 billion in 1987.[37] Cognizant that success in this line of business is closely associated with exchange rate fluctuations, one senior banker interviewed said, with perhaps some exaggeration, "We love volatility."

However, the financial community's stakes in flexible exchange rates go beyond the growth of this concrete business niche. Bankers strongly support the independence of the Federal Reserve, which regulates the banking system and checks inflation in the economy. Banks also have an interest in avoiding domestic interest rate fluctuations. Exchange rate management threatens these interests: it circumscribes the Federal Reserve's autonomy by requiring domestic monetary operations for dollar stabilization purposes, and to the extent that monetary policy is targeted toward exchange rate stability, domestic interest rates will become more volatile. International banks are also vitally interested in

---

37. James V. Houpt, "International Trends for U.S. Banks and Banking Markets," *Federal Reserve Staff Study* 156 (Washington: Board of Governors of the Federal Reserve System, May 1988), table 27, 35. The figure dropped to $1.9 billion in 1988. Foreign-exchange trading became so attractive as to induce even some multinational corporations to bypass their banks and establish their own trading desks.

preventing the imposition of capital controls, toward which fixed exchange rates could be a first step.

Moreover, the large international banks are far better positioned than their clients in the corporate sector to protect themselves from exchange rate fluctuation when it becomes dangerous. To the extent that flexible exchange rates permit or contribute to misalignment of the currency, therefore, the interests of the financial community diverge from the real sector of the economy.

The main point is not that flexible exchange rates per se are a positive attraction for banks; it is rather that the flexible regime is better for banks than the alternatives. Although foreign-exchange trading services certainly prosper under volatility, there is such a thing as too much exchange rate volatility for the international banks. Large losses in foreign-currency speculation have broken some banks and sent panic through their networks of creditor banks. But those instances are relatively rare. When financiers have objected strongly to exchange rate instability to the Treasury and the Fed—as they did in autumn 1978 and in early 1987—they have tended to do so when volatility took the form of a precipitous dollar drop rather than a sharp rise.

As in 1987, most serious conversations between leading bankers and the top officials of the Treasury and the Fed about exchange rate and related policies are held in private. But in the second half of the 1980s some opposition to exchange rate stabilization was expressed in public.[38] This public opposition did not come from those people and institutions to which the Fed and the Treasury are normally most attentive. But because such activity is novel and illustrative of some broadly (but by no means universally) held views within the financial community, it is worth reviewing here.

The Economic Advisory Committee of the American Bankers Association argued that the Louvre Accord was a "mistake," as it contributed to interest rate increases, and they opposed any further development of exchange rate cooperation toward a target zone regime. In 1988, the group strongly recommended that monetary policy not be dedicated to supporting the dollar as a general principle, and it sanctioned foreign-exchange intervention only in exceptional circumstances to correct disorderly market conditions.[39] During congressional testimony, the chairman of the group also expressed grave concern for the Fed's

---

38. Ironically, signals from the financial community contributed to the creation of a stabilization regime, which many later criticized. Bankers reacted to the Treasury's talking the dollar down; Baker took their advice one step further and adopted not a hands-off approach but one of stabilization around provisional target ranges. Since the Louvre Accord, most voices from the financial community have opposed a tightening of the informal exchange rate ranges into a formal target zone system.

39. American Bankers Association, press release, Washington, 4 February 1988; press release, Napa, CA, 1 July 1988.

independence should monetary policy become dedicated to exchange rate stability.[40]

The Chicago Mercantile Exchange is one large nonbank financial institution with a clear-cut interest in floating exchange rates. There, the International Monetary Market (IMM) has been trading futures and options in foreign currencies since the early 1970s. By the description of its founder and chairman of the Exchange, Leo Melamed, the creation of the IMM is "inextricably intertwined with the death of Bretton Woods" and a "necessary by-product" of flexible exchange rate economics.[41] Foreign-currency futures contracts were the first of a series of new financial instruments developed by the IMM. Spurred by exchange rate and interest rate volatility, trading in these instruments grew rapidly from zero in 1972 to 60 million contracts per year by 1986, of which futures and options in currencies accounted for 23.4 million.[42]

Although 1986 was a record year for the IMM, and exchange rate volatility remained high, the Treasury's shift toward more active exchange rate management threatened the long-term growth of currency futures and options trading. Thus, long before the Treasury sought to stabilize the dollar in early 1987, Melamed mounted a public campaign against "fixed exchange foolishness."[43] He formed a group of finance and business representatives and prestigious economists , appropriately named the "American Coalition for Flexible Exchange Rates," dedicated to maintaining the flexible rate system. In its founding statement, the Coalition strongly discouraged direct intervention in the foreign-exchange market and argued that the goal of exchange rate stability (which was probably contrary to the Exchange's interest but which other Coalition members thought desirable) should be achieved through "responsible, consistent macroeconomic policies" instead. It affirmed its support for Secretary Baker's effort to improve coordination at the Tokyo summit.[44]

The Coalition funneled literature extolling the virtues of flexible exchange rates to the public and demonstrated that opposition to foreign-exchange

---

40. See the testimony of Milton W. Hudson in US Congress, House, Committee on Banking, Subcommittee on Domestic Monetary Policy, *Conduct of Monetary Policy in 1987*, hearings, 100th Cong., 2d sess., 17 and 24 March, 1988, 12, 79–93.

41. Leo Melamed, "The International Monetary Market," in Leo Melamed, ed., *The Merits of Flexible Exchange Rates: An Anthology* (Fairfax, VA: George Mason University Press, 1988), 417, 426.

42. Chicago Mercantile Exchange, *IMM 15-Year Commemorative Report* (Chicago: Chicago Mercantile Exchange, 1987), 8; *Annual Report 1985*; and *1986 Statistical Yearbook*, vol. 1, 5.

43. See his editorial in *Wall Street Journal*, 24 April 1986; and Chicago Mercantile Exchange, *Annual Report 1985*, 8–9.

44. American Coalition for Flexible Exchange Rates, "Statement of Purposes and Positions," Washington, August 1986.

intervention was broader than the particular business interests of the Exchange.[45] Some members of the group did express their views to senior administration officials and members of Congress. But beyond this, the activities of the Coalition as a whole were circumscribed by the multiplicity of reasons for supporting flexible exchange rates at that time: among its members were firms (and individuals) whose longer-term interest was in stability but for whom the dollar had not yet fallen enough. The Coalition never met as a full group or, beyond its short initial statement, developed common position papers on an ongoing basis; it is no longer active as of the summer of 1989. Importantly, the principal managers of the large money-center banks have not been Coalition members.

Further support for flexible exchange rates came from the monetarist Shadow Open Market Committee. This group issued repeated statements after early 1985 urging the Fed and the Treasury to cease using monetary policy and intervention to target the dollar's exchange rate. The inspiration behind the nonintervention policy of the Regan-Sprinkel Treasury, these monetarists sharply criticized the change toward activism under Baker. While applauding the slowing of the growth of the money supply in 1987, this group argued that using monetary policy to adjust the exchange rate was mistaken. The group underscored its intellectual commitment to a complete laissez-faire exchange rate policy by advocating that the United States play an "*n*th-currency-country" role.[46]

Summary and Conclusions

The experience of the 1980s suggests several broad observations about the character and pattern of private political activity to influence exchange rate policy and leads us to some conclusions about its impact.

---

45. See, for example, Leo Melamed, ed., *The Merits of Flexible Exchange Rates: An Anthology.*

46. The group argued in March 1985, as the dollar was near its peak, that the recent intervention had been "counterproductive, destabilizing exchange markets" and urged the government to "demand that the Federal Reserve ignore exchange market fluctuations and institute a stable policy of controlling money growth to end inflation." Breaking with mainstream economics, the group also argued, "There is no valid reason for believing that a reduction in the budget deficit will be followed by a fall in the dollar exchange rate." Later, writing just before the stock market crash, the group added, "If the exchange rate is held within a narrow range against major currencies, adjustment of prices and production costs to differences in productivity and saving rates in various countries will occur through other, no less costly, adjustments." See Shadow Open Market Committee, "Policy Statement," New York, 25 March 1985; "An Open Letter to Alan Greenspan: Policy Statement," New York, 14 September 1987; "Policy Statement," New York, 19 September 1988.

Private Political Activity

Despite formidable barriers to lobbying on exchange rate issues, private groups became very active in the mid-1980s. Their activity was responsible for making the dollar a domestic political issue as never before in the postwar period. When lobbying was strong and unanimous on the desirable direction for the dollar, as in 1985, it constrained the Treasury and thereby affected policy. When private lobbying was weak or in conflict, with some groups pressing for depreciation and others for stabilization, as in 1987 and since, the Treasury regained flexibility of action on exchange rate matters.

The bulk of private lobbying activity followed actual movements in the exchange rate with a long lag. Although some particularly exposed corporations responded quickly to the strong dollar, the general outcry against it was deferred. What explains the delay? First, even though many forecasters anticipated that the strong dollar would harm US competitiveness, it is hard to generate broad political action on the basis of projected future events, particularly among groups that previously were inactive. Even for the many groups that had been active on trade matters for some time, international monetary affairs were new territory in the 1980s. Second, the majority of exchange rate forecasters predicted that the dollar would depreciate from each of its successive highs in 1982–84. Potential activists thus had an incentive to "wait and see," until the exchange rate forecasts were proved wrong and the competitiveness projections right. The timing of political action seems best explained, then, not by the rise in the exchange rate itself, or by its anticipated effects on competitiveness, but by the actual impact of the dollar's rise on the real economy. Amid uncertainty, it was the actual shift in people's and businesses' economic fortunes that generated their political response.

Even then, the most influential outside advocates of a change in policy, the large trade-dependent multinational corporations, strongly supported Reagan's overall economic philosophy and policy agenda. Many did not want to oppose or be seen opposing Reagan policies before the 1984 elections. Some corporate officers did challenge the exchange rate policies of the administration at that time, electoral considerations notwithstanding. But others pulled their punches until after Reagan had been safely reelected, at which point they were free to differ publicly with the administration on fiscal and trade as well as exchange rate policy.

Political activity was slowed, and the message watered down, by the mechanisms through which the multifarious economic interests of the private sector were aggregated into privately organized associations. In the larger organizations such as the Business Roundtable, the US Chamber of Commerce, the National Association of Manufacturers, and the AFL-CIO, all of which were originally organized to influence business and economic issues of a domestic character, corporations or unions with international competitiveness concerns are commingled with others having purely domestic interests. Manufacturers are mixed with service industries, commercial enterprises with banks and financial institutions. A crisis had to threaten before these organizations came together and elevated the exchange rate issue to near the top of their agenda. Therefore, although top policymakers might observe the consequences of exchange rate misalignments in the economic statistics, they were not subjected to political pressure until private firms sustained direct damage.

Despite the activity that did take place on the exchange rate issue itself, by far the greatest share of overall lobbying activity by the private sector was still directed toward trade policy. For every attempt to persuade the administration to do something about exchange rates there were numerous attempts, usually not by the same agents, to influence imports (or exports) more directly. There were several reasons for this: the most accessible branch of the government, Congress, had a better handle on trade than on exchange rate policy; successful lobbying there yielded more visible results; and lobbying organizations could better prevent free riding on their efforts in the trade field, where remedies tended to be industry- or sector-specific, than in the monetary arena.[47]

But for those who wanted to correct the trade imbalance, private activity on trade policy was misplaced. Private activity directed toward exchange rate policy offered two important advantages: it promised to improve the overall trade balance, rather than benefit one traded-goods sector at the expense of others, and it could be more closely coupled with advice to correct the ultimate source of the imbalance, namely, the budget deficit. Although perhaps more difficult to organize and yielding more uncertain returns at the firm-specific level, exchange rate activity is a more constructive response than trade activity to an economy-wide trade imbalance. We therefore recommend in the next chapter a private-sector advisory group on exchange rates to help channel private political energy in this more constructive direction.

Finally, it must be noted that despite the nearly unanimous recommendation at mid-decade that the budget deficit be reduced to lower the dollar, private pressure utterly failed to break the political deadlock over fiscal policy. (A separate effort, by the Business Roundtable in particular, to inject competitiveness considerations into the 1986 tax reform process also failed.) More ominously, as the dollar depreciated and import competition weakened, the energy behind business's push for budget deficit reduction dissipated. Without the high dollar and an alarming deterioration in the trade balance as an

---

47. On the greater solubility of dilemmas of collective action in lobbying on trade as compared to monetary policy, see Joanne Gowa, "Public Goods and Political Institutions: Trade and Monetary Policy Processes in the United States," *International Organization* 42 (Winter 1988): 15–32.

inducement to lobby—and without a consensus on the need for tax increases to reduce the deficit—active business advocacy of fiscal responsibility has withered.

Effect of Political Activity on Policy

Responding as it did to an appreciating dollar, political activity on exchange rate policy took time to build in the early 1980s. At the outset of the first Reagan administration there was virtually no private-group political activity on exchange rate policy. As we argued in Chapter 2, political and economic circumstances left those officials immediately in charge with unusually wide latitude within the President's (primarily domestic) economic program to take the lead on exchange rate policy.

The Shift Toward Activism

Nor did political activity have a strong impact on policy during the first phase, from 1981 to 1984, when coalitions supporting change assembled and began to grow. There are several reasons for this. First, although more active during this period than at the very outset of the first Reagan term, the private sector spoke with multiple voices, and the force of this initial effort was diminished by the variety of prescriptions offered. Second, once rebuffed by the Treasury, private groups appealed to a variety of other offices within the government—the White House, other executive agencies, Capitol Hill, and the Fed—making the dollar depreciation movement correspondingly varied and uncertain as to its institutional target. The immediate response of those institutions, which were for the most part outside the closed exchange rate policymaking process, was to rightly state they had little control over exchange rate policy and redirect the petitioner to the Treasury. In some cases, they also stressed the need for cost control and enhancement of productivity, thus deflecting the responsibility for overcoming the competitive disadvantage back upon the private sector itself. Also hampering these early private efforts was the lack of a publicly known timetable for decision making so that advocates of change could know when to press their case to best advantage.

The Yen-Dollar Agreement was a product of private-sector as well as congressional activity in response to Japanese penetration of the US market in the early 1980s. As the initiative was put in terms of capital-market liberalization, the Treasury was much more receptive to this message than to the request for an active exchange rate policy (although it moved only after Secretary Shultz threatened to interfere). However, contrary to the hope of some business leaders that having the government simply focus on this particular exchange rate would cause the markets to lower the value of the US currency, the dollar continued to appreciate (as some analysts had predicted[48]) in the short term. The Yen-Dollar Agreement had beneficial effects in the longer term, helping to sustain capital inflow into the United States during the period of dollar realignment. But their satisfaction with this agreement notwithstanding, private interests certainly did not achieve their specific exchange rate objectives through the accord.

During the second phase of private activism, in 1984 and 1985, the administration could not resist the crescendo of voices calling for policy change. Secretary Baker had been made well aware of the position of senior business leaders while meeting with them as White House chief of staff. He brought this awareness with him to the Treasury, where the movement toward exchange rate policy change was reinforced by numerous private meetings with businessmen during the spring and summer of 1985. Furthermore, the progress the administration sought on trade policy—a new round of trade negotiations and avoidance of protectionist legislation—depended in large measure on private actors' cooperation, which in turn had been clearly linked to progress on the dollar.

The Shift From Depreciation to Stabilization

Private advocacy became less influential as it weakened with the dollar's depreciation during 1985 and 1986 and then split over the question of stabilization. The depreciation of the dollar satisfied many who had been complaining before the Plaza Agreement, although many traded-goods industries considered the dollar still too strong at 140–150 yen and 1.80 marks. Some sectors of the financial community became increasingly disturbed by the Treasury's talking down of the currency, and they communicated this concern to Baker. Others were opposed to stabilization in principle. Thus, in 1987, when considering the future course of exchange rate policy, Baker saw private actors expressing conflicting preferences. In opting for tentative stabilization, Baker was responding principally to the Fed and market conditions rather than to lobbying activity. Pressure for further depreciation clearly exercised diminishing influence on policy between 1987 and 1988, partly because there was less overall activity, and partly because the threat of inflation and financial instability was growing.

---

48. See, for example, Jeffrey A. Frankel, *The Yen/Dollar Agreement: Liberalizing Japanese Capital Markets*, POLICY ANALYSES IN INTERNATIONAL ECONOMICS 9 (Washington: Institute for International Economics, December 1984).

Since 1988 the administration has shown itself complacent in the face of occasional breaching of the target ranges, but this reaction is not the result of activity by proponents of flexible exchange rates. The unwillingness of the Treasury to acknowledge publicly that it was using target ranges in coordination with the other G-7 members might have been motivated, in part, by a wish to minimize criticism from these quarters. But the desire to safeguard its market credibility and to retain flexibility in adjusting target ranges was a more compelling incentive for the Treasury to keep the targets confidential.

Part III

Conclusions and Recommendations

8

Conclusions and Recommendations

In the 1980s the dollar became a first-order issue in US politics. Its value rose by more than 60 percent; the US trade balance deteriorated at an unprecedented pace; and the exchange rate became, for the first time since World War II, a major focus of industry lobbying and legislative entrepreneurship. When in 1985, with the dollar near its peak, the new Secretary of the Treasury James Baker moved to seize the international economic policy initiative, he did so through a dramatic shift in US exchange rate policy. He first initiated an ongoing, multilateral dialogue to bring the dollar down, and later worked with his colleagues to stabilize its value at the substantially lower level it had reached by early 1987.

In one sense, then, the system "worked."[1] Administration policies had produced an international imbalance that brought excruciating economic pressure upon the traded-goods sector. This was in turn translated into political pressure on administration leaders, leading to an adjustment of exchange rate policy. One might conclude, to paraphrase Bert Lance, that the policy process "ain't broke" and hence does not need fixing. But this would be, we are convinced, the wrong conclusion, for three basic reasons. The first is that the rise and fall of the dollar inflicted substantial and irreversible losses on the US industrial economy. The second is that the process of policy change, as it unfolded in the 1980s, involved enormous and unnecessary risks. The third is that the governmental response, impressive and helpful though it was, did not resolve the underlying source of the US trade deficit: the savings-investment imbalance fueled by the federal budget deficit.

Why the Process Needs Fixing

When the dollar rose by 60 percent, US manufacturing firms deferred domestic investments, yielded important markets to imports, shifted production overseas,

---

1. Stephen D. Cohen makes this argument in *The Making of United States International Economic Policy*, 3d ed. (New York: Praeger, 1988), chap. 10.

or did all three—steps they would not have taken in many cases had they known that the dollar would be returning to its 1980 level. These steps forced painful and, over the longer term, economically counterproductive adjustments on US workers and communities. These and other costs of misalignment resulted from the wide divergence of the exchange rate from the level that would produce reasonable balance in the current account.[2]

If there were economic costs, so also were there political risks. The policy shift in 1985 was achieved in part through the threat that trade protectionism would careen out of control. Indeed, had President Reagan been less dedicated to open trade, or had the domestic economy experienced a recession in 1985–86, this might well have occurred. As things happened, Reagan was driven, in the words of his Treasury Secretary, to "grant more import relief to US industry than any of his predecessors in more than half a century."[3] And although the trade legislation passed in 1988 proved more moderate than many had feared, it nevertheless contains provisions that risk exacerbating tensions in major US trade relationships and undermining the global trading system. Nor can the possibility of further compromise of open-trade policies be dismissed as long as the merchandise trade deficit remains at its current high level.

Finally and fundamentally, the central source of the US trade problem, the US budget deficit, has not been corrected. Given the shortfall in US private savings, the result has been the enormous international imbalances that are regularly bemoaned but seldom officially confronted. Domestic economic indicators, particularly the rates of unemployment and inflation, have improved markedly since the early Reagan administration. Complacency thus prevails, despite the fact that this success has been achieved, in important part, by borrowing from the American future.

In sum, if the policymaking system "works" in the 1990s the way it has worked in the 1980s, the consequences could be grave indeed.

A major source of these shortfalls in US policy performance was the *process* by which the US government makes policy affecting exchange rates. There were other important influences, of course, including the views and political strategy of the President on taxes, general macroeconomic conditions, the possibilities of cooperation with foreign governments, and at times the personal views of officials holding key positions. But institutions and processes mediate between these many factors and policy outcomes, and thereby play an important and sometimes independent role in policy determination.

---

2. On this point, see John Williamson, *The Exchange Rate System*, POLICY ANALYSES IN INTERNATIONAL ECONOMICS 5, rev. ed. (Washington: Institute for International Economics, June 1985), 38–44.

3. Remarks of Secretary of the Treasury James A. Baker III at the Institute for International Economics, Washington, 14 September 1987.

Changes in this policy process were far less dramatic than the changes in actual policy during the 1980s. Continuing to hold central responsibility for policy instruments that target the dollar directly—such as declarations, official foreign-exchange market operations, and reliance on the intervention of foreign central banks—was the same Treasury-Fed duopoly that had reigned throughout the postwar period. These institutions did respond, from 1985 on, to the strong pressure from peripheral actors and acted to bring the dollar—and the trade deficit—down. But the very strength and apparent effectiveness of their response served to reinforce the Treasury-Fed dominance that was earlier threatened.

Congress did, in the Omnibus Trade and Competitiveness Act of 1988, broaden its oversight role, and private groups developed a new sense of their stake in the dollar's international price. But the issue cooled, allowing direct executive branch exchange rate policymaking to remain a strikingly closed affair. For no other economic issue of comparable importance are basic policy objectives so narrowly determined in Washington.

Yet the system produced a near catastrophe in the mid-1980s, and the underlying macroeconomic problem remains unresolved. Is the current locus of exchange rate responsibility still desirable as the United States enters the 1990s? Can these proud and capable, but insular institutions, the Treasury and the Federal Reserve, be expected to respond adequately to the strong interests of the real US economy, especially the producers of traded goods?

Even if Treasury-Fed dominance over direct exchange rate policy is desirable, there remains the critical matter of the connection between exchange rate policy and economic policy as a whole. If currency market intervention and declarations are to have lasting effect, they must be reinforced by macroeconomic actions, in the fiscal as well as the monetary area. This is true for achieving the domestic objectives of exchange rate policy. It is equally true when the Treasury is called upon to enforce a target zone system (*de jure* or *de facto*) or any organized international system of currency management.

This chapter addresses these issues, and specifically how reforms in the policy process might facilitate their handling in the decade ahead. We draw particularly upon the experience of the 1980s, because it has been the primary focus of this book, of course, but more importantly because the 1990s are more likely to resemble that decade than those that preceded it.

US policy will not necessarily show the extreme oscillation characteristic of the 1980s, although shifts from neglect to activism have in fact been a staple of US exchange rate policy since the 1960s. It is important, therefore, to bear in mind the experience of prior decades and the dangers of overreacting to specific idiosyncrasies of the Reagan era. But the 1980s are, in most respects, a better guide to the future than preceding periods: the 1990s are likely to resemble the 1980s on such key matters as the magnitude of international capital flows, the rising roles of the Japanese yen and the deutsche mark, and above all, the basic nature of the regime, which remains one of floating rates, managed by governments.

Our specific recommendations treat first, briefly, matters of policy content, and specifically the framework of policy assumptions within which policymaking proceeds. We then offer a more extended treatment of policy processes and institutions.

General Policy Framework

Ours is fundamentally a study of policy process, not policy substance. We have conducted no original research on such matters as how foreign-exchange markets operate or the relationship between exchange rates and trade flows. Instead we have focused on how the US policy process has functioned over the past decade, with the aim of producing recommendations of value to persons who hold a range of substantive views.

Our recommendations will be very useful, however, only to those who believe, as we do, that the international value of the dollar is a major force in the American economy and hence an important concern of public policy. We share this and related substantive views with a wide range of international economic policy specialists, and they form the broad policy framework within which the process adjustments we suggest are likely to prove most useful. It is appropriate, then, to recapitulate these views here.

We begin with what remains the central international economic problem of the United States: the enormous deficit in the current account. Because of an excess of consumption and a deficit of savings relative to investment, the United States has been borrowing, since 1984, an average of $130 billion a year from the rest of the world, or approximately 2.5 percent of current gross national product. The percentages for 1989 and 1990, on current policies, will be similar. Already this new dependence on international capital has transformed the United States from the world's largest creditor nation to the world's largest debtor.

As discussed in Chapter 1, there are circumstances in which it is justifiable, even desirable, for a country to borrow in this manner. In terms of economic welfare, the clearest case occurs when returns to investment in the country are high and foreign borrowing finances an investment boom, which increases national production sufficiently that citizens are better off in the long run even after making the interest payments. But this does not describe the situation in the United States today. Foreign borrowing *has* made possible a higher level of investment than would otherwise have occurred, other things being equal, and there were periods in the 1980s when investment rose sharply: in 1984, for example, and in 1987–88. But for the decade as a whole, investment as a share of US GNP was no greater than in prior periods. Rather, what the massive borrowing facilitated was a consumption boom, bringing Americans a better current living standard at the cost of reducing future welfare and increasing international dependence. In the meantime, high interest rates relative to Europe and Japan tend to depress domestic investment and further weaken the competitive position of the United States among the advanced industrial economies.

The consumption boom could continue for a while longer, as long as foreign creditors are willing to buy dollar assets to finance it. But only an exceedingly short-run conception would see US interests as served thereby. And even if the further erosion of the American economic base were considered acceptable, a continued and growing trade deficit is likely to exacerbate protectionism. Critics will argue that exchange rate adjustment has been tried and has failed to solve the trade problem. Direct, trade-restrictive measures could well follow.

The primary international economic policy goal of the United States, then, must be to sharply reduce, if not eliminate, the US current account deficit over the next few years, and to maintain balance in the current account thereafter. The most important single means to this end is the reduction (and, given the low current rate of US private savings, the elimination) of the federal budget deficit.

Specific attention to the exchange rate is important as well, for two reasons. First, the exchange rate can, under certain circumstances, exert an independent effect on the current account balance, as discussed in Chapter 1. Second, focusing on the exchange rate can be useful in highlighting macroeconomic policy imbalances.

To illustrate this second, "guidepost" function that exchange rates can serve, suppose the Bush administration had sought in early 1989 to bring the dollar down further, in order to reduce the trade deficit, without taking serious action on the budget deficit. The result would have been increased demand for US exports as well as for import-competing US products. In an economy close to full employment and full capacity utilization, the new demand would raise domestic inflation. Were the policy process functioning well, inflation concerns would then initiate a review of fiscal policy. Focusing first on the exchange rate would have served then to highlight the fundamental cause of the imbalance.

How, then, should the US government approach exchange rate policy? We can summarize our answer in five propositions:

■ The United States should set, as a priority international economic goal, a specific current account target, derived from long-term savings-investment and net debtor considerations. This would mean, in practice, sharply reducing if not eliminating the present large current account deficit.

- The US government should treat the international value of the dollar as an important means to this end, because of the exchange rate's direct impact on the trade balance, and because of its value in signaling the need for changes in monetary and fiscal policies.

- The US government should develop, and be prepared to communicate, a general view of what the exchange rate should be: not necessarily that the dollar should be worth 200 or 150 or 100 yen, but at minimum that the current dollar level is either too high, too low, or in the proper range.[4]

- In pursuing its exchange rate goals, the US government should not eschew the levers of direct exchange rate policy: declaration, buying and selling dollars, and encouraging other national monetary authorities to do likewise.[5]

- However, the US government must also recognize the limits of these levers and the need to coordinate their use with US monetary and fiscal measures, whose impact on foreign-exchange markets is likely to prove more durable over the medium and long term.

Judged by these criteria, the substance of US policy, we believe, was particularly deficient between 1981 and 1985. Treasury leaders during that period treated the exchange rate as a market price that government should not seek to affect. They argued that the only way to moderate the strong dollar was to expand monetary policy and threaten inflation. Nor did they acknowledge certain links whose existence was conventional wisdom among mainstream economists: between the US budget deficit and the rise of real interest rates to attract capital to finance it, and between the resulting capital inflow and the rise of the dollar. Rather than moderating exchange-market expectations when the dollar was appreciating, the President and the Treasury Secretary actually cheered market developments; rather than leading the markets they followed them.[6]

---

4. We acknowledge limits to the extent to which the government can publicly call for large changes in the exchange rate. See our discussion later in this section.

5. As discussed in Chapter 1, this study does *not* attempt to resolve the debate over the effectiveness of direct exchange rate policy. However, our conclusions assume that direct exchange rate actions can have significant impact on currency markets, at least in the near term, particularly if reinforced by international coordination.

6. Our critique here presumes the existence of policy alternatives that could have blunted the appreciation of the currency, and its impact on traded-goods producers, without raising inflation or dampening domestic investment. Applying our policy framework outlined above, the best alternative was a different monetary-fiscal mix, which could have averted the stagnation of American manufacturing arising from the loss of trade competitiveness in the early and mid-1980s. But even without changes in monetary and fiscal policy, direct exchange rate policy could have been more constructive. By articulating a long-term view of US interests in the exchange rate and a determination to pursue

In 1985, by the same criteria, policy improved substantially. The Treasury took a view as to an appropriate direction (and later the appropriate level) for the dollar and used public declarations and market intervention to bring it about. Secretary Baker also relied heavily on changes in monetary policy by the Fed and its G-5 counterparts to support his exchange rate policy or, when monetary policy was no longer subject to his influence, to change exchange rate policy toward stabilization.

Even after 1985, however, US exchange rate policy lacked a strong long-term purpose and orientation. Despite some statements, and an effort to institutionalize coordination within the G-7, policy in 1985–89 is best explained by short-term economic and political circumstances. When protectionism threatened to boil over, the Plaza strategy was developed and unveiled. When US growth turned sluggish, as during 1985–86 and as was expected in late 1987, dollar depreciation was encouraged in order to facilitate adjustment. When the economy was feared to be overheating in early 1987, 1988, and early 1989, dollar stabilization was pursued and appreciation countenanced. The central apparent cause of this ad-hockery, moreover, was the policy's gravest flaw: the treatment of the fiscal deficit as given, an exogenous factor, rather than as the central policy needing change. Hence, although reduction in the trade deficit was the stated goal, there was no way that government could credibly target its elimination or even its reduction to a level that could be defended as sustainable.[7]

---

those interests, even if conceding an appreciation of the dollar in the short term, the Treasury could have reduced the damage to traded-goods industries without eviscerating the recovery.

The Treasury might have stated that the long-term equilibrium exchange rate for the dollar was somewhere in the neighborhood of the real effective exchange rate prevailing in 1980–81 and that it expected an eventual return to those levels. Even if administration leaders were not prepared to pressure the Federal Reserve to loosen monetary policy or to propose a fiscal compromise with the Congress, they might have affirmed that reaching those levels was clearly in the long-term US interest. The Treasury might have added that it and the Federal Reserve would intervene in the foreign-exchange markets to prevent rapid appreciation, would review market developments on a daily basis, and would maintain a network of finance ministry and central bank cooperation to moderate appreciation.

This shadow exchange rate policy would not have overwhelmed savings-investment imbalances in the major countries, as far as the effect on exchange rates was concerned. But it probably would have had a significant impact on the financial and exchange markets nonetheless, moderating appreciation enough to at least prevent the speculative bubble of 1984–85, particularly when contrasted with the official cheering of the dollar's rise that actually occurred. In sum, we believe that the Treasury did have alternatives, and the 1985–88 experience supports this assessment.

7. Indeed, there could be no official estimate of what a sustainable current account deficit was, nor of whether that level could be achieved at exchange rates at which the dollar had been stabilized after the Louvre Accord. For the economic logic, on existing policies, was politically unacceptable: a current account deficit below, say, $50 billion could not be forecast on the basis of current policies and exchange rates. See US Department of the

Caution is required, of course, when making public declarations at times of sharp divergence between the dollar's current value and that sought or anticipated by government leaders. Bald declarations that large shifts are needed can provoke excessive market reactions, which in turn drive policymakers to emergency "rescues" they would much sooner avoid. In periods of serious misalignment, leaders face an acute dilemma, as the goals of market direction and market orderliness will to some degree conflict. Nonetheless, direct foreign-exchange operations by the Treasury and the Fed should be based on a long-term conception of US exchange rate interests, one developed as an integral part of overall administration economic policy and explained and defended on Capitol Hill. The Treasury and the Fed should make clear their determination to pursue that policy over the longer term.

But how, precisely, should these policies be developed and managed? This question returns us to the central subject of this book, US government processes and institutions for exchange rate policymaking. It can be divided, in turn, into three central issues. The first concerns exchange rate policy *execution:* at the operational level, who should wield the instruments of direct exchange rate policy—declarations, intervention, and international financial diplomacy? The second involves exchange rate *goal-setting:* how can the administration and Congress best consider and balance competing perspectives and interests? The third focuses on *broad policy linkages:* how can exchange rate policymaking be most effectively coordinated with other, intertwined Washington processes, particularly monetary and fiscal policymaking?

Policy Execution: The Treasury-Fed Relationship

Should the current closed system be maintained? Our answer to this question, based on the analysis in Chapter 5, is that the closed system is appropriate for day-to-day actions but is *not* appropriate for exchange rate goal-setting.

There are major advantages to Treasury-Fed control of policy execution: credibility in international forums and financial markets; the efficiency of a clear, technically competent, institutional focal point; the capacity for secrecy, necessary when operating in potentially volatile financial markets. The Treasury's autonomy facilitated adroit performance during the tenure of James Baker.

Treasury, "Report on Exchange Rates and International Economic Policy," 15 October 1988. For representative projections as of spring 1989, see William R. Cline, *American Trade Adjustment: The Global Impact*, POLICY ANALYSES IN INTERNATIONAL ECONOMICS 26 (Washington: Institute for International Economics, March 1989), 15. The lowest projection for any year by any models was $83 bilion; the highest was $243 billion.

There are also disadvantages to closure of the policy process. The principal one is the danger that the goals pursued will reflect a narrow, biased, or even ideological concept of US policy interests. Closure spawned neglect and delayed policy correction during the tenure of Treasury Secretary Donald Regan. This danger can be minimized in the future, we believe, by improved processes for exchange rate goal-setting.

Assuming that the system of policy execution remains closed, what of the balance of Treasury-Fed responsibility within it? The Treasury clearly shares control over exchange rate matters with the Fed, as discussed in Chapter 5. The anomalous division of responsibility between the two bureaucracies, giving greater formal exchange rate powers to the Treasury but reserving domestic monetary policy for the Fed, poses problems of coordination. Are these successfully managed? Or should both responsibilities be unified under one agency?

There are clear disadvantages to the prevailing institutional interdependence. Shared power gives each agency, in practice, a veto over exchange rate intervention. This creates a bias toward inaction. Moreover, shared power could contribute to a perverse linkage between exchange rate and domestic monetary policy: to the extent that the Treasury's dominance over dollar policy confers influence over monetary policy, that influence could be abused. Or, fearing such assaults on its autonomy in the domestic sphere, the Fed might mute its advocacy of intervention, as it did in the early 1980s. Or the Fed might cease cooperating with the Treasury's exchange rate strategy, as Volcker did in early 1987, inducing Baker to move to stabilization at the Louvre. Effective cooperation is highly dependent, moreover, on the professional and personal relationship between the Secretary and the Chairman.

Shared responsibility also has important strengths, however. When the Secretary-Chairman relationship is constructive, the two officials can cooperate to achieve orderly exchange rate realignments, as Baker and Volcker did at least tacitly in 1985–87. It gives the two leaders and their bureaucracies effective "triangulation" on the markets when using declaratory policy. Joint Treasury-Fed execution of policy also makes possible a fruitful division of labor between the political and technical tasks in exchange rate management.

Shifting broad authority in either direction, to either the Treasury or the Federal Reserve, would create more risks than benefits. Granting the Treasury the power to instruct the Fed to conduct sterilized intervention, for example, would require also giving the Treasury effective dominance over domestic monetary policy. Such a fundamental reversal of the Fed's traditional autonomy in the domestic sphere goes beyond the scope of our study, and we are not prepared to recommend it here. Partial steps in this direction raise their own problems: reducing the Fed's exchange rate role might also reverse its gradual movement toward giving greater emphasis to exchange rate considerations in domestic monetary operations. In any case, it is fiscal, not monetary policy that has been most poorly coordinated with exchange rate strategy in the 1980s.

There are also strong arguments against shifting power from the Treasury to the Fed. Treasury leadership on exchange rates can facilitate linkages to related policy areas, particularly fiscal and trade policy. It also places the political burden for defending exchange rate policy and international monetary agreements before Congress and the general public on an executive agency, where it belongs.

Giving greater exchange rate authority to the Fed could also make the rest of the government lose "institutional interest" in exchange rate management, as warned one former senior Fed official interviewed for this book. If the Fed then sought reinforcement of exchange rate goals through fiscal policy adjustments, for example, it might well be told that the exchange rate was the Fed's problem. And although shifting exchange rate power toward the Fed would facilitate consistency with monetary policy, it could also make the semiautonomous central bank more of a political target and jeopardize the insulation of monetary policy from political pressure.

For these reasons we prefer the present arrangement of interdependent responsibilities, which requires intensive consultation and communication between the two bureaucracies, to unifying exchange rate responsibilities or shifting major authority in either direction. Certain modest adjustments would be constructive, however. First, it would be useful to clarify the legal obligation of the Fed to support a formal international exchange rate stabilization arrangement negotiated by the Treasury with the G-7 and consistent with goals set jointly with other executive agencies and the Congress. In turn, the Fed should be given more discretion in foreign-exchange operations, that is, permission from the Treasury to intervene in larger amounts without having to seek further authorizations. The Fed should also, of course, be included in international negotiations over the stabilization regime.

A clarification of Fed responsibilities might also include an escape clause covering circumstances when US fiscal policy was irresponsible. Exchange rate stabilization should not be used as a mechanism to force the Fed to accommodate US budget deficits.

These adjustments would be particularly useful if the United States decided to stabilize the dollar within broad-banded target zones or via another arrangement, once a sustainable current account balance was achieved. The Treasury and the Fed would have to negotiate an agreement on any proposed target zone system, committing the Fed to support the exchange rate targets with intervention and monetary policy, in consultation with foreign central banks. The Treasury would assume the political responsibility of selling the target zone system to the Congress and the public at large, in particular defending the Fed when the new regime required a tightening of monetary policy, and promoting changes in US fiscal policy when necessary, as well as in macroeconomic policies abroad.

In summary, we see no present need for basic change. In the future, however, the problem will require revisiting, for the US position in the global financial order may make it at once more interested in exchange rate stability and less able to extract cooperation from other governments.[8]

Goal-Setting: Congress, the Executive, and Private Interests

Treasury-Fed dominance of exchange rate policy *execution* needs to be balanced by broader processes to set and review policy *goals*. There are two obvious and appropriate forums for such goal-setting. One is the Congress. The other is the administration.

Congress: Select Committees on the Dollar

Can process changes help Congress focus constructive attention on exchange rate policymaking? Our answer is yes, at the margin.

One reason for this conclusion is that Congress did play a constructive role during the 1980s, as described in Chapter 6. Through hearings and legislative proposals, members of Congress linked the diverse international economic issue areas of trade, exchange rates, and Third World debt at a time when few in the administration were doing so. By threatening to pass legislation requiring exchange rate intervention or imposing trade restrictions, Congress succeeded in persuading the Treasury to reconsider and ultimately to change its policy toward the dollar.[9]

---

8. In the future, the continued internationalization of the US economy, its shrinkage in size relative to the rest of the world, the integration of monetary policy in the European Community, and the persistence of mercantilistic trade and foreign-exchange practices will all sharpen US policy dilemmas. In the past, largely because of its size and closure relative to its trading partners, the United States has been in a strong position to extract foreign assistance for US exchange rate objectives, as illustrated by the heavy intervention by foreign central banks to support the dollar in 1987.

But these trends will make the United States both more interested in the exchange rate and less able to extract cooperation from foreign governments. Under these circumstances, the United States itself will have to carry a larger share of the burden of action in foreign-exchange markets. That is likely to put more stress on the cooperative arrangements, developed in an era of relative closure, between the Fed and the Treasury.

9. Of course, intermittent congressional efforts were not able to force integration of exchange rate and fiscal policy through decisive action on the budget deficit. Senate Republican leaders did work with administration allies to enact modest tax increases in 1982 and 1984, and they spearheaded a major, if ultimately abortive, deficit-reduction effort in the spring of 1985.

Some Congressmen raised the threat of protectionism as a deliberate strategy to force broader action affecting the trade imbalance, especially action on the dollar. For others, direct trade action was a genuine objective. And many favored action on both fronts. Notwithstanding this mix of motivations, the effect of pressure on the trade front was to induce the Treasury to pursue dollar depreciation as a counterstrategy against restrictive import legislation. Thus, the noisy and often chaotic congressional process forced attention to the problem of the trade imbalance, generated alternative proposals to deal with it, and in practice encouraged the administration to adopt responses that were more positive and effective than protectionism. Congress had an independent, constructive impact.

But this outcome is hardly grounds for complacency. The policy change was slow in coming, and the constructive role Congress played in the mid-1980s was premised on the fundamental predisposition of most members of Congress toward open trade and the strong presidential commitment to the same. It is quite possible that neither condition will be satisfied in the future. It would have been far better if attention to the problem had been forced earlier, before so much damage was done to the goods-producing sector. Given the continuing, egregious US current account deficit, the need for attention—and action—remains high.

A place to begin is the steps Congress has taken to enhance its role in exchange rate policy. The 1988 trade bill declared that "a more stable exchange rate for the dollar at a level consistent with a more appropriate and sustainable balance in the United States current account should be a major focus of national economic policy." To advance this goal, the act required multilateral and bilateral negotiations and regular Treasury reporting to the Senate and House banking committees.

The purpose of the reports was to force executive attention to the exchange rate and broader policies affecting it. But as noted in Chapter 6, this process has not proved very effective to date. A key reason is that it does not engage those legislators most concerned about trade and industrial competitiveness (or about overall macroeconomic balances) in the exchange rate oversight process—the members of the banking committees respond to different, primarily financial concerns and constituencies. The separation between these legislators, who possess formal jurisdiction, and the members of the trade committees, who feel the effects of exchange rate misalignment, is one important reason why Congress did not act sooner on exchange rate matters earlier in this decade.

This is a structural problem, and there is no perfect remedy. The basic need is to engage members of Congress concerned about trade and budget matters in the oversight of exchange rates. *To facilitate this, the banking committees should invite representatives of the trade and budget panels to participate in questioning the Secretary of the Treasury on the exchange rate report due in October 1989.* They should be encouraged, in particular, to force attention to the links between the budget and trade deficits and the dollar's international value. The administration should be pressed to set forth, much more explicitly than in previous reports and hearings, the exchange rate and current account implications of current monetary and fiscal policies, and to explain how, in general, it intends to employ direct exchange rate policy instruments. The banking committee hearings should focus mainly on the dollar's relationship to the other major currencies and should not allow the Treasury to divert attention to second-order currency relationships, such as those with the newly industrializing countries.

Over the longer term, this multicommittee participation should be institutionalized through creation, in the House and the Senate, of Select Oversight Committees on the Dollar and the National Economy. [10] Each would include senior representatives of the international finance and monetary policy subcommittees of the banking committees, the trade subcommittees of the Senate Finance Committee and the House Ways and Means Committee, and the budget committees. These committees would not have legislative jurisdiction, but they would have their own small independent staffs and would hold hearings, conduct studies, elicit information from executive agencies, and (as useful) issue reports. The purpose would be to provide forums for integrated consideration of real and financial aspects of exchange rates and the current account balance.

To this end the Select Committees—not the banking committees alone—should receive the biannual Treasury exchange rate reports inaugurated by the 1988 legislation. They should also hear public testimony from the Secretary of the Treasury, the Director of the Office of Management and Budget, and the US Trade Representative on policies to implement exchange rate goals. The Select Committees should also seek ways to solicit the views of the International Monetary Fund and other international financial institutions concerning the impact of US policy on global currency markets. And finally, they should conduct closed-door hearings when they determine that their oversight is more effective in a secret forum.

There is a precedent for these proposed committees in the Select Committees on Intelligence established in the 1970s in the wake of public concern about the use and abuse of covert action overseas. Those committees have effectively monitored the administration in a highly sensitive policy area not amenable to legislation. Their record in handling classified information has been good. Although there are many specific differences in the substantive sphere addressed, the proposed exchange rate committees would focus, like the intelligence panels,

---

10. An alternative would be to give this role to a subcommittee of the Joint Economic Committee. But the administration might take more seriously select committees focused directly on this topic, which draw their members from panels with legislative jurisdiction over the specific policy issues addressed.

on an important policy area previously neglected by Congress, one that involves matters central to no existing committee but within the jurisdiction of several.

In their oversight function, the Select Committees should both challenge their executive counterparts and support them in taking a broad, longer-term view of their responsibilities. Hence they could reinforce the broadened role for the Secretary of the Treasury recommended in the section that follows. The Treasury Department may well be cool toward creation of these committees, as it was toward the exchange rate provisions of the omnibus trade act. But as in that case it could eventually find this reform very useful.

Congress, of course, cannot conduct exchange rate policy itself, just as it cannot conduct intelligence activities. Nor should it, in most instances, demand public statements from the Treasury Secretary or the Fed Chairman about precise exchange rate targets or day-to-day intervention strategies. But it is entirely appropriate, and indeed necessary, for Congress to exercise its oversight role firmly. Members should insist that the administration develop a policy approach that integrates external trade and capital flows with domestic economic performance, and addresses the role to be played by exchange rate and international monetary policy. The Select Committees we recommend should strengthen congressional capacity to play this important oversight role.

An Executive Branch Review

If broad policy on the dollar must be developed by the administration, what processes should it employ? The now-mandated exchange rate report is presented and defended by the Secretary of the Treasury, in proper recognition of his lead role on this and related issues. But such a report should not represent Treasury views alone. Rather, it should reflect an executive-wide policy deliberation leading to an administration stance. The Treasury should lead in this process, but it should invite—and listen to—the views of a range of relevant agencies, particularly those reflecting macroeconomic perspectives such as the Council of Economic Advisers, and those representing producer interests such as the office of the US Trade Representative and the Agriculture and Commerce Departments.

To our knowledge, the Reagan administration never instituted regular executive-branch review processes meeting this description.[11] The 1981 decision to cease intervention was discussed in advance by Reagan's principal economic advisers, but in subsequent years senior officials responsible for

---

11. In previous administrations the process on international monetary issues was centered on an interagency committee at the sub-Cabinet level, headed by the Under Secretary of the Treasury for Monetary Affairs: the Deming Group in the Johnson administration, the Volcker Group under Nixon, and so on.

international trade did not have access to a regular policy review process on the issue. When Baker and Darman reversed the Regan-Sprinkel policy, they did so by designedly *excluding* those who were in opposition, keeping it out of the logical interagency forum, the Economic Policy Council, which Baker chaired. This tactic no doubt enhanced their short-term flexibility but also tended to separate direct exchange rate policy from broader monetary and fiscal policy.

The need for the 1990s will be the opposite, to *connect* policymaking about the desirable level of the exchange rate with policymaking on money, the budget, and trade. *The President should be required by law to include in his annual economic report to the Congress a review of these connections, a desirable current account target, and a calendar for achieving it.* The role of various policy instruments, including the exchange rate, in achieving this objective should be addressed as well. The President's statement should be the product of a broad administration policy review. Exactly how this review operates will depend on general intra-administration relationships, and in particular on broader economic policy coordination procedures treated near the close of this chapter. But one point in particular merits special emphasis at this point. That is the need for producer interests to have a regular input into executive branch goal-setting on exchange rates.

A Private-Sector Advisory Group on Exchange Rates

Despite formidable barriers to lobbying on exchange rate issues, private groups became politically active on exchange rate policy in the 1980s. When private lobbying was strong and one-sided, as it became during 1984 and 1985, it was successful.

But the private response to dollar appreciation lagged considerably behind exchange market developments. Business was not well organized to express its collective views on the matter, and available government channels made it far easier for firms to focus their lobbying on trade policy instruments, even though bringing down the dollar was, if feasible, a far more constructive and relevant remedy to the circumstances American traded-goods producers confronted at mid-decade.

We recommend, therefore, that the government create a forum to encourage the channeling of business lobbying in this direction. It should establish a private-sector Advisory Group on Exchange Rates (AGXR), parallel in structure and functions to those that currently advise the US Trade Representative on trade policy.

Participation should be at the highest level: the chief executive officers of major corporations, for example. Members should be appointed by the President on the recommendation of the Secretary of the Treasury, who should in turn consult with the administration's senior trade and economic officials in putting together the proposed list.[12] The group should be small (10 to 15 members), with financial and service enterprises represented as well as manufacturing and agricultural interests. (It could also include a representative of consumer interests, and an academic exchange rate expert.) It should meet at least twice a year with the Treasury Secretary, with the US Trade Representative and other interested Cabinet-level economic and trade advisers present.

Like its trade policy counterpart, the AGXR would make periodic public reports to the President, the Congress, and the Secretary. These reports should coincide with the Secretary's exchange rate report and provide a basis for private-sector testimony to the Select Committees recommended earlier. This would not, of course, give the group the same leverage as that of the Advisory Committee on Trade Policy and Negotiations in reporting on a trade agreement requiring congressional approval, since the Treasury does not need explicit sanction to conduct exchange rate operations.[13] But the 1985 case where USTR sought private-sector advice on whether to launch a new multilateral trade round is an example of the benefits of having such an advisory group. The strength of the final message not to proceed without parallel discussions of exchange rates was a jolt to the administration, and a constructive one.[14]

In summary, such a group would provide advantages over the present unstructured, ad hoc process by which private views are filtered through to the government. Of course, the Secretary would not be required to act on the board's advice, but he would be expected to listen and respond. This dialogue would also give the Secretary an opportunity to influence these interests and the process through which they are aggregated.

The existence of such an advisory process could rechannel private advocacy in more constructive directions, away from trade-distorting remedies and toward exchange rate (and related macroeconomic) remedies to international imbalances. The group could provide a focal point for lobbying, particularly if attached to a publicized timetable for policymaking, such as the Treasury reports to Congress and G-7 or summit meetings, and if related to specific policy decisions. It would also offer direct access to the Treasury and thus an alternative

---

12. This procedure parallels that provided in the Omnibus Trade and Competitiveness Act of 1988, section 1631, for appointment of an Advisory Committee for Trade Policy and Negotiations.

13. The group may gain leverage, however, from the fact that the market impact of a strong, public exchange rate recommendation could prove significant. The Treasury will fear, quite understandably, that it could prove disruptive. A likely result would be to strengthen the *private* dialogue, since the Treasury will wish either to mute such public impact or to shape the substance of the group's statement so that it reinforces administration exchange rate goals.

14. For an insightful analysis of how private-sector advisory groups helped Robert Strauss negotiate the Tokyo Round, see Gilbert Winham, *International Trade and the Tokyo Round Negotiation* (Princeton, NJ: Princeton University Press, 1986), especially 315–17.

to lobbying Congress. For both of these reasons, the cost of lobbying on exchange rate policy, compared to trade policy, would be reduced, at the margin.

Finally, the group could become one of the mechanisms through which the Treasury seeks general endorsement of exchange rate initiatives it might take in the future. The private-sector advisory process would be a two-way street. The Treasury would inevitably call on the group to support its own policy when that policy is consistent with advice given by the group. That, too, would be constructive. The Treasury will need increased public support because the salience of exchange rates for private groups and Congress has increased. The Treasury would particularly need support for any formalization and enforcement of the now-secret target ranges.

Is there a danger that producer interests would gain too strong a voice on the dollar? History is replete with examples of countries that tailored their exchange rates to bring advantage to their traded-goods sectors. When trading partners reciprocate this mercantilism, competitive devaluations can bring inflation, depression, and related economic ills. Some may see this prescription as leading the United States down that slippery slope, or at least toward its edge.

We cannot dismiss this fear as groundless: the United States did, after all, devalue competitively in 1933. But in the postwar period the problem has been the opposite: the Treasury has responded belatedly to a *deteriorating* trade position of US producers; there is not a single instance of official action driving the currency down to produce a significant international surplus. In 1989, the problem remains a substantial current account deficit, exacerbated by overconsumption, and the balance of political and institutional forces is resistant to change. We see our proposed advisory committee as pushing things in the right direction, and unlikely to be potent enough to institutionalize mercantilism. Until the United States does right its international balances, of course, support for mercantilist approaches to trade and dollar policy is likely to grow. But giving producer interests a legitimate, proportionate role in the policy process will help protect against such a movement getting out of hand.

Linking Exchange Rates and Macroeconomic Policymaking

Last, but assuredly not least, US action on exchange rates needs to be integrated with broader macroeconomic policy. One reason, addressed above, is that direct exchange rate actions affect the macroeconomy. The other, of course, is that macroeconomic policy actions affect exchange rates.

The connections are obvious and straightforward. Monetary policy affects interest rates; fiscal policy influences the savings-investment balance and hence the demand for foreign capital. Both affect the supply and demand for dollars on foreign-exchange markets.

Suppose that the United States has committed itself to a certain value of the dollar—for domestic reasons, and perhaps also to play its role in a target zone system. How is that commitment to be enforced? Declarations and direct market interventions will be helpful, but over the medium and longer term they are unlikely to prove sufficient. Monetary and fiscal action will be necessary.

But monetary and fiscal policy typically give primacy to other goals: combating inflation and averting recession. We can hardly expect these goals to be abandoned, nor would we want them to be. What one *should* want and expect is effective coordination and mutual responsiveness among governmental actors working to reconcile these often-competing values. The connections between exchange rate–specific operations and monetary and fiscal actions must be explicitly recognized and regularly addressed.

The connection between exchange rate goals and overall monetary policy can be maintained, presumably, through Fed-Treasury cooperation, about which we have already spoken at some length. But what of fiscal policy? Specifically, how does one connect action on the budget deficit to desired—and likely—effects on the value of the dollar? The connection must, of course be two-way. We need to ensure that exchange rate target-setting is undertaken in the context of other macroeconomic goals. But in the other direction, we need to make it possible for those who make exchange rate or target zone pledges to deliver on them, by increasing their leverage on the fiscal actions that are so important to their capacity to deliver.

The second Reagan administration, so successful in managing direct exchange rate policy, failed egregiously in making the fiscal connection.[15] In fact, it often seemed that Baker's authority in the former sphere was dependent on his avoiding the latter—staying out of the fiscal thicket his President had made so unrewarding. The Bush administration has tended to compartmentalize fiscal policy also, albeit in a different way. Treasury Secretary Nicholas Brady is involved in the budget negotiations with Capitol Hill. But they are mainly the preserve of Richard Darman, the virtuoso Office of Management and Budget (OMB) Director, whose tactical, insider approach seems aimed at obscuring *all* the broader connections in order, somehow, to get through 1989 with neither Gramm-Rudman-Hollings sequestration nor the sight of presidential lips backing new taxes.

---

15. Nothwithstanding the lack of a serious administration effort, the budget deficit did fall, as a percentage of GNP, from over 5 percent in 1986 to around 3 percent in 1989, as a result of a combination of tax reform, economic recovery, and marginal budgetary changes. But the deficit remains irresponsibly high for a time of full employment, given the low rate of private savings.

One institution that can encourage making such connections is the Congress. Reporting procedures can play a role: the statement now required of OMB and the Congressional Budget Office regarding the impact of the budget on external accounts is a step in the right direction. It would be better, however, if the Secretary of the Treasury and the OMB Director were required to appear *together* before a panel such as the Select Oversight Committees on the Dollar and the National Economy we have recommended, and to set forth there an integrated approach to the budget, the exchange rate, and the current account balance.

A second useful step, and one within the Treasury Secretary's power to implement, would be to give a senior subordinate responsibility for both domestic and international monetary matters. That role was formerly played by the Under Secretary for Monetary Affairs, a position filled in the past by men such as Robert V. Roosa, Paul A. Volcker, Anthony M. Solomon, and Beryl W. Sprinkel, but abolished in the second Reagan administration. Secretary Brady has, to his credit, restored Under Secretary rank to the lead exchange rate official, but unfortunately he has institutionalized an *inferior* arrangement by creating separate under-secretaryships for international and domestic affairs. In view of the need to connect, not separate these two spheres, we recommend that the venerable position of Under Secretary for Monetary Affairs be restored.

Third, greater operational leverage over fiscal policy could be obtained by strengthening the President's ability to win enactment of a balanced budgetary package. This would not, it must be confessed, be a ready remedy for the deficit deadlock of the 1980s. The recent situation has *not* been one of brave Presidents finding their wise fiscal blueprints thwarted by irresponsible legislators. There have been times in the 1980s, in fact, when the pattern was more the reverse. However, *if* the President found it easier to win congressional backing, he might be encouraged to risk responsibility. He would, at a minimum, find it harder to use congressional intransigence as an excuse.

Suppose that the Congress therefore developed a procedure analogous to those employed since 1974 for ratifying trade agreements. *Congress would commit itself in advance to an up-or-down vote, within 90 days, on a presidential proposal to implement a US fiscal policy commitment made at a G-5 or G-7 summit meeting.*[16] The implementing legislation could be very broad (as was, for example, the Trade Agreements Act of 1979 implementing the Tokyo Round accords). It could include (within statutorily defined limits) appropriations cuts, tax increases, changes in laws governing entitlements—whatever was reasonably connected to delivering on the President's international budgetary commitment. The very

---

16. Of course, Congress could omit the requirement of an international deal and simply amend its budget procedures to provide for an up-or-down vote on a presidential deficit reduction package. Presumably, however, Congress would be more likely to make international agreement a precondition.

existence of such an authority would confer on the President (and his Treasury Secretary) greater credibility vis-à-vis foreign leaders, thereby facilitating better international fiscal-monetary–exchange rate bargains. Like the fast-track trade procedures, this authority would likely engage congressional budget leaders in advance negotiations with the administration in shaping the specifics of the international package and the domestic implementing legislation.

Finally, and most important to linking exchange rates with broader policy, the President should enforce a central economic policy process for review of all major issues and actions within this sphere. One model is the Ford administration's Economic Policy Board (EPB), which was chaired (in the President's absence) by the Secretary of the Treasury and staffed by an Assistant for Economic Affairs with direct access to the President. With this dual foundation, Ford's EPB could make it hard on officials and agencies that sought to circumvent it—and with decision procedures widely recognized as fair, it created positive incentives for participation as well.

Following this model, all economic policy, international and domestic, would come under the active jurisdiction of a Cabinet-level Economic Policy Committee led by the Secretary of the Treasury but supported by a White House–based economic policy coordinating staff. President Bush's White House Assistant to the President for Economic and Domestic Policy would be the logical chief of such a staff, and in fact seems to be developing processes generally consistent with those outlined here.

A key aim would be to simultaneously strengthen and broaden Treasury leadership. The Secretary would have a strong and comprehensive mandate; he would be the senior administration player, across the board, on economic policy issues. At the same time, he would be expected to work with—not around—his senior colleagues, through processes that institutionalized their participation. The Treasury Secretary's exchange rate authority could prove a useful lever. He could condition his readiness to subject it to interagency scrutiny on the willingness of his counterparts to bring "their" issues, fiscal policy above all, to the table of the EPC or the informal subgroups it would likely spawn.[17]

---

17. We are grateful to Peter B. Kenen for suggesting this potentiality. Keeping the Treasury in the lead position on exchange rate policy, rather than transferring authority to the Fed, enhances the Treasury's influence over fiscal policy and its ability to coordinate decision making among the other executive agencies.

A step that would carry such reform to its logical extreme would be to move the OMB back into the Treasury Department, reversing the Rooseveltian reform of 1940 and making the Secretary more like his finance minister counterparts, who have budget as well as tax and currency oversight responsibilities. Such a radical shift, however, should be based upon a broader slice of US policy experience than is addressed in this study.

Concluding Thoughts

Like its counterparts in other policy spheres, the closed system of exchange rate policy execution has substantial advantages: efficiency, flexibility, and (at least potentially) a capacity to respond to crises and changing circumstances. There is every reason to maintain these advantages, provided the system can regularly serve the public good. What is needed, therefore, is process reforms to increase the chances that leaders will be responsive to broader economic needs as they pursue their appointed tasks, and to connect them to broader governmental resources so they can achieve government-wide exchange rate goals and deliver on their commitments.

In terms of the priority given exchange rate policy, the United States needs to replicate 1985–88 and avoid 1981–85. But the 1985–88 approach built walls between exchange rate and broader economic policymaking, and this was not unrelated to the primary failure of that period—the failure to address the fiscal deficit seriously and systematically. The consequence is a current account imbalance that remains around $120 billion and threatens to grow further in the absence of major US policy changes. Making such changes, particularly on the fiscal front, remains the nation's foremost international *and* domestic policy priority. Only in that way can we complete the adjustment begun in 1985 and restore America's international balance.

If and when the United States achieves adjustment, the immediate threats posed by the consequences of exchange rate misalignments are likely to dim, and the tendency to relapse into neglect will strengthen. Institutional changes now can help to prevent yet another costly repeat of the cycle from neglect to activism.

Index

Federal Open Market Committee
(FOMC), 12, 52, 62
dollar rebound and, 68
1962 intervention guidelines of, 88
Federal Reserve
autonomy of, 65–66
financial community and, 133–34
threats to, 93–94
Treasury and, 90–91
and Baker-Volcker routine, 52–53
cooperation with Treasury of, 12
dollar rebound and, 68
and inflation suppression, 31, 57, 62
policymaking by, 11–12
Reagan administration policy and, 19
reluctance to challenge nonintervention policy, 30–31
Treasury and, 83-97. See also
Treasury, US
Federal Reserve Act, 87
Feldstein, Martin S., 8n–9n, 27–28, 37,
65, 72n, 127
Finance ministries, 83
Financial sector, 102. See also Private
sector
flexible rates and, 131–36
Fiscal policy, 162. See also Budget defi-
cit, US; Macroeconomic policy
Congress and, 163–64
international spillover of, 18–19
Reagan administration, 78
Fitzwater, Marlin M., 64n
Fixed exchange rates. See also Gold
standard
financial sector and, 133
Flexible exchange rates. See also Target
zone system sympathy for, financial
sector and, 131–36
Fliess, Barbara A., 107n, 114n
Floating exchange rates, 4–5. See also
Exchange rate(s)
FOMC. See Federal Open Market
Committee
Ford administration, Economic Policy
Board of, 164
Foreign borrowing, need for, 26–30,
148–49
Foreign-currency operations
Fed and Treasury interventions,
86–88
Reagan administration and, 2–3
Foreign-exchange markets, 2. See also
International monetary system;
Policy execution
dollar depreciation and, 51–52
sterilized intervention in, 8–9
Fox, Lawrence A., 33n, 125

Franc, 4
France, monetary policies of, 21
Frankel, Jeffrey, 9n, 29n, 140n
Free fall of dollar, 59
Funabashi, Yoichi, 30n, 40n, 42n, 45n,
50n, 58n, 59n, 60, 61n, 76n, 125n

G-3. See Group of Three
G-5. See Group of Five
G-7. See Group of Seven
G-10. See Group of 10
Galvin, Robert W., 125
Garten, Jeffrey E., 69n
General Agreement on Tariffs and
Trade (GATT), 38, 39. See also Multi-
lateral trade negotiations labor and,
123
Gephardt, Richard A., 39, 108
Gephardt amendment, 111
Germany. See also Bundesbank; Mark,
German
dollar rebound and, 72
G-5 talks and, 41
interest rates, 69
and Louvre Accord, 60
Gibbons, Sam M., 89n, 115
GNP. See Gross national product
Goal-setting, 155–61
Gold Commission, 22n
Gold Reserve Act of 1934, 86
Gold standard, 4, 22n, 63n, 99. See also
Bretton Woods system
Gowa, Joanne, 99n, 138n
Gramm-Rudman-Hollings Act, 55, 60
revision of, 64, 64n–65n
Greenspan, Alan, 62, 66, 68, 69n
Greider, William, 28n, 92n, 94n
Gross national product (GNP), US, 2,
57
budget deficit as share of, 60
Group of Five (G-5), 23–24
Baker and, 41, 42
January 1986 meeting and, 51
Louvre Accord and, 60–62
and macroeconomic conflict, 54–55
meetings of
January 1985, 41
January 1986, 51
Plaza Agreement and, 42. See also
Plaza Agreement Germany and, 50
Group of Seven (G-7), 25, 58, 83
Brady Treasury and, 79–80
Christmas 1987 statement, 57, 66–67
conflict in, 63
lack of consensus among, 72
meetings of
1982, 23
1983, 23

May 1986 (Tokyo), 46, 55n
April 1987, 69
Group of Ten (G-10), 23, 25
Group of Three (G-3), 58

Hackley, Howard H., 86n
Hale, David, 69n
Hands-off policy. *See* Laissez-faire
    policy
"Hard landing" of dollar, 59
Hatsopoulos, George, 119n
Henning, C. Randall, 3n, 24n, 42n,
    77n, 96n
Holtham, Gerald, 77n, 96n
Hong Kong, 130
Houpt, James V., 133n
House Banking Committee, 111,
    156–57
    Subcommittee on International
    Finance, 110
House Budget Committee, 156–57
House Ways and Means Committee,
    39, 111
Hudson, Milton W., 135n

Iacocca, Lee A., 125
IMF. *See* International Monetary Fund
IMM (International Monetary Market),
    135
Import ratio, 119–21
Imports, US, 35–36
Import surcharge. *See* Protectionism
Income taxes
    on foreign income, 29
    reform, 55n
Indirect exchange rate policy, 10, 11
Industrial capacity utilization rates, US,
    35–36, 57
Inflation, 2, 19, 57
    dollar depreciation and, 44
    and Louvre Accord, 62
    monetary policy and, in Reagan
    administration, 19, 31
Interest-group politics. *See* Private
    sector
Interest rates
    Federal Reserve role in control of,
    19, 52–53, 83
        exchange rate conflict and, 62–63
    German, 69
    international capital flows and, 27
    Louvre Accord and, 70n
International borrowing, need for,
    26–30, 148–49
International conflict, dollar stabiliza-
    tion and, 53–55
International coordination, breakdown
    of, 72–73

International Monetary Fund (IMF), 2n,
    4, 87, 111. *See also* World Bank–IMF
    meetings
International Monetary Market (IMM),
    135
International monetary system, 3–6. *See
    also* Capital flows, international;
    Foreign-exchange markets;
    Monetary policy, international
Intervention
    Fed and Treasury
        legal rights of, 86–88
        in practice, 88–90
        and tendency toward inaction, 93
        pressures for
            private interests and, 119–31
            shift toward activism and, 139–40
    sterilized v. unsterilized, 8–9
Iran-contra scandal, 56
Islam, Shafiqul, 9n
Issue entrepreneurship, Congress and,
    103–104
Italy, and Louvre Accord, 60

Japan. *See also* Yen
    and Baker-Miyazawa accord, 58–59
    Bank of, 50–51, 53
    capital outflows from, 28n
    influence of, 6
    liberalization of markets in, 24, 29
    and Louvre Accord, 60–61
    trade policy with, 39
J-curve effect, 46–47
Johnson, Manuel H., 37n
Joint Economic Committee, 21, 101,
    157n
Jones, Charles O., 21n

Katzenstein, Peter J., 117n
Kelly, Janet, 118n
Kemp, Jack F., 63n, 110
Kenen, Peter B., 9n, 164n
Kilborn, Peter T., 80n
Knight, Robert H., 86n
Knorr, Klaus, 118n
Kohl, Helmut, 71
Korea, 73–74, 112, 113, 130
Krasner, Stephen D., 117n
Krugman, Paul R., 9n, 119n
Kurland, Philip B., 99n

Labor unions. *See also* Private sector
    Congress and, 102
    and pressure for activism, 122–24
LaFalce, John J., 39, 109n, 110–11
Laissez-faire (nonintervention) policy,
    3

POLICY ANALYSES IN INTERNATIONAL ECONOMICS

24 **United States–Canada Free Trade: An Evaluation of the Agreement**
Jeffrey J. Schott/*April 1988*
$3.95   0–88132–072–2   48 pp

25 **Voluntary Approaches to Debt Relief**
John Williamson/*September 1988, rev. May 1989*
$10.95   0–88132–075–7   80 pp

26 **American Trade Adjustment: The Global Impact**
William R. Cline/*March 1989*
$12.95   0–88132–095–1   98 pp

27 **More Free Trade Areas?**
Jeffrey J. Schott/*May 1989*
$10.00   0–88132–085–4   88 pp

BOOKS

IMF Conditionality
John Williamson, editor/*1983*
$35.00 (cloth only)   0–88132–006–4   695 pp

Trade Policy in the 1980s
William R. Cline, editor/*1983*
$35.00 (cloth)   0–88132–008–1   810 pp
$20.00 (paper)   0–88132–031–5   810 pp

Subsidies in International Trade
Gary Clyde Hufbauer and Joanna Shelton Erb/*1984*
$35.00 (cloth only)   0–88132–004–8   299 pp

International Debt: Systemic Risk and Policy Response
William R. Cline/*1984*
$30.00 (cloth only)   0–88132–015–3   336 pp

Economic Sanctions Reconsidered: History and Current Policy
Gary Clyde Hufbauer and Jeffrey J. Schott, assisted by Kimberly Ann Elliott/*1985*
$45.00 (cloth only)   0–88132–017–X   769 pp

Trade Protection in the United States: 31 Case Studies
Gary Clyde Hufbauer, Diane E. Berliner, and Kimberly Ann Elliott/*1986*
$25.00   0–88132–040–4   371 pp

Toward Renewed Economic Growth in Latin America
Bela Balassa, Gerardo M. Bueno, Pedro-Pablo Kuczynski, and Mario Henrique Simonsen/*1986*
$15.00   0–88132–045–5   205 pp

SPECIAL REPORTS

FORTHCOMING

TO ORDER PUBLICATIONS PLEASE WRITE OR CALL US AT:

Institute for International Economics
Publications Department
11 Dupont Circle, NW
Washington, DC 20036
202-328-9000